The Columbia Book of Chinese Poetry

TRANSLATIONS FROM THE ORIENTAL CLASSICS

The COLUMBIA Book of CHINESE POETRY

Columbia University Press

From Early Times to the Thirteenth Century

Translated and Edited by
BURTON WATSON

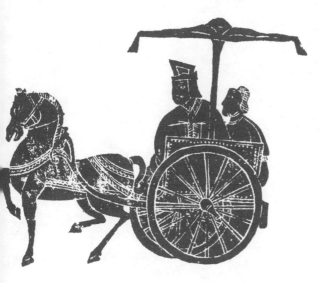

New York

Grateful acknowledgment is made to the following publishers for permission to quote previously published material: to Kodansha International for the poems "Dew on the Leek" and "The Graveyard," from *Meng Ch'iu: Famous Episodes from Chinese History and Legend*, translated by Burton Watson, © 1979 Kodansha International; to Harvard University Press for the poems "Journey to a Village" by Wang Yü-ch'eng; "Written for the Pavilion of the Drunken Old Man at Ch'u-chou," "Calligraphy Practice," and "Distant Mountains" by Ou-yang Hsiu; "Song of Delight" by Shao Yung; "Cold Night" by Ch'en Shih-tao; "Relaxing in the Evening in My Study, the Wo-chih-chai" by Yang Wan-li; "Leaving the City," "From 'Ten Poems Recording Things That Happened at the Year's End,'" and "Weeping for Hsüeh Tzu-shu" by Liu K'o-chuang, from Kōjirō Yoshikawa, *An Introduction to Sung Poetry*, translated by Burton Watson, copyright © 1967 by the Harvard-Yenching Institute.

The illustrations on the jacket, the title page, and within the text are taken from the Chin shih so.
Book designed by Laiying Chong.

Library of Congress Cataloging in Publication Data
Main entry under title.

The Columbia book of Chinese poetry.

(Translations from the Oriental classics)
Bibliography: p.
Includes index.
1. Chinese poetry — Translations into English.
2. English poetry — Translations from Chinese.   I. Watson, Burton, 1925 –   II. Series.
PL2658.E3C66 1984   895.1′1′008   83-26182
ISBN 0-231-05682-6

Columbia University Press
New York   Guildford, Surrey

p 10 9 8 7 6 5 4 3
c 10 9 8 7 6 5 4 3

TRANSLATIONS FROM THE ORIENTAL CLASSICS

CONTENTS

The Columbia Book of Chinese Poetry

PRINCIPAL DYNASTIES OF CHINESE HISTORY

Hsia	2205–1766 B.C.
Shang (Yin)	1765–1122 B.C.
Chou	1122–249 B.C.
Ch'in	221–207 B.C.
Han	206 B.C.–A.D. 220
Former Han	206 B.C.–A.D. 8
Later Han	25–220
Wei	220–264
Chin	265–420
Western Chin	265–316
Eastern Chin	317–420
Northern & Southern Dynasties	420–589
Sui	589–618
T'ang	618–907
Five Dynasties Period	907–960
Sung	960–1279
Northern Sung	960–1125
Southern Sung	1127–1279
Yuan	1234–1368
Ming	1368–1644
Ch'ing	1644–1911

} Six Dynasties Period

INTRODUCTION

POETRY has been many things to the Chinese over the long centuries of their history — a hymn to ancestral spirits, a celebration of the beauties of nature, an expression of friendship or a pleasant accompaniment to a social gathering, a medium for airing political criticisms, for venting grief, for advancing a courtship. It has been composed by emperors and their ladies-in-waiting, by monks and generals, city dwellers and farm folk, but above all by the scholar-officials, men who had received a thorough education in the classics of the language and who, often after passing the civil service examinations, were assigned posts in the complex bureaucracy that governed the vast nation. Whatever level of society it may have sprung from, poetry is woven into the life and history of the Chinese people, and perhaps no other facet of their traditional culture possesses such universal appeal.

Two things about the Chinese poetic tradition are immediately striking — its great antiquity and its remarkable continuity. The earliest works in my selection are taken from an anthology compiled around 600 B.C., and may well date back several centuries earlier. Moreover, they draw upon an oral tradition whose origins are probably as old as the Chinese people themselves. Though there are few works from the centuries immediately following this early anthology, for the period from around 300 B.C. down to the present century, the stream of poetic output is virtually unbroken. The discovery in the first century A.D. of a method of making paper, and the invention of printing about seven centuries later, greatly aided the dissemination and preservation of literary works, with the result that, the Chinese being among the world's most indefatigable compilers and transmitters of texts, the volume of poetry handed down from the past is truly staggering.

To attempt to cover the entire span of such a lengthy and voluminous poetic literature in a single anthology seemed imprudent, and I have instead chosen to deal only with the earlier period, from the time of the oldest extant works to the thirteenth century. I have ended my selection with the thirteenth century because by that time the *shih,* the principal poetic form in use in the early period, had clearly passed the zenith of its development and inspiration. In later centuries, though poetry in *shih* form continued to be written, the focus of interest tended to shift to other poetic forms or to other genres such as drama and fiction.

The history of this early period of poetic development will be outlined in the introductory essays to the individual chapters of the anthology, which will also provide information on major poets and other background material needed by the reader to appreciate the selections. Here I would like first to describe the outstanding characteristics and themes of Chinese poetry as a whole, and then proceed to examine its principal forms in the early period.

One of the first things that is likely to strike the Western reader about Chinese poetry is its remarkable degree of accessibility. To be sure, like any great poetic tradition with a long history of development, that of China has its particular conventions, some of which may seem strange to the reader at first. For example, its treatment of romantic love — a theme it takes up rather less frequently than does the poetry, say, of Europe or Japan — tends, particularly in later centuries, to be presented almost exclusively from the woman's point of view and to place great emphasis upon the pathos and helplessness of her situation. Another set of conventions is found in poetry dealing with the imperial court, in which the ruler is likened to Heaven, his ladies-in-waiting to fairy maidens of the sky, and his favor to the life-giving rain or dew.

In addition to such conventions and stereotypes, Chinese poetry, like that of the West, has its body of myths and legends that it draws upon, and is especially fond of employing allusions to the famous events and personages of the nation's lengthy past. All such mythical and historical allusions, of course, require some degree of explanation to be intelligible to the foreign reader.

But, as has been so frequently remarked, the Chinese poetic tradition is on the whole unusually humanistic and commonsensical in tone, seldom touching on the supernatural or indulging in extravagant flights of fancy or rhetoric. For this reason, even works that are many centuries removed from us in time come across with a freshness and immediacy that is often quite miraculous. The Chinese poetic world is one that is remarkably easy to enter because it concentrates to such a large degree on concerns that are common to men and women of whatever place or time.

Closely allied to this tone of reasonableness that marks Chinese poetry is its air of restraint and decorum. There are no epic poems in the language, and little of the ebullient celebration of heroic deeds and feats of arms that we associate with the epic poetry of India or the West. War and violence are rather seldom touched on, and when they are, it is more often to deplore than to glorify them. Erotic themes likewise are treated in a highly restrained manner. Sexual appeal is suggested by descriptions of dress, makeup, or articles of personal use rather than of the body itself, and anything approaching the indecent is so heavily cloaked in euphemisms that it could be titillating only to the highly initiated. All of this reflects the pervading influence of Confucianism, with its emphasis upon civil rather than military arts and virtues and its somewhat puritanical outlook.

Another important characteristic of Chinese poetry is its frequently personal and occasional nature. The Chinese have for the most part regarded poetry not as the product of any one particular group in society or personality type, not as the fruit of rare genius or divine inspiration, but as something that almost anyone with a grasp of the rules of prosody and a genuine desire for self-expression can compose. Particularly among scholars and government officials, poetry was an indispensable accompaniment of daily life. Poems were customarily composed as part of the entertainment at banquets and outings or exchanged among friends at times of parting. At other times, one might write poems to describe the events of his daily life, to record the scenes of a journey, to give vent to grief or frustration, or simply to dispel boredom or polish up one's literary skills. The practice of drawing lots to determine what rhymes one was to use when composing poems with a group of friends, or of "harmonizing" with the rhymes of someone else's poem — either employing the same rhyme categories as the original poem, or using the exact same rhyme words — added an element of challenge to the composing of poetry and gave it a gamelike quality.

Chinese occasional poetry — that is, poetry inspired by or written to commemorate a particular occasion — is much like the occasional poetry of the West. But whereas the Western poet in such circumstances usually tries to invest his poem with some sense of a universal truth transcending the occasion, the Chinese poet is more often content to try to capture the particular truth or sentiment that came to him on that occasion. For this reason, he frequently prefaces his poem with a headnote describing the precise time, place, and circumstances that prompted its composition. There is less sense than in the West of a poem as possessing a life of its own apart from that of its creator, more of the poem as a form of autobiography, shedding light on the life of the poet and at the same time yielding up its full meaning only when read in the context of that life. The poem is the voice of the poet not self-consciously addressing posterity or the world at large, but speaking quietly to a few close friends, or perhaps simply musing to himself.

But, although there is this very important personal and intimate side to Chinese poetry, and it is the side which, because of its engaging understatement and freedom from pretension, is likely to appeal most to present-day Western readers, there is also a more public side to poetry in China. The earliest anthology of Chinese poetry, the *Shih ching* or *Book of Odes,* was believed to have been compiled by the sage Confucius, who made clear that what he valued in poetry were its moral and didactic elements. From early times, Confucian scholars have seen poetry as playing a vital role in the ordering of the state, functioning as a vehicle through which the officials and common people might celebrate the virtue of a just ruler or, as is more likely to be the case, decry the hardships inflicted by an unjust one. This view of poetry as a medium for social and political complaint has led to the composition of many moving and impassioned works, realistic descriptions of the griefs of the tax-burdened farmers, outcries against military conscription and the ills of war, and attacks on social injustice in its many guises.

According to Confucian theory, the ruler was expected to welcome such complaints as expressions of loyal concern on the part of his subjects. But in an authoritarian governmental system such as that of imperial China, reasonable complaint was in practice all too often interpreted as treasonable impertinence, and countless officials found themselves summarily demoted and "exiled" to minor office in some remote province as a result of their poetic criticisms. It is a tribute to the courage and integrity of the Chinese poet-officials that, in spite of such risks, so many of them continued over the centuries to pour out their remonstrances in poetry.

The fondness of the Confucian scholars for poetry of didactic and political import at times led them to discover political meaning in places where it was almost certainly never intended. Thus, for example, they interpreted the simple love and courtship songs of the *Book of Odes* as allegories of the loyal minister's devotion to his sovereign, or saw in the crude ditties sung by children in the street the prophecies of impending events in the world of politics. On the other hand, countless Chinese poems were in fact intended to have political significance, even though it may not be immediately apparent in the surface meaning of the poem. Thus, for example, the poem by Chiang Lu on p. 191 seems to be no more than an objective description of a wrecked riverboat. But the poet's biography in *Nan shih*, chapter 36, reveals that in fact it was written as a rueful comment on the writer's own frustrated official career. Such allegorical levels of meaning are often difficult to identify, particularly at this far remove in time. But it is well to keep in mind that a seemingly ingenuous poem of objective description may have had a quite different significance for the poet and his associates. Most Chinese poets of early times wrote not for the reading public at large, but primarily for the members of their own coterie, and it was enough if the members of that group grasped the full import of the work.

Another important theme of traditional Chinese poetry to be

touched on here is that of the beauties of nature, particularly as seen in remote mountain areas, a theme that is of prime importance in Chinese painting as well. Here again there are conventions and symbolisms at work which we should be aware of. Thus, to give a few examples at random, pines and cranes are traditionally suggestive of longevity; orchids — the modest, unshowy Oriental variety — stand for the retiring gentleman of upright character; plum blossoms, because they open so early in the spring, symbolize fortitude; bamboos symbolize integrity, etc.

In the very early period of Chinese history, when large areas of the country were still in a state of wilderness, the natural landscape was often looked on as dark and threatening, the abode of fierce beasts and nature spirits of doubtful benignancy. But as more lands were opened up for cultivation and population pressures built up, the more isolated mountain and valley regions came to seem increasingly inviting. In contrast to the cities, which represented wealth, power, and the corrupting influences that seem inevitably to accompany them — the world of "red dust," as the Chinese call it — the mountains offered a realm of safety, serenity, and freedom from care, where one might savor the unspoiled grandeur of the landscape, pursue the life of a Taoist or Buddhist practitioner, or search for medicinal herbs to prolong life. It is no wonder that the poet-officials, shackled to their posts and ever in danger of encountering sudden reversals of fortune or even execution, should have dreamed so often of escaping to these carefree realms. And when, as frequently happened, civil strife erupted in the nation or foreign invaders swept down from the north or west, flight to the hills became almost the only hope for survival.

All these connotations — safety, longevity, spiritual peace, emancipation — underlie the traditional Chinese attitude toward nature and the life that is lived in the midst of natural surroundings. And added to these, as in the West, is an element of mysticism and religious feeling, a sense that in such a setting one is on the threshold of the supernatural. But, whereas the Western poet customarily looks upon nature as the eloquent handiwork of a Supreme Being who exists above and apart from his creation, the Chinese poet, imbued with the nondualism of Taoism and Buddhism, sees nature as the embodiment of the Absolute itself. Every element in the landscape, from the most sublime to the lowliest, is equally a manifestation of the Tao. And man, far from being the lord and caretaker of creation, is simply another one of the elements in it.

Finally, a word must be said about the theme of death. Though the poems in the *Book of Odes,* as will be noted later, are almost superstitious in their avoidance of the subject, by Han times the terrifying brevity and uncertainty of human life and the fear of death — the "claw coming out of the earth," to borrow Robert Payne's striking phrase[1] — had become a major theme in Chinese poetry.

In the face of such fear, many writers could only urge that we make the most of the little time given us. As one of the famous series of anonymous poems known as "The Nineteen Old Poems of the Han" puts it: "If the day is short and you hate the long night,/why not take the torch and go wandering?" In time, however, more thoughtful poets came forward with three possible ways to solve, or in some sense alleviate, the problem of human mortality.

The first, drawing upon ancient beliefs of the folk religion, particularly those associated with popular Taoism, suggests that, through the use of rare herbs or other semimagical means, one can attain the status of a *hsien* or immortal spirit, or at least greatly prolong the span of life. The art and literature of early China abound in descriptions and depictions of such immortals, cavorting in the mountain fastnesses that are their habitat or winging to the sky on the back of a white crane.

Confucianism, with its stress on humanism and rationalism, understandably took a dim view of such beliefs. Confucian-minded writers offered in their place more sober and socially responsible kinds of immortality, that achieved biologically through the perpetuation of the family, and the less certain hope of being remembered by posterity because of one's outstanding deeds or character. "A shining name — let that be the prize!" declares another of the poems in the series just mentioned.

1. Robert Payne, ed., *The White Pony: An Anthology of Chinese Poetry* (New York: The New American Library, 1947), p. xi.

But virtue, as the poets themselves glumly noted, too often fails to receive its just recognition, and the Chinese annalists, for all their proverbial diligence, can hardly be counted on to get down all the names of those who deserve remembrance. Thus in time a third solution to the problem began to take shape, one that is far subtler than the others and founded on the Taoist and Buddhist concepts of nondualism already alluded to above. The individual is indeed fated to perish when his allotted years come to an end. But if he can somehow transcend or set aside his individuality and merge himself with the ceaselessly recurring life of nature as a whole, he can in a sense free himself from bondage to the conventional concepts of life and death and become as eternal as the universe itself.

Sometimes, as in T'ao Yüan-ming's poem "Substance, Shadow, and Spirit," such philosophical ideas are set forth in a systematic manner, though more often, particularly in the case of the last view mentioned, they are merely hinted at. Many Chinese poems are frank celebrations of the sensual pleasures of life, albeit conscious of how fleeting such pleasures may prove to be. Others are works of high moral and artistic seriousness, intended in some way to better the state of mankind, and at the same time to insure a measure of literary immortality to the author. But others — often among the finest works in the language — are quite different from these in nature, exercises in quietude and anonymity in which the poet deliberately seeks to divest himself of his personality, even of his humanity, in an effort to become one with the countless other forms of being around him.

The question of just how satisfactory any of these solutions I have outlined may have been to the poets who embraced them is outside the scope of our inquiry here. But we ought to be aware of these varieties of philosophical orientation so that we can properly appreciate the tenor of a given poet's work, and not look for moralizing from someone who is concerned only with sensibility, or displays of ego from one whose whole aim is the shedding of ego.

Having noted some of the principal themes and characteristics of Chinese poetry, I would like to say something about its forms.

Nearly all the works contained in the present anthology, which covers the first two thousand years of Chinese poetry from about 800 B.C. to A.D. 1200, employ the *shih* form, a term we have already encountered in the title of the earliest anthology, the *Shih ching* or *Book of Odes*. It was originally a song form, and continued in later centuries to be essentially lyric in nature, though at times employed for narrative and descriptive poetry as well.

In its earliest form in the *Book of Odes*, it customarily uses a line made up of four characters. Since one character represents one syllable, and since classical Chinese is basically monosyllabic, this means in effect that there are usually four words to a line. Lines tend to be end-stopped, with few run-on lines except in the final couplet, so that the effect is of a series of brief and compact utterances or images.

In later centuries, the old four-character line of the *Book of Odes* for the most part dropped out of use, being replaced by versions of the *shih* that use a five-character or seven-character line. Rarely, poems with a three-character or six-character line are found, as well as those in the so-called "mixed line" form that uses lines of varied lengths. In the headings to the poems in the anthology that follows, form and line length will be noted.

End rhyme is employed from the earliest times, usually appearing at the end of the even-numbered lines. Occasionally rhymes on the odd-numbered lines are also used, as well as rhymed couplets. In short poems a single rhyme is customarily used throughout; in longer poems the rhyme may change as often as the poet wishes. In addition to end rhyme, much use is made of alliteration, internal rhyme, and onomatopoetic words descriptive not only of sounds but of actions and moods as well.

Though Chinese was probably a tonal language from very early times, we are not certain what role tone played in the prosody of ancient Chinese poetry. From around the sixth and seventh century, a new type of *shih* poetry evolved that took careful account of the tone of the words used in composition. This new, tonally regulated type of verse came to be known as *chin-t'i-shih* or "modern style *shih*," and the older, unregulated type was referred to as *ku-shih* or "old style" *shih*. (For these and other technical terms, see the glossary on pp. 373-375.)

For purposes of prosody, the four tones of medieval Chinese were classified into two categories: level tones, in which the voice remains on an even level, and deflected tones, in which the voice dips or rises in pronouncing the syllable. The rules for tonal regulation, or tonal parallelism, as it is sometimes called, are highly complex and need not be described in detail here. In principal they decree that a single line shall not have more than two, or at the very most three, syllables or words in succession that belong to the same tonal category, and that in the second line of a couplet the words in key positions shall be opposite in tone to the corresponding words in the first line of the couplet. This latter results in the second line of the couplet producing, in terms of tone, a mirror image of the first line.

All of these rules and devices no doubt insured that traditional Chinese poetry had a highly patterned and pleasing aural effect. However, because of the extensive changes that have taken place in pronunciation over the centuries, it is difficult to reconstruct the exact effect today.

Along with such euphonic devices as rhyme and tonal parallelism, Chinese poetry employs numerous rhetorical devices such as simile, metaphor, personification, etc. in the manner of Western poetry, though usually with greater restraint, and makes extensive use of verbal parallelism. Such parallelisms customarily appear in the form of couplets in which both lines follow exactly the same syntactical pattern; thus nouns, verbs, adjectives, etc. in the upper line are matched by identical parts of speech in the lower line, number words are matched with number words, color words with color words, etc.

Let me illustrate some of these points by quoting a typical poem in *shih* form. It is by Liu Tsung-yüan (773-819), a well-known T'ang official, poet, and prose writer, and is entitled "River Snow." The poem is in the *chüeh-chü* or quatrain form, one of the "modern style" or tonally regulated forms which consists of four lines made up of five, seven, or in rare cases six characters each. This particular example uses a five-character line. The transcription of the original given here represents the pronunciation used in modern standard Chinese, which is quite different from the pronunciation of T'ang times, when the poem was written. For example, in T'ang pronunciation, the rhyme words *chüeh, mieh,* and *hsüeh* all ended in a final "t," giving them a gently plosive effect that is lost in modern pronunciation. The mark ○ indicates syllables that belong to the level tone category, the mark ▲, those that belong to the deflected category.

As will be seen, the first two lines observe strict verbal parallelism. Interestingly, the poet summons up images of flying birds and well-traveled paths, only to negate them by telling us that they have been obliterated by the heavy snow. The third line is a run-on line, requiring the final line to complete the sense. Against a background of all-enveloping gray, the old man, muffled up in straw cloak and broad hat, sits alone in his little boat, apparently so immersed in his fishing and so at home on the river that he does not even notice the cold. The poem, because of its hushed atmosphere and air of mystery, has been a favorite subject for illustration by Chinese painters.

Liu Tsung-yüan, River Snow (5-ch. *chüeh-chü*)

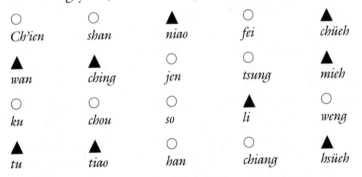

○	○	▲	○	▲
Ch'ien	*shan*	*niao*	*fei*	*chüeh*
▲	▲	○	○	▲
wan	*ching*	*jen*	*tsung*	*mieh*
○	○	○	▲	○
ku	*chou*	*so*	*li*	*weng*
▲	▲	○	○	▲
tu	*tiao*	*han*	*chiang*	*hsüeh*

From a thousand hills, bird flights have vanished;
on ten thousand paths, human traces wiped out:
lone boat, an old man in straw cape and hat,
fishing alone in the cold river snow.

In addition to the *shih,* there are two other poetic forms that were of importance during the period treated here. The first is the *fu* or rhyme-prose form, which came to prominence in the second century B.C. and continued to be of major significance down to T'ang times. The *fu* employs lines of varying lengths, arranged usually in blocks of lines of a uniform length that alternate with one another. A strong preference for four-character and six-character lines is apparent, and many poems are made up entirely of such lines. The poem often begins with an introduction in prose and contains prose interludes; in many cases it concludes with a reprise or recapitulation in verse. End rhyme is used throughout in the verse portions, as well as extensive alliteration and assonance. Many of the early *fu,* written by poets associated with the court, are given over to lavish depictions of imperial hunts and entertainments or the splendors of the capital cities, and run to considerable length. My selection includes seven well-known shorter works, some personal and meditative in tone, others pieces of objective description. Rhetorical devices such as parallelism and allusion abound in the *fu,* and the language tends to be learned and ornate; in my translations I have accordingly used a rather more elevated style of English than that which I ordinarily employ for translations of the *shih.*

Around the ninth and tenth centuries, a new poetic form came into vogue, the *tz'u* or "lyric meter." The earliest *tz'u,* anonymous works that originated on the popular level, were lyrics composed to fit Chinese tunes or tunes imported from Central Asia, and usually dealt with romantic lovers or other themes common in the folk song tradition. Later, the form was taken up by members of the educated class and used to treat a variety of subjects. In chapter 12, I have presented a selection of works in *tz'u* form from the T'ang and Sung periods that will convey an idea of the distinctive mood and literary appeal of the form and show how it differs from the *shih.* The formal characteristics of the *tz'u* are described in the introduction to the chapter.

As pointed out by David Lattimore, among others, classical Chinese poetry was only successfully translated into English when

CHAPTER ONE

The *Book of Odes*

THE *Shih ching* or *Book of Odes,* an anthology traditionally believed to have been compiled by Confucius, consists of 305 poems, the oldest extant examples of Chinese poetry. The poems probably date from around 1000 to 600 B.C., or the early centuries of the Chou dynasty. Most, if not all, were intended to be sung, though the musical settings were lost long ago.

Many of the shorter poems appear to be folk songs and are attributed to various feudal states of Chou period China. They have apparently been revised to make them conform to a standard system of rhymes, and perhaps refined and polished in the process. Other poems are designed to accompany the rituals and entertainments of the aristocracy or are recitals of dynastic legends or hymns for use in the ancestral temples.

The songs center on daily activities. We see people farming, hunting, gathering food plants, building, courting, feasting, performing sacrifices, going off to war. The imagery is that naturally associated with such activities, concrete and commonsensical. There is no imagery that appears to be designedly exotic, and no interest in the beauties of nature for their own sake. The poems concentrate on youth, beauty, and vigor, with considerable attention to the misfortunes that trouble the young. Little mention is made of sickness, old age, or death, though these were later to become major themes in Chinese poetry. Children, likewise, aside from indications that they are to be desired in great number, are largely ignored, as though to note their existence might place their lives in jeopardy. Many of the songs are festive and lighthearted in tone, but others complain bitterly of unhappy love affairs or marriages, misrule or the hardships of soldiering.

The songs employ a line made up of four characters or syllables, though lines of other lengths occur at times. One line usually constitutes a single syntactical unit. The lines are arranged in stanzas, usually of four, six, or eight lines each. End rhyme is used in almost all the songs, the rhyme customarily coming at the end of the even-numbered lines. Rhymed couplets occur but are infrequent. Alliteration and internal rhyme are also used. Many of the songs, particularly those of the folk song type, are highly compressed and elliptical and employ repetitions and refrains. Economy, even starkness of expression is a characteristic of the anthology as a whole.

A large number of the poems begin the stanza with an image drawn from nature such as a particular species of bird, insect, or plant. These natural creatures and their appearance, cry, or behavior are meant in some sense to parallel, or at times to contrast with, the human feelings and activities depicted in the succeeding lines. The use of such metaphorical imagery adds greatly to the literary impact of the poems, though it is difficult for us, many centuries removed from the world of the originals, to guess just what connotations such images may have had for the people of ancient China. One may note that the happier songs tend to be sparing in their use of such metaphorical imagery and to express their feelings directly. It is the unhappy singer who turns most often to metaphor to assist him in depicting the quality and intensity of his pain.

Because of its great antiquity and the fact that it was believed to have been compiled by Confucius, the *Book of Odes* was numbered among the Five Confucian Classics and became a basic text in the traditional style Chinese education. Numerous commentaries were written describing what could be known or surmised about the historical background of the poems and purporting to elucidate their ethical and political significance. In later centuries, much philological study was done on the text, while in recent times the techniques of comparative literature have helped to throw new light on the origin and nature of the poems. Though many of the passages of the anthology remain obscure, there can be no doubt about its importance in the shaping of the Chinese poetic tradition or its standing as a classic of world literature. Its voices, simple, impassioned, and timeless, speak to us across the centuries with almost disquieting force and clarity.

In my selection, I have concentrated on the short folk songs or folk song type works that occur in the early part of the anthology, since these are of the greatest literary interest and have had the most influence on later Chinese literature. The numbers are those of the poems in the Mao text, the standard version of the *Odes*.

No. 1. Gwan! Gwan! Cry the Fish Hawks

(Said to be a wedding song for a member of the royal family; the fish hawks are symbolic of conjugal affection.)

Gwan! gwan! cry the fish hawks
on sandbars in the river:
a mild-mannered good girl,
fine match for the gentleman.

A ragged fringe is the floating-heart,
left and right we trail it:
that mild-mannered good girl,
awake, asleep, I search for her.

I search but cannot find her,
awake, asleep, thinking of her,
endlessly, endlessly,
turning, tossing from side to side.

A ragged fringe is the floating-heart,
left and right we pick it:
the mild-mannered good girl,
harp and lute make friends with her.[1]

A ragged fringe is the floating-heart,
left and right we sort it:
the mild-mannered good girl,
bell and drum delight her.

1. The bride is welcomed into the groom's house.

No. 5. Grasshopper Wings

Grasshopper wings,
swarms and swarms of them:
right that your sons and grandsons
should prosper and thrive!

Grasshopper wings,
files and files of them:
right that your sons and grandsons
should carry on the line!

Grasshopper wings,
droves and droves of them:
right that your sons and grandsons
should make up a throng!

No. 6. Peach Tree Young and Fresh

Peach tree young and fresh,
bright bright its blossoms:
this girl's getting married,
she'll do well in her home.

Peach tree young and fresh,
plump are its fruits:
this girl's getting married,
she'll do well in her rooms.

Peach tree young and fresh,
its leaves lush and full:
this girl's getting married,
she'll do right by her people.

No. 14. Chirp Chirp the Katydids

Chirp chirp the katydids,
hop hop the hoppers:
before I've seen my lord,
my grieving heart quails,
but once I've seen him,
once I've laid eyes on him,
then my heart is calm.

I climb that southern hill,
there pick its ferns:
before I've seen my lord,
my grieving heart is pained,
but once I've seen him,
once I've laid eyes on him,
then my heart is glad.

I climb that southern hill,
there pick its ferns:
before I've seen my lord,
my heart is hurt and sore,
but once I've seen him,
once I've laid eyes on him,
then my heart's at rest.

No. 16. That Broad and Spreading Sweet Pear

That broad and spreading sweet pear,
don't hew it, don't hack it —
Lord Shao camped there.

That broad and spreading sweet pear,
don't hew it, don't harm it —
Lord Shao stopped there.

That broad and spreading sweet pear,
don't hew it, don't fell it —
Lord Shao rested there.[1]

No. 20. The Plum Tree Drops Its Fruit

The plum tree drops its fruit,
its fruits are seven:
all you men who court me,
move while the time is lucky!

The plum tree drops it fruit,
its fruits are three:
all you men who court me,
may you make your move now!

The plum tree drops its fruit,
I fill my slanting basket:
all you men who court me,
I ask you to speak up!

No. 23. In the Meadow There's a Dead Deer

(A girl secretly seduced is compared to a deer stealthily shot and concealed with rushes; the last stanza depicts the seduction.)

In the meadow there's a dead deer,
with white rushes cover it:
there's a girl with thoughts of spring
and a fine man who tempts her.

1. Tradition says that Lord Shao is Chi Shih, the duke of Shao, an early Chou period statesman mentioned in historical texts.

In the woods are the scrub oaks,
in the meadow a dead deer:
in white rushes wrap and bind it.
There's a girl fair as jade.

Go slow — gently, gently!
Don't muss my waist cloth,
don't make the dog bark!

No. 26. That Cypress Boat Is Drifting

That cypress boat is drifting,
drifting with the flow:
fretful, fretful, I cannot sleep,
as if from a painful grief,
though I've no lack of wine
to ease and amuse me.

My heart is not a mirror,
you can't just peer into it!
I too have brothers,
though not the kind to rely on.
I go to them with pleas,
only to meet their anger.

My heart is not a stone,
you can't tumble it around;
my heart is not a mat,
you can't just roll it up!
My conduct was pure and proper,
you cannot fault me there.

My grieving heart pains and sorrows,
I'm hated by those petty people.
Trouble — I've seen plenty;

suffered insults — not a few.
Silently I brood on it,
awake, beating my breast.

You sun, you moon,
why do you take turns hiding?
Sorrow around my heart
like an unwashed robe —
silently I brood on it,
helpless to rise and fly away.

No. 41. Cold Is the North Wind

Cold is the north wind,
the snow falls thick.
If you are kind and love me,
take my hand and we'll go together.
You are modest, you are slow,
but oh, we must hurry!

Fierce is the north wind,
the snow falls fast.
If you are kind and love me,
take my hand and we'll go home together.
You are modest, you are slow,
but oh, we must hurry!

Nothing redder than the fox,
nothing blacker than the crow.
If you are kind and love me,
take my hand and we'll ride together.
You are modest, you are slow,
but oh, we must hurry!

No. 46. Thorn Vine on the Wall

Thorn vine on the wall
must not be stripped:
words in the chamber
must not be told.
What could be told
would be the ugliest tale!

Thorn vine on the wall
must not be pulled down:
words in the chamber
must not be recited.
What could be recited
would be the longest tale!

Thorn vine on the wall
must not be bundled off:
words in the chamber
must not be rehearsed.
What could be rehearsed
would be a shameful tale!

No. 52. See the Rat — at Least It's Got a Hide

See the rat — at least it's got a hide,
but a man with no manners,
a man with no manners —
why doesn't he just die!

See the rat — at least it's got teeth,
but a man with no decorum,
a man with no decorum —
what's keeping him! why doesn't he die!

See the rat — at least it's got legs,
but a man without courtesy,
a man without courtesy —
why doesn't he hurry up and die!

No. 61. Who Says the River Is Wide?

(Reproving a lover who makes excuses.)

Who says the river is wide?
On a reed you can cross it!
Who says Sung is far?
On tiptoe you can see it!

Who says the river is wide?
It won't hold a sliver of a boat!
Who says Sung is far?
You can get there before the morning's out!

No. 66. My Lord's Gone to Service

(A farm wife thinks of her husband on military duty.)

My lord's gone to service,
I don't know for how long.
When will he come home?
The chickens roost in their nooks,
it's the evening of the day
and the sheep and cows come down.
My lord's gone to service —
how can I not think of him?

My lord's gone to service,
not for a day, not for a month.
When will I see him again?
The chickens roost on their perches,
it's the evening of the day
and the sheep and cows make their way down.
My lord's gone to service —
may he never hunger or thirst!

No. 67. Merry, Merry Is My Lord

Merry, merry is my lord,
his left hand holding a reed-organ,
his right calling me from my room —
oh the fun of it!

Jolly, jolly is my lord,
his left hand holding a feather-stick,
his right calling me from the dance ground —
oh the fun of it!

No. 76. Please, Chung Tzu

(A young woman pleads with an overzealous suitor.)

Please, Chung Tzu,
don't leap into my village,
don't break the willows they planted.
Not that I mind about them —
I'm afraid of my father and mother.

You're a love, Chung,
but the word of my father and mother —
that's something to be scared of!

Please, Chung Tzu,
don't jump over my wall,
don't break the mulberries they planted.
Not that I mind about them —
I'm afraid of my older brothers.
You're a love, Chung,
but the word of my older brothers —
that's something to be scared of!

Please, Chung Tzu,
don't jump into my garden,
don't break the spindle trees they planted.
Not that I mind about them —
I'm afraid of a lot of talk from others.
You're a love, Chung,
but a lot of talk from others —
that's something to be scared of!

No. 77. Shu Has Gone Hunting

Shu has gone hunting,
in our lanes there're no dwellers.
How could there be no dwellers?
But there're none like Shu,
so handsome and kind!

Shu has gone after game,
in our lanes there're no wine-drinkers.
How could there be no wine-drinkers?
But there're none like Shu,
so handsome and good!

Shu is off to the uplands,
in our lanes there're no horse-drivers.
How could there be no horse-drivers?
But there're none like Shu,
so handsome and brave!

No. 81. Walking the Wide Road

Walking the wide road
I catch hold of your sleeve.
Do not hate me,
so quickly forgetting the old times!

Walking the wide road
I catch hold of your hand.
Do not despise me,
so quickly forgetting the good times!

No. 82. She Says, Cocks Are Crowing!

She says, Cocks are crowing!
He says, It's barely dawn!
Then get up and look at the night —
the morning star is shining!
You must go roaming and roving
to shoot wild ducks and geese.

When you've shot them and downed them,
then I'll dress them for you,
dress them, and we'll drink wine —

you and I growing old together,
harps and lutes at our mealtime,
nothing not peaceful and good.

If I know when you're coming,
I'll give you assorted belt-stones for a gift.
If I know that's agreeable,
I'll call on you with assorted belt-stones.
If I know that you love me,
I'll repay you with assorted belt-stones.

No. 85. Dry Leaves, Dry Leaves

Dry leaves, dry leaves,
the wind tosses you about:
brothers, oh brothers,
as you sing so must I follow.

Dry leaves, dry leaves,
the wind blows you along:
brothers, oh brothers,
as you sing so must I too.

No. 87. If You Think Kindly of Me

If you think kindly of me,
I'll hike up my skirt and wade the Chen.
But if you've no thoughts for me,
are there no others,
you most foolish of foolish boys?

If you think kindly of me,
I'll hike up my skirt and wade the Wei.
But if you've no thoughts for me,
are there no other men,
you most foolish of foolish boys?

No. 91. Blue Blue Your Collar

Blue blue your collar,
sad sad my heart:
though I do not go to you,
why don't you send word?

Blue blue your belt-stone,
sad sad my thoughts:
though I do not go to you,
why don't you come?

Restless, heedless,
I walk the gate tower.
One day not seeing you
is three months long.

No. 97. "How Quick You Are!"

"How quick you are!"
You met me in the region of Mount Nao,
side by side we chased a pair of boars.
You bowed to me and said, "You're the one who's nimble!"

"What a fine figure you cut!"
You met me on the road to Nao,
side by side we chased a pair of bucks.
You bowed to me and said, "You're the one who's handsome!"

"How good you are at it!"
You met me on the sunny side of Nao,
side by side we chased a pair of wolves.
You bowed to me and said, "You're the one who's expert!"

No. 110. I Climb That Barren Ridge

I climb that barren ridge,
gaze far off toward my father:
my father says, "Ah, my boy,
off to service, day and night no rest —
just make sure of this:
come home, don't let them hold you captive!"

I climb that grassy knoll,
gaze far off toward my mother:
my mother says, "Ah, my youngest,
off to service, day and night no sleep —
just make sure of this:
come home, don't let them leave you there!"

I climb that little hill,
gaze far off toward my older brother:
my older brother says, "Ah, little brother,
off to service, day and night always with the others —
just make sure of this:
come home, don't die out there!"

No. 113. Big Rat, Big Rat

(A complaint against rapacious officials.)

Big rat, big rat,
don't eat my millet!
Three years I've served you
but you won't care for me.
I'm going to leave you
and go to that happy land,
happy land, happy land
where I'll find my place.

Big rat, big rat,
don't eat my wheat!
Three years I've served you
but you do me no good.
I'm going to leave you
and go to that happy realm,
happy realm, happy realm —
things will be right for me there.

Big rat, big rat,
don't eat my sprouts!
Three years I've served you
but you give me no comfort.
I'm going to leave you
and go to those happy fields,
happy fields, happy fields,
who will moan there for long?

No. 124. The Kudzu Spreads Till It Darkens the Brier

(A woman swears to be faithful to her absent lover until the grave.)

The kudzu spreads till it darkens the brier,
the bindweed blankets the fields.
My beautiful one — he's not here —
who would I live with, if not alone?

The kudzu spreads till it darkens the thorn tree,
the bindweed blankets the graves.
My beautiful one — he's not here —
who would I sleep with, if not alone?

My pillow of horn gleams brightly,
my brocade coverlet glows,
my beautiful one — he isn't here —
who would I greet the dawn with, if not alone?

Days of summer,
winter nights:
after a hundred years have passed,
I'll join you in your dwelling.

Nights of winter,
summer days:
after a hundred years are over,
I'll join you in your room.

No. 132. Swift Is That Falcon

Swift is that falcon,
dark that northern wood:
I have not seen my lord,

my grieving heart is pained.
Why is it, why is it
you forget me so often!

Thick oaks grow on the mountain,
in the damp places, magnolia:
I have not seen my lord,
my grieving heart knows no joy.
Why is it, why is it
you forget me so often!

There are thick cherries on the mountain,
in the damp places, wild pear:
I have not seen my lord,
my grieving heart feels drunk.
Why is it, why is it
you forget me so often!

No. 140. Willow by the Eastern Gate

Willow by the eastern gate,
its leaves are lush and full:
we were to meet at twilight —
now the morning star is shining.

Willow by the eastern gate,
its leaves are dense and dark:
we were to meet at twilight,
but now the morning star gleams.

No. 167. We Pick Ferns, We Pick Ferns

(Men on duty guarding the country from the Hsien-yün tribes of the north.)

We pick ferns, we pick ferns,
for the ferns are sprouting now:
oh to go home, to go home
before the year is over!
No rooms, no houses for us,
all because of the Hsien-yün,
no time to kneel or sit down,
all because of the Hsien-yün.

We pick ferns, we pick ferns,
the ferns now are tender:
oh to go home, to go home!
Our hearts are saddened,
our sad hearts smolder and burn.
We are hungry, we are thirsty,
no limit to our border duty,
no way to send home for news.

We pick ferns, we pick ferns,
now the ferns have grown tough:
oh to go home, to go home
in the closing months of the year!
The king's business allows no slacking,
no leisure to kneel or rest.
Our sad hearts are sick to death,
this journey of ours has no return!

What splendor is here?
The splendor of cherry flowers.
What chariot is this?
The chariot of our lord.
The war chariot is yoked,
four stallions sturdy and strong.
How would we dare to stop and rest?
In one month, three engagements!

We yoke those four stallions,
four stallions stalwart and strong,
for our lord to ride behind,
for lesser men to shield.
Four stallions stately,
ivory bow-ends, fish-skin quivers:
could we drop our guard for a day?
The Hsien-yün are fearfully swift!

Long ago we set out
when willows were rich and green.
Now we come back
through thickly falling snow.
Slow slow our march,
we are thirsty, we are hungry,
our hearts worn with sorrow,
no one knows our woe.

No. 192. How Is the Night?

How is the night?
The night's not yet ended.
Courtyard torches are lit;
our lord is coming,
his bridle-bells make tinkling sounds.

How is the night?
The night's not yet over.
Courtyard torches shimmer and shine:
our lord is coming,
his bridle-bells make jangling sounds.

How is the night?
The night gives way to dawn.
Courtyard torches are glimmering:
our lord is coming,
I can see his banners!

No. 206. Don't Walk Beside the Big Carriage

Don't walk beside the big carriage,
you'll only get yourself dusty.
Don't brood on a hundred worries,
you'll only make yourself sick.

Don't walk beside the big carriage,
the dust will blacken and blind you.
Don't brood on a hundred worries,
you'll never reach a brighter land.

Don't walk beside the big carriage,
the dust will swallow you up.
Don't brood on a hundred worries,
you'll only weigh yourself down.

No. 219. Buzz Buzz, the Blue Flies

Buzz buzz, the blue flies,
lighting on the fence:
my joyous and gentle lord,
don't listen to slanderous words!

Buzz buzz, the blue flies,
lighting on the thorn:

slandering men know no limits,
they destroy every state around!

Buzz buzz, the blue flies,
they light on the hazel:
no end to slanderers' doings —
they set the two of us to quarreling!

No. 220. When Guests First Take Their Seats

When guests first take their seats,
left and right they move in order.
Baskets and platters are ranged in rows,
foods and pitted fruits set forth.
The wine is well blended and tasty,
we drink wine in perfect accord.
Bells and drums are put in place,
host and guest exchange cups pleasantly.
The great target is erected,
bows are strung with arrows,
the archers disposed in groups:
Now show your skill!
Shoot at the mark,
earn your cup of reward!

With flutes they dance to reed-organ and drum,
musicians playing in harmony,
offering delight to illustrious forebears,
rounding out the hundred rites.
When the hundred rites are perfect,
possessed with largeness and grandeur,
they confer on you great blessing,
causing sons and grandsons to rejoice,
to rejoice and be happy,

so let each of you display your art.
The guests take their partners in hand,
the host enters once more,
fills the cup of good ease,
"because you showed us a hit!"

When guests first take their seats,
mild mild is their courtesy;
before they've gotten drunk,
their deportment is solemn and grave.
But once they've gotten drunk,
their deportment is frightful, frightful!
They leave their seats, move about,
insist on dancing round and round.
Before they've gotten drunk,
sedate sedate is their deportment;
but once they've gotten drunk,
it's scandalous, scandalous!
Once they've gotten drunk
they lose all sense of order.

The guests have gotten drunk,
shouting, brawling;
they upset our baskets and platters,
insist on dancing — stagger stagger.
Once they've gotten drunk,
they no longer know their blunders,
with crooked caps sliding off
they insist on dancing on and on.
If those who are drunk would only go,
they'd have their blessing with the rest.
But so long as they refuse to leave
they spoil the power of the feast.
Drinking wine is a great delight,
but only when done with deportment!

Among all those drinking wine,
some get drunk, some don't.
So we set up a supervisor,
at times a scribe to assist him.
When drunks do something unsightly,
those not drunk feel embarrassed for them.
Don't encourage them,
don't let them be too careless!
What is not to be uttered, don't utter!
What is not to be encouraged, don't mention!
Encourage the words of a drunken man
and he turns into a young ram!
Three cups and you don't know what you're doing —
how would you think of drinking more!

No. 228. Swampland Mulberries Are Lovely

Swampland mulberries are lovely,
their leaves have a fullness.
I have seen my lord —
how great is my delight!

Swampland mulberries are lovely,
their leaves have a sheen.
I have seen my lord —
how could I not delight?

Swampland mulberries are lovely,
their leaves are somber.
I have seen my lord —
his virtue is vast and firm.

In my heart I love him —
why should I not speak out?
I store him deep in my heart,
what day will I forget him?

No. 245. She Who First Bore Our People

(The birth of Hou Chi or "Lord Millet," legendary founder of the Chou royal family and the god of agriculture.)

She who first bore our people
was Lady Yüan of Chiang.
How did she bear them?
She knew how to make *yin* and *ssu* sacrifices
so she would not be childless.
She stepped in the footprint of God's big toe and was quickened,
she was magnified, she was blessed,
she was stirred to pregnancy, quickly it came.
She bore him, she nurtured him:
this was Hou Chi.

She fulfilled her months
and her first-born came forth.
There was no rending, no tearing,
no injury, no harm,
showing that it was divine.
Did the Lord on High not give her ease?
Did he not receive her sacrifices?
Effortlessly she bore her child.

They laid him in the narrow lane,
but the oxen and sheep stood about to shelter him.
They laid him in the forest of the plain,
but he was found by woodcutters of the forest.
They laid him on the cold ice,
but the birds covered him with their wings.
When the birds had departed,
Hou Chi began to wail.

Long he cried, loud he cried,
that voice of his was huge.
Then he began to crawl,
he could straddle, he could stand firm
to seek food for his mouth.

And he planted big beans,
big beans that grew like banners,
rich rich the rows of grain,
luxuriant the hemp and wheat,
plump plump the young melons.

Hou Chi's husbandry
had ways to help the growing.
He cleared the rank grasses,
planted his yellow treasure,
it filled the field, abundant.
Once planted, it grew,
it flowered, it formed ears,
it was firm, of fine quality,
drooping and full-kerneled.
And then he made his home in T'ai.

He bestowed on us good grain,
black millet, double-kerneled black millet,
red millet, white millet.
The black millet he planted far and wide,
reaped it, took it by the fieldful.
The red and white he planted far and wide,
shouldered it, bore it on his back,
took it home to commence the sacrifices.

What are our sacrifices like?
Some pound the grain, some scoop it,
some winnow it, some trample it.
We soak it, slosh slosh,
we steam it, hiss hiss.
We plan carefully, we ponder,
we gather sagebrush, offer up fat,
choose a ram for the spirits of the road.
We roast, we broil
in order to begin the coming year.

We heap high the platters,
the platters and earthen vessels.
When the fragrance begins to rise,
the Lord on High rests contented —
how timely is the sweet aroma!
Hou Chi commenced the sacrifices
and without error or reproach
they've been carried on till today.

No. 279. Rich Is the Year with Much Millet and Rice

(Hymn for the ancestral temple.)

Rich is the year with much millet and rice,
and we have tall granaries
with hundreds and thousands and millions of sheaves.
We make wine and sweet spirits
to offer to ancestor and ancestress,
thus to fulfill the hundred rites
and bring down blessings in abundance.

CHAPTER TWO

The *Ch'u Tz'u*

THE *Book of Odes* is a product of the culture of northern China, that of the ruling Chou dynasty with its court at Lo-yang, and of the feudal states surrounding it in the area of the Yellow River. By contrast, the next group of poems to come down to us from ancient China are associated with Ch'u, a large state located to the south in the central valley of the Yangtze. The poems, entitled *Ch'u Tz'u* or "Words of Ch'u," were compiled in their present form in the first century A.D., apparently on the basis of a somewhat earlier collection. The earliest and most important works in the collection, those that we will be examining here, date from around the fourth century B.C.

Ch'u was very different in customs and culture from the states of northern China, which in fact tended to look down on it as a semibarbarous region. For one thing, shamanism seems to have played a more important role in the religious life of the people than it did in the north, which is perhaps one reason why the poetry of Ch'u is more rhapsodic in tone, richer and more fantastic in imagery, than the rather sober-minded poetry of the north. Among the earliest works in the *Ch'u Tz'u* is a group of poems entitled "Nine Songs," actually a set of eleven poems, which are largely inspired by shamanism. The songs deal with various male and female deities, most of them associated with the general region of Ch'u but a few whose cults were centered in the north. It is not known exactly how the songs came to be compiled as a group, though it has been suggested that a poet or poets, drawing on materials from the folk religion, shaped them into a series of masques for performance at the Ch'u court.

Certainly the form of the poems is suggestive of drama, and some commentators have even attempted to arrange the texts as libretti with lines assigned to various speakers. In the poems, a male or female shaman, depending upon the sex of the deity to be addressed, dons elaborate costume and makeup and, singing and dancing, invites the god to an amorous encounter. In most cases, the deity seems to make only a fleeting appearance, vanishing quickly and leaving the worshiper pining in frustration and despair.

In form the "Nine Songs" use a four-, five-, or six-character line, broken in the middle by the insertion of a breathing particle or carrier sound represented by a character pronounced *hsi* in modern Chinese. Rhyme occurs at the end of most lines. From its use in the "Nine Songs," the form has come to be referred to as "song style" and, as we shall see in the next chapter, was frequently used in the early centuries of the succeeding Han period.

Aside from the "Nine Songs," the most important work in the *Ch'u Tz'u* is a 374-line narrative poem, the longest in pre-Han literature, entitled *Li Sao* or *Encountering Sorrow*. The work, like the "Nine Songs" and a number of other poems in the anthology, has traditionally been attributed to a nobleman of Ch'u named Ch'ü Yüan (dates uncertain) who served as a high minister to King Huai of Ch'u (r. 328-299 B.C.). He became estranged from the king as a result of the slanders of court rivals and was finally banished to the south by King Huai's son and successor, King Ch'ing-hsiang (r. 298-63 B.C.). There he is said to have drowned himself in a fit of despair in the Mi-lo, a tributary of the Yangtze.

Though modern scholars have questioned this attribution, the poem does indeed appear to be about a man of aristocratic birth who complains of slanderous opponents and alienation from his sovereign (whom he refers to by such epithets as "Fair One" or "Godly One"), mourns the relentless winging of time, and repeatedly stresses his unwavering loyalty and the matchless qualities that make him uniquely suited for his lord's service. To bolster his arguments, he employs a device much favored by early Chinese philosophers and rhetoricians, the lesson from history, citing examples from the annals and legends of the past to prove that the ruler who employs upright ministers is bound to prosper, and that he who fails to do so will meet with downfall.

These political and didactic elements in the poem, which ally it with the *Book of Odes* and other works of the Confucian tradition, are very much what we would expect in a work written by a disconsolate statesman who felt he had suffered unjust treatment at the hands of an undiscerning sovereign. But interspersed with these are elements of a quite different nature, themes and modes of expression that are clearly related to the shamanism of the "Nine Songs." Thus, for example, the protagonist decks himself out with the same precious stones and fragrant plants as those sported by the shaman invokers, and his relationship to the ruler is frequently couched in erotic language similar to that used by the shamans in adddressing their divine lovers. At some points in the poem the hero seems to change sex, imagining himself as one of the women in the king's harem; at other times he is seen earnestly searching for a beautiful woman to be his companion, this quest for an ideal mate presumably symbolizing his longing for a ruler who will recognize his true worth. In addition, the poem makes use of the journey motif so common in the literature of shamanism, picturing the hero as borne in a carriage drawn by dragons and attended by the gods of the wind and rain, roaming the universe and visiting spots famous in myth and legend. The poem as a whole, in fact, could perhaps best be described as a rich and rather chaotic combination of disparate themes and symbols, lush in imagery, passionate in tone, sweeping the reader forward with its eloquence and air of moral conviction while often leaving him baffled as to its precise meaning. We are not sure just who the hero is, why his endeavors seem to fare so badly, or exactly what message underlies his fretful allegories; yet for all that, his anguish strikes us as very real.

The poem employs a line of six or seven characters. Around the middle of the line occurs a grammatical particle that is more lightly stressed than the words around it, thus relieving the monotony of the line and giving it rhythmic variation. The carrier sound *hsi* appears at the end of the odd-numbered lines, the rhyme at the end of the even-numbered ones.

My selection from the *Ch'u Tz'u* includes the second, eighth, ninth, and tenth of the "Nine Songs" and the complete text of the *Li Sao*. The remaining poems in the anthology, though containing occasional passages of great beauty, are mainly imitations of the *Li Sao* or elaborations of the Ch'ü Yüan legend, and are of less literary importance.

SELECTIONS FROM THE "NINE SONGS"

The Lord Among the Clouds

I bathe in orchid water,
   wash my hair with scents,
put on colored robes,
   flower-figured.
The spirit, twisting and turning,
   poised now above,
radiant and shining
   in endless glory,
comes to take his ease
   in the Temple of Long Life,
and with the sun and moon
   to pair his brilliance.
Riding his dragon chariot,
   drawn like a god,
he hovers and soars,
   roaming the vastness;
spirit majestic,
   but now descended,
swiftly rising
   far off to the clouds.
He looks down on Chi-chou,[1]
   the regions beyond,
crosses to the four seas;
   what land does he not visit?
I think of you, Lord,
   sighing.
You afflict my heart
   sorely, sorely!

1. Designation for a region in north China, one of the Nine Provinces of ancient China.

Lord of the River

(Ho-po, the Lord of the River, is the god of the Yellow River. The Yellow River, rising in the fabled K'un-lun Mountains of the far west, flowed into the sea in nine channels known as the Nine Rivers.)

I sport with you
    by the Nine Rivers.
Fierce winds rise,
    billowing waves.
I ride a water chariot
    with lotus canopy,
drawn by two dragons
    between a pair of river serpents.
I climb K'un-lun
    and gaze at the four quarters,
my heart bounding upward,
    restless and astir.
Though the sun is setting,
    in my grief I forget to go.
Thinking of that distant shore,
    I lie awake longing.
Of fish scales is his house,
    with dragon halls,
gates of purple cowrie,
    palaces of pearl.
What does the Spirit do
    down in the water?
He rides a white turtle,
    by speckled fish attended.
I sport with you
    among the river isles.
Wild are the waters
    that come rushing down.
You take my hand
    and journey east,

escorting your fair one
   to the southern shore.
Waves, surge on surge,
   come to greet us;
fishes, shoal on shoal,
   to be my bridesmaids.[1]

The Mountain Spirit

(Though the subject of individual lines is a matter of dispute, in this song the deity
rather than the shaman appears to be the one who pines and waits in vain.)

There seems to be someone
   by the bend of the hill,
dressed in cassia,
   ground-pine for a sash.
She has cast shy glances,
   appropriate smiles.
"You yearn for me,
   you are modest and fair."
She rides a red leopard,
   striped lynxes attending,
her carriage of mountain magnolia
   trimmed with cinnamon banners.
She dons rock orchids,
   a sash of asarums,
breaks off sprays of fragrant scent
   to send to the one she loves.
"I live among the dark bamboo;
   nowhere can I see the sky.
The way is hard and perilous,
   late and alone I've come."

1. The last section of the poem may refer to the old custom of sacrificing a young girl
each year as a "bride" for the Lord of the River. She was placed on a couch and left to
float down the river until the couch overturned and she drowned.

She stands all alone
   on top of the mountain,
billowing clouds
   spread out below her,
gray and lowering,
   darkening the day.
East winds bluster,
   the goddess sends down rain.
"I'll make my lovely one linger,
   so contented he forgets to go.
But once the year has ended,
   who will favor me then?"
She gathers three-blossomed iris
   in the cleft of the hill,
rocks heaped all around,
   kudzu tendrils trailing.
"I think in anger of my lord,
   in my sorrow I forget to return.
You long for me,
   Yet you spare me no time!"
She is there in the mountain
   fragrant with sweet flag.
She drinks from a rocky spring
   overshadowed by cypress and pine.
"You long for me,
   yet you have doubts!"
Thunder rolls and rumbles,
   dark rains come down,
monkeys shrill and chatter,
   apes cry in the night.
The wind howls mournfully,
   the trees whisper and sigh.
"I long for my lord
   and all I encounter is grief!"

Those Who Died for Their Country

We take up the halberds of Wu,
   put on rhino hide armor.
Chariots clash, hub against hub,
   short swords parry.
Banners blot out the sun,
   the enemy come on like clouds.
Arrows fall in answering volleys,
   warriors vie for the lead.
They have broken through our formations,
   trampled over our lines.
The trace-horse on the left has fallen,
   the right one is slashed with knives.
The chariot wheels are dug in,
   teams of four horses entangled.
We seize our jade drumsticks,
   beat a call on the drums.
But Heaven's season frowns on us,
   the awesome gods are angry.
Our stalwart ones are all slaughtered,
   cast away on field and plain.
They set out, never to come back;
   went, never to return.
The level plains are distant,
   the road stretches on and on.
They buckled on their long swords,
   shouldered the bows of Ch'in.
Though heads are parted from bodies,
   their hearts have no regret.
Truly they were courageous,
   true men of arms as well.
To the end fierce and unyielding,
   they could never be cowed.
Though in body they have died,
   their spirits take on divinity.
Valiant are their souls,
   they are heroes in the realm of ghosts.

Encountering Sorrow

Descendant of the ancestor Kao-yang,
Po-yung was my honored father's name.
When the constellation She-t'i pointed to the first month,
on the day *keng-yin* I was born.[1]
My father, observing the aspects of my birth,
divined and chose for me auspicious names.
The personal name he gave me was Upright Model;
the formal name was Godlike Balance.
Having from the first this inborn beauty,
I added to it fine talents as adornments,
picking river sage and rare angelica to wear,
twisting autumn orchids for a belt.[2]
I hurried on, as though I could never catch up,
fearful that the years would leave me behind.
Mornings I gathered mountain magnolia,
evenings I picked winter grasses on the shoals.
Days and months sped by, never halting;
springs and autumns gave way to each other.
I thought how the grass and trees wither and go bare,
and feared that my Fair One too would grow old.
Hold fast to youth, cast off what is foul!
Why won't you change your ways?
Harness your fine steeds, gallop abroad!
Come, I'll go before you to lead the way.

So pure the virtue of those three ancient lords

---

1. Kao-yang is the divine ancestor of the royal house of Ch'u. *Keng-yin* is the 27th day in the 60-day cycle used for calculating dates; unfortunately, the year of the hero's birth cannot be determined.

2. Here and elsewhere the plant names, usually of aromatic or efficacious plants, are probably intended to represent actual adornments to the hero's dress and at the same time to symbolize his talents and superior moral qualities.

that all fragrant things flocked around them.[3]
With the pepper of Shen they mingled dwarf cinnamon,
had more than mere heliotrope and angelica.
And Yao and Shun, shining in splendor —
they followed the Way, found the right road;
but Chieh and Chou in depravity
hurried by bypaths, stumbling at each step.[4]
Men of that ilk enjoy stolen pleasures,
their road dark and shadowy, peril all around.
It's not that I tremble for my own safety,
I dread the overturn of my lord's carriage!
Swiftly I will run before and behind it
till we find ourselves in the tracks of former kings.
But he fails to perceive my inner feelings;
instead, heeding slander, he turns on me in rage.
My frank counsels bring me only trouble, I know,
but I must endure it, I cannot desist.
I point to the ninth heaven as witness of my uprightness —
all this I do solely for my Godly One.
Once he talked to me in open words,
but later regretted it and took to other ways.
I'm not afraid to be cut off from him,
only sorrow that my Godly One should be so fickle.

In the past I planted nine acres of orchids,
sowed a hundred fields with heliotrope,
set out peonies and cart-halt flowers,
mixed them with asarums and fragrant angelica,
hoping their stems and leaves would flourish and grow firm,
looking for the time when I could reap them.
Though they wither and die, how would that pain me?

3. Yü, T'ang, and Wu, founders of the Hsia, Shang, and Chou dynasties respectively. For easier reading, I have divided the translation into sections on the basis of content, though there are no such divisions in the original poem.

4. Yao and Shun are sage rulers of the time before Yü. Chieh and Chou are the evil last rulers of the Hsia and Shang dynasties respectively.

But I grieve to see these fragrant ones treated like foul weeds.
Others outdo themselves in avarice and greed;
discontent with all they have, they go grasping for more,
indulgent with themselves, expecting others to be the same,
each nursing a heart full of jealousy and spite.
I too race off in pursuit,
but my heart races after different goals.
Old age draws near me step by step
and I fear I will never win a name for goodness.
Mornings I drink the dew that drips from the magnolias,
evenings feed on fallen petals of autumn chrysanthemum.
While my feelings are truly pure and steadfast,
what harm if I grow lank and pale with hunger?
I twine tree roots with angelica,
string them with fallen stamens of cassia,
gather dwarf cinnamon and plait it with heliotrope,
loop it with long long strands of creeper.
I pattern myself on worthy men of long ago,
not the kind the vulgar world applauds.
Though I may not move in harmony with the men of today,
I long to follow the model that P'eng Hsien left us.[5]

With repeated sighs I wipe my tears,
grieved that this life should be so thick with woes.
I do what is just and good, yet they tie and bind me;
I give admonitions at dawn, by evening I am banished.
Banished, I fashion a sash of heliotrope,
add to it angelica I've gathered.
So long as my heart tells me this is right
I will die nine deaths with no regret.
But it wounds me that my Godly One should be so rash and heedless;
never will he look into a person's heart.
His other women envy my moth eyebrows;
gossiping, slandering, they say I love wicked ways.[6]

5. Said to be a shaman ancestor who lived in the Shang dynasty and drowned himself.
Just what P'eng Hsien's "model" is we do not know, though some commentators take it
to mean his suicide.
6. Moth eyebrows are eyebrows shaped like moth antennae, a mark of feminine
beauty. In this passage the hero imagines himself as a beautiful woman.

The clever carpenters who follow the times
reject rule and t-square to fashion their own measure,
turn their back on chalk and line in favor of the crooked,
make accommodation their only rule.
Bitterly downcast in my frustration,
in such times I alone suffer hardship and want.
Better to die at once as a wandering exile —
I could never bear to do what those others do!

The swift-winged bird does not travel with the flock;
from times past this has been so.
How can square and round be made to fit together,
how can those who travel different roads plan for one another?
But to humble the heart and curb the will,
suffer censure, put up with shame,
hold fast to purity and whiteness, die for the right —
this the ancient sages heartily extolled.

Regretting that I had not plotted my course with greater care,
I stood in hesitation, about to turn back.
I wheeled my carriage around, took the old road
before I could go too far in a false direction.
I let my horse amble by orchid-grown marshes,
galloped over pepper hills, rested there awhile.
Advancing, I found no entrance, only met with blame;
retiring, I began to make clothes to my old design,
fashioning water-chestnut and lotus for a coat,
gathering mallows to be my mantle.
Others do not understand me? — let it be;
enough if my motives are in no way foul.
I'll sport a cap that's peaked and towering,
a long sash that dangles and trails,
trimmed and embellished with scent and sparkle,
all of glowing substance, without the slightest flaw.
Suddenly I looked around, letting my eyes wander,
thinking to go and view the four regions,
my belt richly loaded with adornments,
fragrance pouring forth more pungent than before.
Each man has that which he delights in;

for me the love of beauty is my constant concern.
Though my limbs be torn apart, I'll never change;
my heart — how could it be shaken?

Then the Woman, her breath coming in gasps,
chided and berated me again and again.[7]
"Kun in his steadfastness forgot his own safety
and in the end perished on the plain of Yü.[8]
Why be so proud, so fond of beauty?
Why must you alone have such fine adornments?
Thorns and weeds fill the palace chambers now;
why stand aloof and refuse to bend?
Can you go from door to door convincing others?
Will you say to them, 'Look into my heart!'?
If others band together and love their cliques,
why must you stand alone, deaf to my advice?"

But I take the ancient sages as my inner guide.
Sighing, vexed in heart, I went on as before.
Fording the Yüan and Hsiang, I journeyed south,
visited Ch'ung-hua and stated my case.[9]
"Ch'i's Nine Arguments and Nine Songs —
these the Hsia rulers loved, indulging their desires.
They failed to heed danger, to consider the ages to come,
and so Wu-kuan brought contention to the ruling house.[10]
Yi wandered recklessly, too eager for the chase;
he loved to shoot the big foxes.
But wild and disorderly ways seldom end right,

---

7. The identity of the Woman — or Women — is unknown. Early commentators take
it to be an older or younger sister of Ch'ü Yüan, while others interpret it to refer to the
hero's women in waiting. One recent writer has seen it as the voice of the feminine
principle.

8. Kun was the father of Yü, the founder of the Hsia dynasty. He tried unsuccessfully
to combat the floods that his son eventually brought under control, and was put to death
for his failure.

9. The Yüan and Hsiang rivers in Ch'u south of the Yangtze. Ch'ung-hua is another
name for the sage ruler Shun, said to be buried near the Hsiang.

10. Ch'i was a son of Yü, founder of the Hsia dynasty. He visited Heaven and brought
back the pieces of music mentioned here. Wu-kuan was a son of Ch'i.

and Han Cho was there to covet his wife.[11]
Chiao dressed himself in stout armor,
gave way to desires without restraint,
daily losing himself in sport and pleasure,
until his head came tumbling down.[12]
Chieh of the Hsia violated the norms
and thus in the end encountered disaster.
Lord Hsin pickled the flesh of others
and hence the rule of Yin lasted no longer.[13]
T'ang and Yü were solemn, pious, respectful;
Chou expounded the Way and committed no error;
they promoted men of worth, employed the able,
followed the chalk and line without partiality.[14]
August Heaven shows no favoritism;
it sees men's virtue and apportions its aid accordingly.
Only the sages and wise men flourish in action;
they indeed are worthy to rule these lands below.
I have viewed what went before, scrutinized what came after,
observing the standards that guide men's conduct.
Who, if not righteous, can ever rule,
who, if not good, can oversee affairs?
I have placed myself in peril, drawn close to death,
but as I look back at my former ways I have no regret.
Trying to shape a peg without thought for the hole it must fit —
even the ancient worthies met misfortune that way.
I sigh in my gloom and melancholy,
sad that the times I live in are so uncongenial.

---

11. Yi, noted as a skilled archer, usurped power from the Hsia rulers but spent all his time hunting and neglected government affairs. In time the high minister Han Cho had him murdered and married Yi's wife.

12. Chiao was the son of Han Cho and Yi's wife. Though he wielded power for a time, he was overthrown by a prince of the Hsia dynastic line.

13. Lord Hsin is another name for Chou, the evil last ruler of the Shang or Yin dynasty. Pickling the flesh of his associates was only one of the many heinous deeds he is charged with.

14. Chou here is the dynasty founded by the sage kings Wen and Wu to succeed the Shang dynasty, not the last ruler of the Shang, whose name is written with a different character.

Picking tender heliotrope, I wipe away the tears,
tears that wet my collar in wave on wave."

So I knelt on the hem of my robe, pouring out these words —
how patently clear it was that I had acted justly!
Then, yoking four jade dragons to a phoenix carriage,
I rose swiftly on the wind, venturing aloft.
I unchocked my wheels at dawn, set out from Ts'ang-wu;
by evening I had reached the Hanging Gardens.[15]
I wanted to rest awhile by its spirit gates,
but the sun hurried on in its setting.
I ordered Hsi-ho to slacken his pace,
to linger above Yen-tzu and not press on.[16]
Long long the road, distant the journey,
but I must go on searching high and low.
I watered my steeds in the Lake of Hsien,
tied the reins to the Fu-sang tree,
broke a branch from that tree to strike the sun with,
to make him loiter and delay there awhile.[17]
Wang Shu I sent to ride before me,
with Fei Lien racing behind to bring up the rear.[18]
Luan birds went ahead to warn of my coming,
but the Thunder Lord informed me he was not ready yet.
I ordered the phoenixes to fly aloft,
and so we continued morning and night.
Whirlwinds gathered around, clinging together;
with clouds and rainbows trailing, they came in greeting,
joining and parting in wild confusion,
rising and dipping in jumbled array.
I commanded Heaven's porter to open for me,

15. Ts'ang-wu is the region where Ch'ung-hua is buried. The Hanging Gardens are in the K'un-lun Mountains in the far west.

16. Hsi-ho is the charioteer of the sun. Yen-tzu is the mountain where the setting sun enters the earth.

17. The Lake of Hsien is a constellation. The Fu-sang is a tree that grows in the far east, where the sun rises. Some commentators take these to be the actions of Hsi-ho, the charioteer of the sun.

18. Wang Shu is the charioteer of the moon, Fei Lien the lord of the wind.

but he leaned on the gateway and eyed me with scorn.
The day grew darker, drawing to a close;
twining rare orchids, I stood in hesitation.
In this foul and muddy world, heedless of distinctions,
they love to malign beauty, treat it with jealous spite!

In the morning I made ready to cross the White Waters,
then climbed Lang-feng and tethered my horses there.[19]
Suddenly I looked around and tears began to flow —
I sighed that on this high hill there was no woman with me.
In haste I visited the spring temple there,
broke a branch of carnelian to tie to my girdle.
While the flower of youth has not yet faded,
I will seek some modest woman to give it to.
I ordered Feng Lung to ascend the clouds,
to discover the place where Fu-fei dwells.[20]
I doffed my sash to use as pledge for my words,
commanded Chien Hsiu to act as go-between.[21]
First came a flurry of meetings and partings,
then suddenly there was discord, no agreement could be reached.
Evenings the goddess returned to lodge on Ch'iung-shih,
mornings washed her hair in the waters of Wei-p'an.[22]
She guarded her beauty, arrogant and proud,
daily indulging in wanton games.
Lovely as she is, she lacks decorum.
Come, let her be! I'll look somewhere else!

I gazed everywhere, to the end of the four directions,

19. The White Waters is one of the four rivers that flow out of the K'un-lun Mountains, each of a different color; later we will encounter the Red Waters. Lang-feng is a peak in the K'un-lun range.

20. Feng Lung is a god of the rain and thunder. Fu-fei is the lovely goddess of the Lo River.

21. Chien Hsiu has been identified by commentators as a minister of the mythological ruler Fu Hsi, Fu-fei's father. The name means "Lame Beauty" and Hawkes speculates that it is a kenning for Nü Kua, a goddess with a snake's body who is associated with marriages.

22. These place names appear to be associated with the K'un-lun region. Some commentators take the hero himself to be the subject of these two lines rather than the goddess.

circled the bounds of heaven and then descended,
surveyed the steep heights of Jasper Terrace
and there spied a lovely daughter of the land of Sung.[23]
I dispatched the falcon to be my matchmaker
but he reported that she was not beautiful at all.[24]
Then the grosbeak set off to cry my message —
I hated the glib and clever way he chattered.
In my mind I was doubtful, undecided,
wanting to go myself, though I knew that wouldn't do.
The phoenixes had already accepted marriage gifts —
I feared that Kao Hsin had gotten there before me.[25]
I wanted to fly far away, but there was nowhere to rest;
I wandered distractedly, never pausing.
If Shao K'ang has not wedded them,
perhaps I could linger with the two fair ladies of Yü,[26]
but my pleaders are ineffectual, my matchmakers clumsy —
I fear the talks would never reach accord.
The world is foul and muddy, envious of worth;
it delights in maligning beauty, praises ugliness instead.
Deep within his palace chambers
the wise king slumbers and will not wake.
I must hold back my thoughts and not speak out,
yet how can I go on like this forever?

I gathered bindweed, bamboo slips for divination,
commissioned Ling Fen to tell my fortune.[27]
"Two beautiful ones are certain to come together," he said.

23. Chien Ti, ancestress of the rulers of the Shang dynasty. She was confined to a tower but became pregnant when she ate the egg of a swallow sent to her by Ti K'u, the ancestor of the Shang.

24. The bird translated "falcon" is the *chen*, noted for the deadly poison contained in its feathers. Commentators, ignoring the question of why the hero should choose such an inappropriate creature to press his love suit, assert that it functions here as a symbol for slandering and sycophantic ministers.

25. Kao Hsin is another name for Ti K'u in note 23 above.

26. Shao K'ang is the prince of the Hsia dynasty who overthrew Chiao in note 12 above. He obtained employment with the lord of Yü and married the lord's two daughters.

27. Ling Fen is identified as an ancient expert in divination. Stalks were bound together and then broken to perform the divination.

"Who is truly fair and yet lacks admirers?
Consider the breadth and vastness of these Nine Provinces —[28]
why should you think of those women only?
Dare to range farther afield, put off doubt —
who in search of beauty would pass you by?
What region is without its fragrant grasses?
Why must you pine for your old land?"
But the age is benighted, blinded and confused;
who claims it can discern the good and bad in me?
People may differ in likes and dislikes,
but these cliquish ones — they're a breed apart!
Each one sports mugwort stuffed in his waist
and avers that rare orchids are not fit to wear.
If they're so blind in their discernment of plants,
how could they gage the worth of precious gems?
They scoop up rotten earth to fill their scent bags
and claim that the pepper of Shen lacks aroma.

I wanted to trust Ling Fen's auspicious augury,
but in my mind I was hesitant and uncertain.
The Shaman Hsien was to descend at evening,
so I wrapped pepper and rice balls and went to greet him.[29]
A hundred spirits hovered over, descending in escort,
Nine Peak Mountain loomed up, welcoming him as well.[30]
Blazing in august brightness, he sent forth his godly light,
then cited for me these propitious lessons from the past:
"Take care to search for her high and low;
look for one who shares your standards and norms.
T'ang and Yü with due gravity sought for companions,
and Yi Yin and Kao Yao were able to gratify their desires.[31]

28. The nine provinces of ancient China and, by extension, the world at large.

29. Wu Hsien or Shaman Hsien is one of ten ancient shamans who live on a holy mountain in the west, from which they descend at times.

30. Nine Peak Mountain, sometimes translated Nine Doubt Mountain, is the burial place of the sage ruler Shun.

31. Yi Yin and Kao Yao were chief ministers to the sage rulers T'ang and Yü respectively. Here and below the acquisition of an able minister is being likened to the finding of a suitable mate.

If your inner feelings are true and beautiful,
what need have you for matchmakers?
Fu Yüeh labored pounding earth at Fu-yen
yet Wu Ting employed him and had no misgivings.[32]
Lü Wang wielded a butcher's knife
but when he met Wen of Chou he was raised to high office.[33]
Ning Ch'i sang his songs of complaint;
Duke Huan of Ch'i heard him and made him his aide.[34]
Act now, while the years are still before you,
while time has not yet run out.
Quickly, before the nightjar sounds his autumn note
and the hundred grasses have lost their fragrance!"

How rich the rare jewels I wear at my sash,
but the crowd conspires to darken and conceal them.
Among such partisans, none can be trusted;
I fear in their envy they'll smash my treasures.
The times are discordant, too easily they shift —
how can I linger any longer?
Orchid and angelica have changed and lost their fragrance,
sweet flag and heliotrope have turned to mere grass.
Why have the fragrant plants of bygone days
now all gone to common mugwort and wormwood?
How could it be for any other reason?
The fault's that no one cares for beauty!
I thought that orchid could be trusted,
but he proved to have no substance, nothing but boasts.[35]
He spurns beauty to run with the crowd,
yet expects to be ranked with the fragrant ones.

32. The Shang ruler Wu Ting dreamed of a worthy minister and had a picture painted of him so messengers could be sent throughout the country to search for the man in the picture. He was found in the person of Fu Yüeh, a laborer at Fu-yen who was pounding earth to make walls.

33. Lü Wang worked as a butcher before he was discovered by King Wen, one of the founders of the Chou dynasty, and made his chief minister.

34. Ning Ch'i was a merchant, and for a time an ox herder, when Duke Huan of Ch'i (r. 685-43 B.C.), one of the leading feudal rulers of the Chou period, heard his song of complaint and raised him to office.

35. Commentators have attempted to identify "orchid," "pepper," and the other plants censured in this passage with persons at the Ch'u court, though with little evidence to go on.

Pepper is all flattery and insolence,
and even prickly ash thinks he can fill a scent bag!
They strive to advance, work to gain admittance,
but what fragrance are they fit to offer?
Yet such, to be sure, is the current of the times —
who can fail to be affected?
If I see pepper and orchid behaving thus,
what can I expect from cart-halt and river sage?
Only this girdle of mine is worthy of respect;
others scorn its beauty, but I go on as before.
Its teeming fragrance never falters,
its aroma to this day has yet to fade.
I will compose myself, think of my own pleasure,
go rambling once more in search of a mate.
Now while my adornments are at their finest
I'll seek her through every land high and low.

Ling Fen had already told me his auspicious augury;
I would choose a lucky day and commence my journey.
I broke a branch of carnelian to serve as food,
pounded carnelian fragments to make rations for the road.
I had flying dragons to draw my vehicle,
a carriage inlaid with jasper and ivory.
How could I band with those of different mind?
I would go far away, remove myself from them.
I turned my course toward the K'un-lun Mountains,
over distant roads rambling on and on,
hoisting clouds and rainbows to shield me from the sun,
sounding the tinkle of jeweled carriage bells.
In the morning I set off from the Ford of Heaven,[36]
by evening I had reached the westernmost limit.
Phoenixes reverently bore my banners,
soaring and dipping in solemn flight.
Suddenly my route took me to the Flowing Sands;
I traced the Red Waters, ambling at my ease.[37]

36. A constellation in the eastern portion of the sky.

37. The name Flowing Sands probably refers to the desert areas north and west of China; on the Red Waters, see note 19 above.

I beckoned dragons and horned dragons to bridge the ford for me,
commanding the Western Sovereign to let me pass over.[38]
But the trail was long and rank with dangers
so I summoned a host of carriages to come and attend me.
Passing Pu-chou Mountain, I veered to the left,[39]
pointing to the western sea as our destination.
I marshalled my chariots, a thousand in number,
their jeweled hubs aligned as they raced side by side,
my eight dragons drawing me, writhing and turning,
my cloud pennants fluttering and streaming on high.
I tried to curb my will, to slacken my pace,
but my spirit soared upward into distant regions.
I played the Nine Songs, danced the Shao music, [40]
stealing a brief day for enjoyment.
But as I ascended the bright reaches of heaven,
suddenly I looked down and saw my old home.
My groom was filled with sadness, and the horses in their longing
pulled about in the reins and refused to go on.

Luan[41]

It's over! In this land there's no one, no one who knows me!
Why must I long for my old city?
Since there's no one I can join with in administering just rule,
I will seek out P'eng Hsien in the place where he dwells.[42]

38. The Western Sovereign is the mythical ruler Shao Hao, who in Chinese cosmology presides over the western direction.

39. Pu-chou Mountain serves as a pillar holding up heaven in the northwest sector. When Kung Kung, contending for power with the mythical ruler Chuan Hsü, butted his head against the mountain in rage, he caused heaven to tilt toward the northwest and the earth to sag in the opposite direction.

40. The Nine Songs of Ch'i; see note 10 above.

41. *Luan* appears to have been a musical term designating the concluding section of a musical selection. Here and in other works that imitate the *Li Sao* it denotes a reprise or summation of the poem.

42. Since P'eng Hsien is supposed to have committed suicide by drowning, commentators have traditionally taken the last line to refer to the hero's determination to do likewise. Ch'u culture abounds in legends of persons who drowned themselves in a river and thereafter became the tutelary deity of the river, and the hero of the *Li Sao* perhaps hopes for a similar apotheosis.

CHAPTER THREE

Early Songs, Poems in Rhyme-Prose Form, and *Yüeh-fu* Ballads

THOUGH the rule of the Chou dynasty nominally lasted until 249 B.C., the Chou kings had many centuries earlier ceased to wield any real power, being permitted to retain the title of Son of Heaven only because of the ritual and religious significance of their role. Actual power was in the hands of the larger feudal states, which vied to expand their territories and gain mastery over the empire. One of them, the state of Ch'in in the west, eventually succeeded in conquering its rivals and abolishing the last traces of Chou sovereignty. In 221 B.C., the Ch'in king proclaimed the founding of a new dynasty, the Ch'in, with himself as First Emperor.

The harsh measures that the Ch'in employed to suppress opposition and bring unity to the nation were said to have aroused widespread hatred, and the new dynasty, that was to have lasted for ten thousand years, barely outlived its founder. His son and heir, the Second Emperor, was summarily overthrown, and in 206 B.C., another dynasty known as the Han was founded. A brief period of dynastic eclipse divides the life of the dynasty into two parts, the Former or Western Han (206 B.C. to A.D. 8), when the capital was at Ch'ang-an, and the Later or Eastern Han (A.D. 25 to 220), when the capital was moved east to Lo-yang.

Literature and learning flourished during the Han's long years of relative peace and stability, encouraged by the founding of a state university and the beginnings of the famed civil service examination system. In the field of poetry, much energy went into the writing of long descriptive works in the *fu* or rhyme-prose form, many of them ornate depictions of imperial hunts or outings or of the Han capitals written for the delectation of the rulers. Two examples, shorter and more personal in tone, are included in my selection, the "Rhyme-Prose on the Owl," a Taoist-minded meditation on death, and the lament of an imperial concubine fallen from favor.

Shorter works of a lyrical nature were often cast in the song form that derived from the "Nine Songs" of the *Ch'u Tz'u,* using a six- or seven-character line broken in the middle by the breathing particle *hsi.* To give a famous example, in 202 B.C., when Hsiang Yü, the military leader who had challenged the founder of the Han for control of the empire, was surrounded by his enemies and faced certain defeat, he is said to have composed the following song in farewell to his horse Dapple and his beautiful companion, Lady Yü:

> My strength plucked up the hills,
>   my might shadowed the world.
> But the times were against me
>   and Dapple runs no more.
> When Dapple runs no more,
>   what then can I do?
> Ah Yü, my Yü,
>   what will your fate be?

The victor in the struggle for power, Liu Pang, the founder and first emperor of the Han, writing in a very different vein, composed the following poem in song style in 196 B.C. when he visited his native village in his old age and reflected upon his accomplishments:

> A great wind came forth,
>   the clouds rose on high.
> Now that my might rules all within the seas,
>   I have returned to my old village.
> Where will I find brave men
>   to guard the four corners of my land?

The selection that follows includes two other examples of works in the song style, one by Liu Pang's descendant, Liu Ch'e or Emperor Wu of the Han, the other by a princess whose sad fate it was to become a pawn in the game of Han diplomacy.

Most of these works in song style are preserved in histories of the period where, as the examples above suggest, they are given a specific historical context and assigned to a known author. Quite different in nature are the poems that follow these in my selection, anonymous folk songs attributed to the Han period that are referred to by the term *yüeh-fu.* These works take their name from a government office called the Yüeh-fu or Music Bureau that was set up around 120 B.C. by Emperor Wu. One of its duties was to collect folk songs from various parts of the empire, and hence the term *yüeh-fu* came to be used to designate such early folk songs.

Whether the ballads we have today are the actual songs collected by the Music Bureau we cannot say, though they seem to be genuine folk songs of the early period and reflect the lives and hardships of the common people. Some use lines of irregular length, perhaps because they were written to fit tunes imported from Central Asia. Others are predominantly or entirely in five-character or seven-character lines, and thus indistinguishable in form from the type of *shih* poetry we will be examining in the following chapters. In later times, poets often wrote imitations of the early *yüeh-fu* ballads, treating the old themes but embellishing them according to their fancy. Such *yüeh-fu* imitations are usually in regular meter and, unlike the original ballads, were not intended to be sung.

The last poem in my selection, the long narrative work entitled "Southeast the Peacock Flies," is not customarily classified as a *yüeh-fu* ballad, but I have included it here because of its anonymous authorship and balladlike character.

ANONYMOUS

Ground-Thumping Song

(Reputed to be a song of very early times sung by peasant elders as they beat on the ground to keep time. Irregular.)

When the sun comes up we work,
when the sun goes down we rest.
We dig a well to drink,
plow the fields to eat —
the Emperor and his might — what are they to us!

CHIA YI *(201–169* B.C.*)*

Rhyme-Prose on the Owl

(Written in 174 or 173 B.C., this is the earliest poem in *fu* or rhyme-prose form whose authorship and date of composition are reasonably certain. The poet, a scholar-official, had been banished to a minor post in Ch'ang-sha in the south and was suffering from depression and ill health. When a hoot-owl one day flew into his lodge and perched on a corner of his mat, he took the occurrence as an omen of impending death and composed the following poem to console himself.)

In the year *tan-o,*
fourth month, first month of summer,
the day *kuei-tzu,* when the sun was low in the west,
an owl came to my lodge
and perched on the corner of my mat,
phlegmatic and fearless.

Secretly wondering the reason
the strange thing had come to roost,
I took out a book to divine it
and the oracle told me its secret:
    "Wild bird enters the hall;
    the master will soon depart."
I asked and importuned the owl,
"Where is it I must go?
Do you bring good luck? Then tell me!
Misfortune? Relate what disaster!
Must I depart so swiftly?
Then speak to me of the hour!"
The owl breathed a sigh,
raised its head and beat its wings.
Its beak could utter no word,
but let me tell you what it sought to say:
All things alter and change,
never a moment of ceasing,
revolving, whirling, and rolling away,
driven far off and returning again,
form and breath passing onward,
like the mutations of a cicada.
Profound, subtle, illimitable,
who can finish describing it?
Good luck must be followed by bad,
bad in turn bow to good.
Sorrow and joy throng the gate,
weal and woe in the same land.
Wu was powerful and great;
under Fu-ch'a it sank in defeat.
Yüeh was crushed at K'uai-chi,
but Kou-chien made it an overlord.
Li Ssu, who went forth to greatness, at last
suffered the five mutilations.
Fu Yüeh was sent into bondage,

yet Wu Ting made him his aide.[1]
Thus fortune and disaster
entwine like the strands of a rope.
Fate cannot be told of,
for who shall know its ending?
Water, troubled, runs wild;
the arrow, quick-sped, flies far.
All things, whirling and driving,
compelling and pushing each other, roll on.
The clouds rise up, the rains come down,
in confusion inextricably joined.
The Great Potter fashions all creatures,
infinite, boundless, limit unknown.
There is no reckoning Heaven,
nor divining beforehand the Tao.
The span of life is fated;
man cannot guess its ending.
Heaven and earth are the furnace,
the workman, the Creator;
his coal is the yin and yang,
his copper, all things of creation.
Joining, scattering, ebbing and flowing,
where is there persistence or rule?
A thousand, a myriad mutations,
lacking an end's beginning.
Suddenly they form a man:
how is this worth taking thought of?
They are transformed again in death:
should this perplex you?
The witless takes pride in his being,
scorning others, a lover of self.
The man of wisdom sees vastly

1. Wu and Yüeh were rival states in the southeast during Chou times, and Fu-ch'a and Kou-chien the rulers who led them to defeat and glory respectively. Li Ssu, prime minister to the First Emperor of the Ch'in, later fell from favor and was executed. Wu Ting was a ruler of the Shang dynasty who dreamed of a worthy minister and later discovered the man of his dream in an ex-convict laborer, Fu Yüeh.

and knows that all things will do.
The covetous run after riches,
the impassioned pursue a fair name;
the proud die struggling for power,
while the people long only to live.
Each drawn and driven onward,
they hurry east and west.
The great man is without bent;
a million changes are as one to him.
The stupid man chained to custom
suffers like a prisoner bound.
The sage abandons things
and joins himself to the Tao alone,
but the multitudes in delusion
with desire and hate load their hearts.
Limpid and still, the true man
finds peace in the Tao alone.
Discarding wisdom, forgetful of form,
transcendent, destroying self,
vast and empty, swift and wild,
he soars on wings of the Tao.
Borne on the flood he sails forth;
he rests on the river islets.
Freeing his body to Fate,
unpartaking of self,
his life is a floating,
his death a rest.
In stillness like the stillness of deep springs,
like an unmoored boat drifting aimlessly,
never looking on life as a treasure,
he embraces and drifts with Nothing.
Comprehending Fate and free of sorrow,
the man of virtue heeds no bounds.
Petty matters, weeds and thorns —
what are they to me?

LIU CH'E, EMPEROR WU OF THE HAN *(157–87 B.C.)*

Song of the Autumn Wind

(Song style)

Autumn wind rises,
　white clouds fly,
plants, trees yellow and shed their leaves,
　wild geese go south again.
The orchid has its beauty,
　the chrysanthemum its scent;
I long for my lovely one,
　powerless to forget.
We launch the towered boat,
　cross the Fen River,
cutting through the current,
　stirring up white waves.
Pipes and drums echo,
　oarsmen's songs ring out.
When joy is at its highest,
　sad thoughts run rife —
youth and strength, how short they last,
　how hopelessly we age!

ANONYMOUS

Song of Sorrow

(Around 107 B.C. Liu Hsi-chün, the daughter of a prince of the Han imperial family who had plotted revolt and committed suicide, was given the title of princess and sent to be the bride of the aging chieftain of the Wu-sun, a nomadic tribe living northwest of China with whom the Han dynasty wished to establish friendly relations. She is said to have composed the following song to express her grief. Song style.)

My family has married me
in this far corner of the world,
sent me to a strange land,
to the king of the Wu-sun.
A yurt is my chamber,
felt my walls,
flesh my only food,
kumiss to drink.
My thoughts are all of my homeland,
my heart aches within.
Oh to be the yellow crane
winging home again!

PAN CHIEH-YÜ *(1st cen.* B.C.*)*

Poem in Rhyme-Prose Form

(Lady Pan, a favorite concubine of Emperor Ch'eng (r. 32–7 B.C.), is known by
her court title *Chieh-yü* or Beautiful Companion, her personal name being un-
known. She bore the emperor two sons but both died in infancy. Later, when she
lost favor and was slandered by rivals, she asked permission to take up residence in
the eastern palace, the Palace of Lasting Trust, where she waited on the empress
dowager. In the following untitled poem in *fu* form, she gives vent to her sadness.)

Virtue of ancestors handed down
bestowed on me precious life as a human being,
allowed me, humble creature, to ascend to the palace,
to fill a lower rank in the women's quarters.
I enjoyed the holy sovereign's most generous grace,
basked in the radiance of sun and moon.
Burning rays of redness shone on me,
I was granted highest favor in the Tseng-ch'eng Lodge.
Already receiving blessings beyond what I deserved,
I yet ventured to hope for more happy times,
sighing repeatedly, waking or asleep,

undoing my girdle strings with thoughts of the past.[1]
I spread out paintings of women, made them my mirror,
looked to my instructress, queried her on the *Odes;*
I was moved by the warning of the woman who crows,
pained at the sins of the lovely Pao-ssu;
I praised Huang and Ying, wives of the lord of Yü,
admired Jen and Ssu, mothers of Chou.[2]
Though I'm foolish and uncouth, no match for these,
would I dare turn my thoughts away, let them be forgotten?
The years pass in sorrow and apprehension;
I grieve for lush flowers that no longer flourish,[3]
weep for the Yang-lu Hall, Hall of the Wild Mulberry,[4]
babes in swaddling clothes who met with woe.
Surely it was due to no error of mine!
Heaven's decrees — can they never be changed?
Before I knew it, the bright sun had veiled its light,
leaving me in the dusk of evening,
but still the ruler's kindness sustains and shelters me;
in spite of faults, I have not been cast off.
I serve the empress dowager in her eastern palace,
take my place among lesser maids in the Palace of Lasting Trust;
I help to sprinkle and sweep among the curtains,
and shall do so till death brings my term to a close.
Then may my bones find rest at the foot of the hill,
a little shade of pine and cypress left over for my grave.

Recapitulation:
Hidden in the black palace, gloomy and chill,

1. When a girl was about to be married, her father fastened the strings of her girdle and gave her words of instruction and warning; Lady Pan is recalling that time.

2. A hen that crows at dawn in place of the rooster is an ancient symbol for a domineering woman; the specific reference here is to Ta-chi, concubine of the evil last ruler of the Shang dynasty. The beautiful but treacherous Pao-ssu brought about the downfall of King Yu of the Chou. O-huang and Nü-ying were daughters of the sage ruler Yao; he gave them in marriage to his successor to the throne Shun, the lord of Yü. T'ai-jen and T'ai-ssu were the mothers of kings Wen and Wu respectively, the founders of the Chou dynasty. Most of these women are mentioned in the *Book of Odes* and were no doubt depicted in the paintings that Lady Pan was perusing for her instruction.

3. The flowers are her own fading youth and beauty.

4. The halls are the places where she bore her two sons.

main gates bolted, gates to inner quarters barred,
dust in the painted hall, moss on marble stairs,
courtyards rank with green grass growing,
spacious rooms shadowy, curtains dark,
chamber windows gaping, wind sharp and cold,
blowing my skirts, stirring their crimson gauze,
flapping, rustling them, making the silk sound.
My spirit roams far off to places secret and still;
since my lord departed, who finds joy in me?
I look down at red flagstones, remembering how he trod them,
look up at cloudy rafters, two streams of tears flowing;
then I turn to left and right, my expression softening,
dip the winged wine cup to drive away care.
I reflect that man, born into this world,
passes as swiftly as though floating on a stream.
Already I've known fame and eminence,
the finest gifts the living can enjoy.
I will strive to please my spirit, taste every delight,
since true happiness cannot be counted on.
"Green Robe" — "White Flower" — in ancient times as now.[5]

Song of Regret

(The poem is of uncertain date, though it has traditionally been attributed to Lady Pan. *Yüeh-fu* style, 5-ch.)

To begin I cut fine silk of Ch'i,
white and pure as frost or snow,
shape it to make a paired-joy fan,
round, round as the luminous moon,

5. The song in the *Odes* entitled "Green Robe," no. 27, is said to describe a wife whose place has been usurped by concubines; "White Flower," no. 229, is traditionally interpreted as censuring King Yu of the Chou for putting aside his consort Queen Shen in favor of the evil Pao-ssu. Lady Pan compares herself to these unfortunate women of antiquity.

to go in and out of my lord's breast;
when lifted, to stir him a gentle breeze.
But always I dread the coming of autumn,
cold winds that scatter the burning heat,
when it will be laid away in the hamper,
love and favor cut off midway.

ANONYMOUS

Dew on the Leek

(*yüeh-fu,* irregular)

Dew on the leek,
how quickly it dries!
Dew that dries
will fall again tomorrow,
but a man once dead and gone —
when will he come again?

The Graveyard

(*yüeh-fu,* irregular)

The graveyard — who makes his home in that land?
Gathered ghosts, wise and foolish alike.
Lord of spirits, why must you hurry us so!
Man's life allows not a moment of lingering.

By Heaven!

(*yüeh-fu,* irregular)

By Heaven!
I will be your comrade,
and may our friendship never fail.
When mountains have no peaks
and rivers run dry,
when thunder rolls in winter
and summer snow falls —
only then will I desert you!

They Fought South of the Wall

(*yüeh-fu,* irregular)

They fought south of the wall,
died north of the outworks,
lie dead in the fields unburied,
fine food for the crows.
Tell the crows for me,
weep for these strangers!
Dead in the field, if no one buries them,
how can their rotting flesh hope to escape you?
Waters are deep, swift and strong,
rushes and reed banks cluster darkly;
the brave horsemen have fought and died,
their weary mounts wander here and there, neighing.
On the bridge they built sentry huts —
how could we go south? how could we go north?
And if we do not gather in the grain and millet,
what will our lord have to eat?
We want to be loyal subjects, but what can we do?

I think of you, good subjects,
good subjects, how I remember —
at dawn you set off to battle;
night fell, but you never came back.

Sad Song

(*yüeh-fu*, irregular)

Can a sad song take the place of crying?
Can peering in the distance take the place of going home?
I think with longing of the old village,
my spirits downcast, fretful and forlorn.
I want to go home but there's no one there,
I want to cross the river but there is no boat —
thoughts in my heart I can find no words for,
like cartwheels going round in my belly!

There's Someone I Think Of

(*yüeh-fu*, irregular)

There's someone I think of
and he's south by the great sea.
What shall I send you?
Tortoiseshell hairpins[1] with a pair of pearls;
I'll use a jeweled cord to tie them.
But I hear you've set your heart on someone else
so I break, I smash, I burn them.
I smash and burn them

1. Men used hairpins to fasten their cap to their topknot.

and fling the ashes to the wind.
From now on I will not think of you,
my thoughts of you are all ended!
Cocks crow, dogs bark,
my older brother and his wife will know of this!
Ai-yah!
The autumn wind moans and moans,
the falcon flies swiftly.
In a moment the east will brighten and then they will know!

At Fifteen I Went Off to the Army

(*yüeh-fu*, 5-ch.)

At fifteen I went off to the army;
I was eighty when they let me come home.
Along the road I met a villager,
asked him, "Who's left at my homestead?"
"Look there — there's your homestead!" —
pine and cypress growing by a heap of graves.
Rabbits came in through the dog holes,
pheasants flew down from the rafters.
In the courtyard, grain was growing that had seeded itself,
by the well were self-sown mallows.
I pounded the grain to make some gruel,
picked the mallows and made soup,
but when the soup and gruel were ready,
I couldn't think who to give them to.
I went out the gate, gazing eastward,
tears falling, wetting my clothes.

Southeast the Peacock Flies

(A brief preface of unknown date states that the following poem, which concerns a government clerk of Lu-chiang in Anhwei named Chiao Chung-ch'ing and his young wife Liu Lan-chih, is based on an actual event that took place in the Chien-an era [196–220]. 5-ch. *shih*.)

Southeast the peacock flies,
and every five li it hesitates in flight.

"At thirteen I knew how to weave plain silk,
at fourteen I learned to cut clothes;
at fifteen I played the many-stringed lute,
at sixteen recited from the *Odes* and *Documents*.
At seventeen I became your wife,
but in my heart there was always sorrow and pain.
You were a clerk in the government office,
I guarded my virtue and was never untrue.
At cockcrow I began my work at the loom,
night after night never resting.
In three days I turned out five measures of cloth,
but the Great One[1] grumbled at my slowness.
It's not that I'm so slow at weaving,
but it's hard to be a bride in your home.
The work is more than I can cope with —
what use in my staying any longer?
So I beg of your honored mother,
let her send me away at once!"

When the clerk heard this,
he ascended the hall, addressed his mother:
"Your son is blessed with little fortune,
but luckily I've found this wife.
From the time we bound our hair,[2] we've shared pillow and mat,
and we'll go together to the Yellow Springs.[3]
But it's scarcely been two or three years,

1. The groom's mother.
2. Men bound up their hair at 20, women at 15, as a sign they had reached maturity.
3. The land of the dead.

no time at all since we married.
There's nothing wrong in the woman's conduct —
why do you treat her so harshly?"

His mother said to the clerk,
"How can you be so foolish and doting!
This wife knows nothing of propriety,
her actions are selfish and willful.
For a long time I've found her infuriating —
how dare you try to have your own way!
The family east of us have a virtuous daughter —
Ch'in Lo-fu is her name,
beautiful in form, no one to rival her —
your mother will arrange it for you.
This other must be sent away at once.
Send her off and don't dare detain her!"

The clerk, humbly kneeling, replied,
"I beg to say this to my mother,
if this wife of mine is sent away,
till death I will never have another!"
His mother, hearing this,
pounded on her chair in a fit of rage.
"Little one, have you no caution?
How dare you speak up for your wife!
I've wasted kindness enough on her already —
you'll never have my permission for this!"
The clerk was silent, unspeaking;
he bowed once more, then returned to his room,
started to tell his wife what had happened
but sobs choked him till he couldn't speak.
"I'm not the one who's sending you away —
my mother forces me to it.
Just go home for a little while.
I must report to my office,
but before long I will return
and then I will surely come and fetch you.

Let these words of mine calm your fears,
take care and do not disobey them!"

The young wife said to the clerk,
"No more of this muddling talk!
Once in the past, in early spring,
I left my family, came to your noble gate,
did all I could to serve your honored mother —
when was I ever willful in my ways?
Day and night I kept at my duties,
though ache and exhaustion wrapped me around.
I know of no fault or error of mine —
I strove only to repay the great debt I owe her.
And now I'm being driven away —
how can you speak of my coming again?
I have an embroidered vest
so lovely it shines with a light of its own.
I have double bed curtains of scarlet gauze
with scent bags hanging from each of the four corners.
I have boxes and hampers, sixty or seventy,
tied with cords of green and turquoise and blue.
Each is a little different from the rest,
and in them are articles of all kinds.
But if a person is lowly, her things too must be worthless —
they would never do for the one who comes after.
But I leave them so they may be used for gifts.
From now on we won't be meeting again —
look at them sometimes if it should please you,
and over the long years, do not forget me!"

Cocks crowed, outside the dawn was breaking;
the wife rose, dressing herself with care,
put on her lined embroidered skirt,
going through each motion four or five times.
On her feet she wore silken shoes,
on her head shone a tortoiseshell comb;
round her waist she wrapped some flowing white gauze,
in her ears fastened moon-bright pearls.

Her fingers were slim as scallion roots,
her mouth as though lined with vermilion or cinnabar.
Lithely she walked, with delicate steps,
in loveliness unequalled in all the world.
She ascended the hall, knelt before the mother;
the mother agreed to let her go, did nothing to stop her.
"In the past when I was a child,
being born and bred in the countryside,
I had no proper training or instruction,
and added to my disgrace by entering your noble family.
I've received from you numerous coins and bolts of cloth,
yet have never succeeded in serving you well.
Today I go back to my old home,
though I fear my departure may leave your household short-
　　handed."
Then she went to take leave of her little sister-in-law,
tears falling like strands of pearls.
"When I first came here as a bride,
you could barely stand up by holding to the bed,
yet today, when I'm being sent away,
you're fully as tall as me!
Be diligent, take good care of your mother,
and look out for yourself as well.
When the seventh and the twenty-ninth come round,
remember the games and good times we had together."[4]
Then she went out the gate, mounted the carriage and left,
her tears falling in a hundred streams or more.

The clerk had ridden off on horseback,
the wife set out later by carriage;
bump-bump, rumble-rumble went the wheels,
when the two chanced to meet at the entrance to the highway.
The clerk dismounted, climbed into the carriage,
lowered his head and spoke into her ear,

4. On the 7th and 29th days of the month, women were allowed to rest from their work. Some commentators take the 7th to refer to the festival of the Herdboy and the Weaving Maiden held on the night of the 7th day of the 7th month, when girls prayed for skill in weaving and needlework. See p. 100.

"I swear I will never leave you —
only go home for a little while.
I must be off to the government office
but before long I will be back.
I swear to Heaven I won't be untrue!"

The young wife said to the clerk,
"I am grateful for your kind concern.
If indeed you think so much of me,
I may hope you will come before long.
You must be like the solid boulder,
I like a rush or a reed.
Rushes and reeds can be strong as well as pliant,
just so the boulder does not move.
But I have a father and older brother
with tempers as violent as thunder.
I doubt they will let me have my way —
just thinking of it makes my heart blanch!"
They lifted their hands in endless endearments,
two souls bound by a single longing.

Through the gate, into her house went the young wife,
not knowing how to face her family.
Her mother slapped her palms together:
"I never expected *this* child to return!
At thirteen I taught you to weave,
at fourteen you knew how to cut clothes;
at fifteen you played the many-stringed lute,
at sixteen understood the rules of decorum.
At seventeen I sent you to be a bride,
thinking you would never betray your vows.
But now, if you haven't committed some fault,
why have you come home unsummoned?"
Lan-chih was ashamed before her mother,
"Truly, I've done nothing wrong!"
and her mother felt great pity for her.

When she had been home ten days or so,

the magistrate sent his matchmaker:
"It concerns the magistrate's third son,
a handsomer young man nowhere in the world,
just turned eighteen or nineteen,
clever in speech, a boy of many talents —"
The mother said to her daughter,
"Here is a proposal worth answering!"
But her daughter, tear-choked, replied,
"When I came home this time,
the clerk pleaded with me again and again,
and we made a vow that we'd never part.
Today if I went against those feelings,
I fear nothing lucky could come of it!
Let us break off these negotiations,
or say we need time to think it over slowly."
The mother informed the matchmaker,
"This child of our poor and humble home
has just been sent back from her first marriage.
If she wasn't fit to be the wife of a clerk,
how could she be suitable for a magistrate's son?
I beg you to make inquiries elsewhere —
we could never give our consent."

A few days after the matchmaker left,
an aide came from the governor with a like request,
saying that Lan-chih's family
for generations had served as officials,
that the governor's fifth son,
a favorite child, was as yet unmarried,
that the aide had been sent as go-between,
had come with a secretary to open discussions.
"In the governor's family," he reported,
"there's this fine young gentleman —
they wish to conclude a marriage alliance
and hence have sent me to your honored house."
The mother apologized to the matchmaker:

"My daughter has given her word elsewhere —
what can an old woman like me say?"

When Lan-chih's older brother heard of this,
he was troubled and angry in heart.
He went and said to his little sister,
"How thoughtless a way to plan things!
Formerly you were married to a clerk,
now you could marry this gentleman.
Your lot would be as different as heaven from earth —
you could assure yourself of a brilliant future!
If you do not marry this fine gentleman,
how do you intend to get along?"
Lan-chih lifted her head and answered,
"What you say is quite reasonable, brother.
I left my family, went to serve a husband,
but midway came back to my brother's house.
Your wishes should rule in this matter —
how could I hope to have my way?
Though the clerk and I made our promises,
I seem fated never to see him again.
Let us give our consent at once
and get on with the marriage arrangements."

The matchmaker got down from his seat,
with "Yes, yes," and then "Fine, fine!"
He returned and reported to the governor,
"Your servant has carried out his task —
the talks have ended in splendid agreement."
When the governor heard this,
his heart was filled with delight.
He looked at the calendar, consulted his books,
decided that this month was just right.
"The six accords are right now in agreement,[5]
the thirtieth is an auspicious day.
Today is already the twenty-seventh —

5. The "six accords" may refer to the positions of the sun, moon, and four stars in the Big Dipper, though the meaning is uncertain.

go again and arrange the wedding!"

Talks were held, preparations rushed,
unceasing bustle like streams of floating clouds.
Green sparrow and white goose boats,
dragon pennants at their four corners
fluttering gracefully in the wind,
golden carriages with jade-trimmed wheels,
dapple-gray horses stepping slowly,
gold-threaded saddles with colored pompons,
a wedding gift of three million cash,
all the coins strung on green cords,
three hundred bolts of cloth in assorted hues,
rare seafoods purchased in Chiao and Kuang,[6]
attendants, four or five hundred,
all setting out in droves from the governor's gate.
The mother said to her daughter,
"You have received the governor's letter.
Tomorrow they will come to fetch you —
why aren't you making the clothes you'll need?
Don't go and spoil things now!"
The daughter was silent, unspeaking,
her handkerchief muffling her sobs,
her tears coming down in cascades.
She moved her crystal-studded couch,
placed it in front of the window,
in her left hand took her knife and ruler,
in her right hand held her satins and gauzes.
By morning she had finished her lined embroidered skirt,
by evening she had finished her unlined gauze jacket,
and as the day wore away and darkness fell,
with somber thoughts she went out the gate weeping.

When the clerk heard of this change in matters,
he asked leave to go home for a while,
and when he was still two or three li away,

6. The provinces of Chiao-chou and Kuang-chou on the far southern seacoast.

his weary horse began to neigh sadly.
The young wife recognized the horse's neigh,
stepped into her shoes, went out in greeting,
peering into the distance anxiously,
and then she knew that her husband had come.
Raising her hand, she beat on the saddle,
with sobs that tore at her heart.
"Since I took leave of you,
unimaginable things have happened!
I can no longer be true to my former promise,
though I doubt you will understand why.
I have my parents to think of,
and my brother has pressed me as well,
making me promise myself to another man —
how could I be sure you would return?"
The clerk said to his wife,
"I compliment you on your rise in the world!
The boulder is square and solid —
it can last for a thousand years.
But the rush or the reed — its moment of strength
lasts no longer than dawn to dusk!
You will grow mightier, more exalted daily —
I will go alone to the Yellow Springs."
The young wife said to the clerk,
"What do you mean by such words!
Both of us were forced against our will,
you were, and so was I!
In the Yellow Springs we will meet again —
no betraying the words I speak today!"
They clasped hands, then went their separate ways,
each returning to his own family.
Still alive, they were parted as though by death,
with grief and regret beyond describing,
thinking now to take their leave of the world,
knowing that their lives could last no longer.

The clerk returned to his home,

ascended the hall, bowed to his mother:
"Today the winds blow fierce and cold,
the cold winds break the tree limbs,
and harsh frost collects on the orchids in the garden.[7]
Your son today goes into darkness,
leaving you behind all alone.
I do this bad thing of my own will —
do not rail at the gods or spirits.
May your years be like the rock on the southern mountain,
your four limbs sturdy and straight."
When his mother heard this,
her tears fell in time to her words:
"You are the son of a great family
who have served in high government office.
Don't be foolish and die for this woman,
when she is so far beneath you!
The family to the east have a virtuous daughter,
her beauty the boast of the whole city.
Your mother will arrange for you to have her,
it will be done in the space of a day!"
The clerk bowed once more and withdrew,
in his empty bedroom sighed unendingly,
then made his plan, determined to see it through,
turned his head, looked toward the door,
grief pressing in on him more cruelly than ever.

That day the cattle lowed, the horses neighed,
when the bride entered the green enclosure.[8]
And after the darkness of evening had come,
when all was still and people had settled down,
she said, "My life will end today,
my soul take leave, my body remaining."
She lifted her skirt, stepped out of her silken shoes,
and threw herself into the clear pond.
When the clerk heard of this,

7. His wife's name, Lan-chih, means Orchid Plant.
8. A curtained enclosure that the bride enters as part of the wedding ceremony.

he knew in his heart they must part forever.
He circled the tree in the garden,
then hanged himself from the southeast limb.

The two families agreed to bury them together,
to bury them by the side of Flower Mountain.
To east and west they planted pine and cypress,
left and right set out parasol trees.
The branches came together to make a canopy,
leaf entwined about leaf.
And in their midst a pair of flying birds,
the kind called mandarin ducks,
raised their heads and cried to each other
night after night till the hour of dawn.
Travelers halted their steps to listen,
widows got up and paced the room.
And this I say to you of later ages:
take warning and never forget this tale!

Poems of the Han and Wei

THE middle years of the Han dynasty saw a highly significant development in the history of Chinese poetry, the appearance of a new kind of *shih* poetry that employs a five-character or five-syllable line rather than the four-character line typical of the *Book of Odes*. The new form seems to have been of popular origin and was perhaps influenced by changes in the music of the time. By the first century A.D. it had been taken up by the literati, and soon became the favorite vehicle for lyric expression. A variant of the form employing a seven-character line appeared about the same time but did not gain wide acceptance until several centuries later.

Among the finest works in the new five-character *shih* form are the set of poems known as "The Nineteen Old Poems of the Han." They are anonymous works of uncertain date, though in diction, imagery, and content they closely resemble works by known writers of the late second century. Some deal with love and marriage, others with friendship, feasting, or the quest for fame and fortune. For the most part they are somber in tone, no doubt reflecting the troubled social conditions of the time, and dwell much on the themes of distance, separation, and the dreadful brevity and uncertainty of human life. Thirteen of the set of nineteen have been included in my selection, along with two other anonymous works that appear to belong to the same general period.

A similar tone of brooding melancholy informs most of the *shih* poems by known writers of the late Han, and of its brief successor, the Wei dynasty (220-264). These writers include Ts'ao Ts'ao, the powerful military leader who opened the way for his son Ts'ao P'i to ascend the throne as the first emperor of the Wei, and his younger son Ts'ao Chih, one of the finest poets of the period. Flourishing under the patronage of the Ts'ao family were the so-called Seven Masters of the Chien-an Era (196-220), represented in my selection by Hsü Kan, Wang Ts'an, Ch'en Lin, and Liu Cheng, all of whom, it may be noted, died in an outbreak of plague in 217.

The works of these men for the most part mirror the harsh realities of the period, depicting in realistic detail the civil strife, unrest, and political intrigue that accompanied the downfall of the Han dynasty. In some, such as Ch'en Lin's poem on the Great Wall, the poet borrows a persona from the *yüeh-fu* ballad tradition; in others he speaks in his own voice, as in Ts'ao Chih's long and moving farewell to his younger brother.

The decay and collapse of the Han served in some degree to discredit the Confucian doctrines that had formed the official foundation of the state and to clear the way for a revival of interest in the transcendental thought of the Taoist philosophers Lao Tzu and Chuang Tzu. This new intellectual trend is represented in the Taoist-flavored, spiritedly anti-Confucian work by Chung-ch'ang T'ung in my selection. This poem, as well as one by Ts'ao Ts'ao on the sea, employs the old four-character *shih* form, which continued in sporadic use.

At the same time, as disease, warfare, peasant uprisings and the sudden shifts in political power made life increasingly perilous for members of the ruling class, there was growing speculation concerning the possibilities of employing drugs or dietary regimen to prolong life or even perhaps achieve the state of a *hsien* or immortal spirit, a figure often depicted in Taoist writings. True, the old rationalistic habits of thought nurtured by Confucianism militated against the acceptance of such beliefs, at least among the educated class. One of the "Nineteen Old Poems" alludes scornfully to the frequency with which people poisoned themselves by imbibing such "immortality potions," which were usually concocted of highly toxic ingredients such as lead, arsenic, or mercury. And the emperor-poet

Ts'ao P'i, invoking the names of two legendary figures who were alleged to have become *hsien,* Prince Ch'iao and the Master of the Red Pine, declares cynically, "Prince Ch'iao — false information bequeathed us; / Red Pine — empty words handed down!" ("Song of the Broken Willow").

Nevertheless, despite such skepticism, the thought persisted that somehow one might discover a means to escape the horrors of the human condition, or at least might insure a longer and less harrowing life by removing oneself from the more immediate dangers of the social and political scene. In the centuries that followed, as we shall see, the themes of reclusion and the dream of flight to some freer, happier realm constitute one of the major concerns of Chinese poetry.

ANONYMOUS

Selections from the "Nineteen Old Poems of the Han"

(5-ch.)

I.
On and on, going on and on,
away from you to live apart,
ten thousand li and more between us,
each at opposite ends of the sky.
The road I travel is steep and long;
who knows when we meet again?
The Hu horse leans into the north wind;
the Yüeh bird nests in southern branches:
day by day our parting grows more distant;
day by day robe and belt dangle looser.
Shifting clouds block the white sun;
the traveler does not look to return.
Thinking of you makes one old;
years and months suddenly go by.
Abandoned, I will say no more
but pluck up strength and eat my fill.

2.
Green green, river bank grasses,
thick thick, willows in the garden;
plump plump, that lady upstairs,
bright bright, before the window;
lovely lovely, her red face-powder;
slim slim, she puts out a white hand.

Once I was a singing-house girl,
now the wife of a wanderer,
a wanderer who never comes home —
It's hard sleeping in an empty bed alone.

3.
Green green the cypress on the ridge,
stones heaped about in mountain streams:
between heaven and earth our lives rush past
like travelers with a long road to go.
Let this measure of wine be our merriment;
value it highly, without disdain.
I race the carriage, whip the lagging horses,
roam for pleasure to Wan and Lo.
Here in Lo-yang, what surging crowds,
capped and belted ones chasing each other;
long avenues fringed with narrow alleys,
the many mansions of princes and peers.
The Two Palaces face each other from afar,
paired towers over a hundred feet tall.[1]
Let the feast last forever, delight the heart —
then what grief or gloom can weigh us down?

4.
We hold a splendid feast today,
a delight barely to be told in words.
Strike the lute, raise joyful echoes,
new notes of ghostly beauty.
Let the talented sing fine phrases;
he who knows music will understand.
One in mind, we share the same wish,
though the thought within remains unspoken:
Man lives out his little sojourn,
scudding by like a swirl of dust.
Why not whip up your high-stepping horses,

1. The Two Palaces are those of the emperor and the heir apparent situated in the northern and southern sectors respectively of Lo-yang, the capital of the Eastern or Later Han.

be first to command the road to power?
What profit to stay poor and unhonored,
floundering forever in bitterness!

5.

Northwest the tall tower stands,
its top level with floating clouds,
patterned windows webbed in lattice,
roofs piled three stories high.
From above, the sound of strings and song;
what sadness in that melody!
Who could play a tune like this,
who but the wife of Ch'i Liang?[1]
The clear *shang* mode drifts down the wind;
halfway through, it falters and breaks,
one plucking, two or three sighs,
longing, a grief that lingers on —
It is not the singer's pain I pity,
but few are those who understand the song!
If only we could be a pair of calling cranes,
beating wings, soaring to the sky!

7.

Clear moon brightly shining in the night,
crickets chirring by eastern walls;
the jade bar points to early winter;[1]
crowding stars, how thick their ranks!
White dew soaks the wild grasses,
cycle of the seasons swiftly changing;
autumn cicadas cry among the trees;

---

1. Ch'i Liang, a man of the state of Ch'i, was killed in battle in 550 B.C. According to legend, his grief-stricken wife committed suicide by throwing herself into the Tzu River. She is often described as playing a lute just before her death. In one version of the legend, her pitiful cries cause the city wall to collapse. The *shang* mode mentioned in the next line is one of the five modes or keys of traditional Chinese music, that associated with autumn and sadness.

---

1. The "jade bar" seems to refer to the handle of the Big Dipper, whose position now indicates the approach of winter.

dark swallows, where did they go?
Once we were students together;
you soared on high, beating strong wings,
no longer recalling the hand of friendship;
you've left me behind like a forgotten footprint.
Southern Winnow, Dipper in the north,
Draught Ox that will not bear a yoke —[2]
truly, with no rock to underpin them,
what good are empty names?

8.
Frail frail, lone-growing bamboo,
roots clasping the high hill's edge;
to join with my lord now in marriage,
a creeper clinging to the moss.
Creepers have their time to grow,
husband and wife their proper union.
A thousand miles apart, we made our vow,
far far — mountain slopes between us.
Thinking of you makes one old;
your canopied carriage, how slow its coming!
These flowers sadden me — orchis and angelica,
petals unfurled, shedding glory all around;
if no one plucks them in blossom time
they'll wilt and die with the autumn grass.
But if in truth you will keep your promise,
how could *I* ever be untrue?

2. An allusion to *Odes*, no. 203:

Bright shines that Draught Ox
but one yokes it to no wagon;...
South there is the Winnow
but it can't be used to sift with;
north there is the Dipper
but no wine or sauce it ladles.

I.e., though these constellations in the sky bear impressive names, they are in fact as useless as the vows of friendship that the fellow students had once exchanged.

9.

In the garden a strange tree grows,
from green leaves a shower of blossoms bursting.
I bend the limb and break off a flower,
thinking to send it to the one I love.
Fragrance fills my breast and sleeves,
but the road is far — it will never reach you.
Why is such a gift worth the giving?
Only because I remember how long ago we parted.

10.

(The following poem concerns the legend of the Herdboy and the Weaving Maiden,
constellations that correspond roughly to Aquila [Herdboy] and Vega and the Lyre
[Weaving Maiden]. The Weaving Maiden, daughter of the Emperor of Heaven
and an expert at weaving, married the Herdboy, but after her marriage she neglected
her weaving. To punish her, her father placed the couple on opposite sides of the
River of Heaven, as the Milky Way is called in China. They are permitted to meet
only once a year, on the night of the seventh day of the seventh lunar month, when
sympathetic magpies form a bridge for them over the stream of stars.)

Far far away, the Herdboy Star;
bright bright, the Lady of the River of Heaven;
slim slim, she lifts a pale hand,
clack clack, plying the shuttle of her loom,
all day long — but the pattern's never finished;
welling tears fall like rain.
The River of Heaven is clear and shallow;
what a little way lies between them!
Only the span of a single brimming stream —
they gaze and gaze and cannot speak.

11.

I turn the carriage, yoke and set off,
far far, over never-ending roads.
In the four directions, broad plain on plain;
east wind shakes the hundred grasses.
Among all I meet, nothing of the past;
what can save us from sudden old age?

Fullness and decay, each has its season;
success — I hate it, so late in coming!
Man is not made of metal or stone;
how can he hope to live for long?
Swiftly he follows in the wake of change.
A shining name — let that be the prize!

13.
I drive my carriage from the Upper East Gate,[1]
scanning the graves far north of the wall;
silver poplars, how they whisper and sigh;
pine and cypress flank the broad lane.
Beneath them, the ancient dead,
black black there in their long night,
sunk in sleep beneath the Yellow Springs;
a thousand years pass but they never wake.
Times of heat and cold in unending succession,
but the years Heaven gives us are like morning dew.
Man's life is brief as a sojourn;
his years lack the firmness of metal or stone.
Ten thousand ages come and go
but sages and wise men discover no cure.
Some seek long life in fasts and potions;
many end by poisoning themselves.
Far better to drink fine wine,
to clothe ourselves in soft white silk!

15.
Man's years fall short of a hundred;
a thousand years of worry crowd his heart.
If the day is short and you hate the long night,
why not take the torch and go wandering?
Seek out happiness in season;
who can wait for the coming year?
Fools who cling too fondly to gold
earn no more than posterity's jeers.

1. The northernmost of the three gates in the east wall of Lo-yang.

Prince Ch'iao, that immortal man—
small hope we have of matching him![1]

17.
First month of winter: cold air comes,
north winds sharp and cruel.
I have many sorrows, I know how long the night is,
looking up to watch the teeming ranks of stars.
Night of the fifteenth: a bright moon full;
twentieth night: toad and rabbit wane.[1]
A traveler came from far away,
put a letter into my hand;
at the top it spoke of "undying remembrance,"
at the bottom, of "parting long endured."
I tucked it away inside my robe;
three years—not a word has dimmed.
With whole heart I offer my poor love,
fearful you may not see its worth.

ANONYMOUS

Old Poem

(5-ch.)

She went up the hill to pick angelica;
she came down the hill and met her former husband.
She knelt and asked her former husband,
"How do you find the new wife?"
"The new wife I would say is fine,

---

1. Wang-tzu Ch'iao or Prince Ch'iao was believed to have become a *hsien* or immortal spirit.

---

1. In the light and dark areas of the moon the Chinese see a toad and a rabbit.

but she lacks the old wife's excellence.
In face and complexion they're much alike,
but quite unlike in skill of hand.
When the new wife came in the gate,
the old wife left by the side door.[1]
The new wife is good at weaving gauze,
the old wife was good at weaving plain stuff.
Weaving gauze, one does a bolt a day,
weaving plain stuff, five yards or more.[2]
And when I compare the gauze with the plain stuff,
I know the new wife can't equal the old!"

Old *Chüeh-chü*

(The dodder is a parasitic vine that grows on trees. 5-ch.)

The dodder vine trails with the long wind,
but its roots never break from the trunk they cling to.
If even these unfeeling things shun separation,
how could we, who have feelings, bear to part?

---

1. Some commentators take these two lines as the words of the wife, questioning her husband's sincerity by reminding him of how he treated her. I take them as an indirect admission by the husband that he acted badly.

2. One bolt or *p'i* is equivalent to four yards or *chang*.

TS'AO TS'AO *(155-220)*

Song on Enduring the Cold

(The poem was probably written in 206 when Ts'ao Ts'ao, the most powerful military leader of the time, was crossing the T'ai-hang Mountains in northern Shansi to attack a rival. *Yüeh-fu* style, 5-ch.)

North we climb the T'ai-hang Mountains;
the going's hard on these steep heights!
Sheep Gut Slope dips and doubles,
enough to make the cartwheels crack.

Stark and stiff the forest trees,
the voice of the north wind sad;
crouching bears, black and brown, watch us pass;
tigers and leopards howl beside the trail.

Few men live in these valleys and ravines
where snow falls thick and blinding.
With a long sigh I stretch my neck;
a distant campaign gives you much to think of.

Why is my heart so downcast and sad?
All I want is to go back east,
but waters are deep and bridges broken;
halfway up, I stumble to a halt.

Dazed and uncertain, I've lost the old road,
night bearing down but nowhere to shelter;
on and on, each day farther,
men and horses starving as one.

Shouldering packs, we snatch firewood as we go,
chop ice to use in boiling our gruel —
That song of the Eastern Hills is sad,
a troubled tale that fills me with grief.[1]

---

1. Eastern Hills, *Odes* no. 156, describes the hardships of a military campaign similar to the one Ts'ao Ts'ao was engaged in.

Viewing the Ocean

(The Chieh-shih Mountains are on the coast of northern China overlooking the Gulf of Pohai. 4-ch.)

East looking down from Chieh-shih,
I scan the endless ocean:
waters restlessly seething,
mountained islands jutting up,
trees growing in clusters,
a hundred grasses, rich and lush.
Autumn wind shrills and sighs,
great waves churn and leap skyward.
Sun and moon in their journeying
seem to rise from its midst,
stars and Milky Way, brightly gleaming,
seem to emerge from its depths.
How great is my delight!
I sing of it in this song.

HSÜ KAN *(171-217)*

The Wife's Thoughts

(5-ch.)

Clouds that drift so far and free
I'd ask to bear my message,
but their whirling shapes accept no charge;
wandering, halting, I long in vain.
Those who part all meet once more;
you alone send no word of return.
Since you went away,
my shining mirror darkens with neglect.
Thoughts of you are like the flowing river –
when will they ever end?

WANG TS'AN *(177-217)*

Seven Sorrows

(Two from a set of poems written around A.D. 195 when the poet fled from Ch'ang-an, the Western Capital, and journeyed south to the semibarbarian region of Ching in the upper Yangtze valley. The "wolves and tigers" of the second line are rebel leaders preparing to attack the city. 5-ch.)

1.

The Western Capital in lawless disorder;
wolves and tigers poised to prey on it:
I'll leave this middle realm, be gone,
go far off to the tribes of Ching.
Parents and kin face me in sorrow,
friends running after, pulling me back.
Out the gate I see
only white bones that strew the broad plain.
A starving woman beside the road
hugs her child, then lays it in the weeds,
looks back at the sound of its wailing,
wipes her tears and goes on alone:
"I don't even know when my own death will come —
how can I keep both of us alive?"
Whip up the horses, leave her behind —
I cannot bear to hear such words!
South I climb the crest of Pa-ling,
turning my head to look back on Ch'ang-an.
I know what he meant — that falling spring —
sobbing racks my heart and bowels.[1]

2.

Tribes of Ching — that's not my home;
how can I stay for long among them?
My two-hulled boat ascends the great river;

---

1. "That falling spring" is a phrase from *Odes,* no. 153, a song of sorrow and nostalgia for the capital of the Chou dynasty which, like Ch'ang-an, had fallen on evil days. It employs the refrain, "Cold the waters of that falling spring!"

the sun at evening saddens my heart.
On mountain and ridge, a last ray of light,
slope and embankment in deepening gloom;
foxes and raccoon dogs hurry to their lairs,
flying birds go home to the woods they know.
Sharp echoes wake from the roaring torrents,
monkeys peer down from the cliffs and cry.
Strong winds flap my robe and sleeves,
white dew soaks the collar of my cloak.
I can't sleep at night alone
but get up, put on a robe, and play the lute;
strings and paulownia wood know how I feel;
for me they make a sorrowful sound.
On a journey that has no end,
dark thoughts are powerful and hard to bear!

CH'EN LIN *(d. 217)*

Song: I Watered My Horse at the Long Wall Caves

(A conscript laborer assigned to work on the Great Wall. *Yüeh-fu* style, 5-ch. & 7-ch.)

I watered my horse at the Long Wall caves,
water so cold it hurt his bones;
I went and spoke to the Long Wall boss:
"We're soldiers from T'ai-yüan — will you keep us here forever?"
"Public works go according to schedule —
swing your hammer, pitch your voice in with the rest!"
A man'd be better off to die in battle
than eat his heart out building the Long Wall!
The Long Wall — how it winds and winds,

winds and winds three thousand li;
here on the border, so many strong boys;
in the houses back home, so many widows and wives.
I sent a letter to my wife:
"Better remarry than wait any longer —
serve your new mother-in-law with care
and sometimes remember the husband you once had."
In answer her letter came to the border:
"What nonsense do you write me now?
Now when you're in the thick of danger,
how could I rest by another man's side?"
(HE)   If you bear a son, don't bring him up!
       But a daughter – feed her good dried meat.
       Only *you* can't see, here by the Long Wall,
       the bones of the dead men heaped about!
(SHE) I bound up my hair and went to serve you;
       constant constant was the care of my heart.
       Too well I know your borderland troubles;
       and I — can I go on like this much longer?

LIU CHENG *(d. 217)*

Poem Without a Category

(5-ch.)

Office work: a wearisome jumble;
ink drafts: a crosshatch of deletions and smears.
Racing the writing brush, no time to eat,
sun slanting down but never a break;
swamped and muddled in records and reports,
head spinning till it's senseless and numb —
I leave off and go west of the wall,

climb the height and let my eyes roam:
square embankments hold back the clear water,
wild ducks and geese at rest in the middle —
Where can I get a pair of whirring wings
so I can join you to bob on the waves?

CHUNG-CH'ANG T'UNG *(179-220)*

Speaking My Mind

(4-ch.)

The Great Way — simple as it is,
few spy out its secrets.
Follow the will and you do no wrong;
go along with things — none are in error.
From times past, ties and entanglements,
cricks and coils, this petty lot,
these hundred worries — what are they?
All that's most important rests in you!
Hand your woes to the sky above,
bury your troubles in the ground,
flout and discard the *Five Classics*,
put an end to the *Odes.*
And those muddled scraps that are the hundred philosophers —
consign them please to the flames!
Lift your ambitions to the hills and westward,
let your mind wander east of the sea.
With the Primal Breath as your boat,
the little winds for a rudder,
sail and soar in the Great Purity,
do what you want to, handsome and blithe!

MIU HSI *(186-245)*

Poem in the Form of a Coffin-Puller's Song

(5-ch.)

In life I stroll the capital city,
in death I am cast in the midst of the plain.
At dawn I step forth from the high hall,
at dusk to lodge beneath the Yellow Springs.
The white sun sinks into the Gulf of Yü,[1]
its chariot halted, its four steeds at rest.
The Creator, for all his godly glory,
cannot restore me to wholeness again!
Body and face slowly losing shape,
teeth and hair bit by bit falling away —
since time began it has been like this for all —
who's the man could ever break away?

TSO YEN-NIEN *(3rd cen.)*

Call to Arms

(*yüeh-fu* style, 5-ch.)

How bitter for these border men!
One year, three calls to arms;
three sons sent to Tun-huang,
two sons in Lung-hsi now.
Five sons gone to distant battle,
five wives, every one with child.

1. The place where the charioteer of the sun goes to rest at evening.

TS'AO P'I *(187-226)*

Lotus Lake

(5-ch.)

By hand-drawn cart, an excursion at evening,
a carefree stroll in the Western Gardens.[1]
Double conduits pour water into the lake,
rare trees line the streams that pass through,
their low limbs brushing my feathered carriage top,
their tall branches sweeping the azure sky.
A sudden wind lifts the carriage hubs,
flying birds start up before me.
The red of sunset flanks the bright moon,
gleaming stars come out between the clouds —
the heavens send down their shining colors,
their five hues fresh and clear!
Mine is not the long life of Sung or Ch'iao;[2]
who can hope to be immortal like them?
With pleasures I will ease my heart,
take care to live out my hundred years!

TS'AO CHIH *(192-232)*

Written on Parting from Mr. Ying

(The first of two poems with this title. The Lo-yang palaces had been burned in
190 by the rebel leader Tung Cho and the city suffered terribly in the civil strife
that ensued. 5-ch.)

1. The gardens in the old Wei capital at Yeh.
2. The immortals Sung or the Master of the Red Pine and Prince Ch'iao.

On foot I climb Pei-mang Slope,
looking far off at Lo-yang's hills:
Lo-yang — how still and desolate,
palaces and chambers all gutted and charred,
every wall and fence row gaping and torn;
thorns and brambles reach up to the sky.
No sight of the old men who used to be;
all I meet are unknown youths.
I try to pick a foothold but no path goes through;
overgrown fields lie unplowed.
The wanderer has been so long from home
he no longer recalls the grid of streets.
The plains around — how bleak and bare,
a thousand li and no smoke of cooking fires.
Thinking of the place I used to live,
my breath chokes up and will not let me speak.

The Forsaken Wife

(5-ch.)

The pomegranate grows in the garden front,
pale green leaves that tremble and turn,
vermilion flowers, flame on flame,
a shimmering glory of light and hue;
light that flares like the ten-colored turquoise,
fit for holy creatures to sport with.
Birds fly down and gather there;
beating their wings, they make sad cries.
Sad cries — what are they for?
Vermilion blossoms bear no fruit.
I beat my breast and sigh long sighs;
the childless one will be sent home.

She with children is a moon that sails the sky;
the childless one, a falling star.
Sky and moon have end and beginning,
but the falling star sinks in spiritless death.
She whose sojourn fails of its rightful goal
falls among tiles and stones.
Dark thoughts well up;
I sigh till the dawn cocks crow,
toss from side to side, sleepless,
rise and wander in the courtyard outside.
I pause and turn to my room again;
chamber curtains swish and sigh;
I lift them and bind my girdle tighter,
stroke the strings of a white wood lute;
fierce and pleading, the tone lingers on,
soft and subtle, plaintive and clear.
I will dry my tears and sigh again;
how could I turn my back on the gods?
The star Chao-yao waits for frost and dew;[1]
why should spring and summer alone be fertile?
Late harvests gather good fruit—
if my lord will only wait with trusting heart!

Presented to Piao, the Prince of Pai-ma

(The Prince of Jen-ch'eng was Ts'ao Chang, an older brother of the poet; the Prince of Pai-ma was Ts'ao Piao, a younger half brother. All three brothers had journeyed to Lo-yang to pay respects to their eldest brother, Ts'ao P'i, who in 220 had ascended the throne as ruler of a new dynasty, the Wei. Both Ts'ao Chih and Ts'ao Piao had to travel east to return to their respective fiefs, but the emperor evidently wished them to travel separately so they would have no opportunity to plot against him. 5-ch.)

1. Chao-yao is the first star in the handle of the Big Dipper; when the handle points west-southwest, it signals the beginning of autumn.

Preface: Huang-ch'u 4th year (A.D. 223), 5th month. The
Prince of Pai-ma, the Prince of Jen-ch'eng, and I together went to
attend court at the capital on the occasion of the seasonal gathering
After we had reached Lo-yang, the Prince of Jen-ch'eng passed
away. In the 7th month, the Prince of Pai-ma and I prepared to
return to our territories. Presently, however, those in charge of
such matters decided that in returning to our fiefs it was proper
that we should stop at separate places along the road. I was vexed
and grieved at this, for it meant that in the space of a few days we
had to take leave of each other for a long time to come. Herein I
have laid bare my feelings in farewell to the Prince, making a poem
of my resentment.

Audience with the emperor, Hall of Inherited Brilliance;
now to return to my old domain,
in clear dawn departing the imperial city,
at sundown past Shou-yang Hill.
The Yi and Lo are broad and deep;
I want to cross over but there's no bridge.
The bobbing boat leaps giant waves;
I hate the longness of this eastern road,
look back fondly at the city gates,
stretching my neck, within me thoughts of sorrow.

Great Valley — how vast and wild,
mountain trees thick in blue blue gloom;
endless rains turn the trail to mud,
swollen streams spill to left and right.
The road breaks midway, ruts washed out;
I veer into a new path, drive up the tall hill,
a long slope that climbs to clouds and sun,
my black horses yellowing with strain.

Yellow with strain, they still push on,
but my thoughts are tangled fast in gloom;
tangled in gloom — what do I think of?
That near and loved one far away.
At first we thought to keep each other company;

it changed — we couldn't go together.
Kites and owls screech at the carriage yoke,
jackals and wolves lurk by the way;
blue flies with their muck turn white to black,
glib talk and lies put kinsmen apart.
I want to go back but the road is cut off;
reins in hand, I halt in indecision.

Undecided, but how can I stay?
Thoughts of you will never be done.
Autumn wind brings a subtle chill,
cold cicadas cry by my side;
upland moors — how bleak and bare,
the white sun all at once lost in the west.
Homing birds head for the tall trees,
p'ien-p'ien go their swift wings flapping;
a lone animal seeks its mate,
grass in its jaws, no time to eat.
Moved by these creatures, my thoughts are dragged down;
I strike my heart and give a great sigh.

A great sigh — what will that do?
Heaven's decrees are set against me!
What good to think of my mother's son?[1]
Once gone, his body returns no more,
his lonely soul on wing to old haunts,
his coffin at rest in the capital.
The living — how quickly they pass,
their bodies rotting away in death.
Man lives his single age,
gone like morning dew that dries.
The year rests between Mulberry and Elm,[2]
a shadow, an echo, not to be pursued.
To think I am not made of metal or stone,
and in an instant — it grieves my heart.

1. Ts'ao Chang, who had the same mother as the poet.
2. Constellations, here representing the closing of the year and, by extension, of one's lifetime.

Grieves my heart and moves my soul —
but lay it aside and say no more!
A brave man's eyes are set on the four seas;
ten thousand miles are next door for him.
Where love and bounty are not lacking,
distance will bring us closer each day.
Why must we share quilt and curtain
before we can bare our deepest concerns?
Fretting till you make yourself sick and feverish —
this is mere childish, womanish love!
Yet suddenly parted from flesh and blood,
can I help brooding in bitterness and pain?

Bitterness and pain — what are my thoughts?
The decrees of Heaven bear no trust.
Useless to seek the ranks of immortals;
Master Sung has deceived us too long!
Change and mishap are here in a moment;
who can live out his hundred years?
We part — it may be forever;
when will I clasp your hand again?
Prince, be cautious of that worthy body;
together let us live to see the white-haired years.
I wipe back the tears and take my long road;
the brush I hold bids you farewell for now.

Rhyme-Prose on the Goddess of the Lo

(Though the preface gives the third year of the Huang-ch'u era as the date of the
events that inspired the poem, this is probably a mistake for the fourth year of the
era, A.D. 223, when, as we have seen in the preceding poem, the poet had been in
Lo-yang to pay respects to his elder brother Ts'ao P'i, the emperor of the Wei
dynasty. Though the poem would appear to be a simple exposition of the poet's
ideal of feminine beauty and virtue, some critics give it an allegorical interpretation,
seeing it as a declaration of loyalty addressed by the poet to his brother the emperor.)

In the third year of the Huang-ch'u era, I attended court at
the capital and then crossed the Lo River to begin my journey
home. Men in olden times used to say that the goddess of the river
is named Fu-fei. Inspired by the example of Sung Yü, who
described a goddess to the king of Ch'u,[1] I eventually composed a
fu which read:

Leaving the capital
to return to my fief in the east,
Yi Barrier at my back,
up over Huan-yüan,
passing through T'ung Valley,
crossing Mount Ching;
the sun had already dipped in the west,
the carriage unsteady, the horses fatigued,
and so I halted my rig in the spikenard marshes,
grazed my team of four at Lichen Fields,
idling a while by Willow Wood,
letting my eyes wander over the Lo.
Then my mood seemed to change, my spirit grew restless;
suddenly my thoughts had scattered.
I looked down, hardly noticing what was there,
looked up to see a different sight,
to spy a lovely lady by the slopes of the riverbank.

I took hold of the coachman's arm and asked, "Can you see
her? Who could she be – a woman so beautiful!"

The coachman replied, "I have heard of the goddess of the
River Lo, whose name is Fu-fei. What you see, my prince – is it not
she? But what does she look like? I beg you to tell me!"

And I answered:

Her body soars lightly like a startled swan,
gracefully, like a dragon in flight,

1. A reference to the "Rhyme-Prose on the Goddess" attributed to Sung Yü (3rd cen.
B.C.), in which the poet describes to King Hsiang of Ch'u a woman of supernatural beauty
who visited him in a dream; the work was apparently one of the principal models for Ts'ao
Chih's poem.

in splendor brighter than the autumn chrysanthemum,
in bloom more flourishing than the pine in spring;
dim as the moon mantled in filmy clouds,
restless as snow whirled by the driving wind.
Gaze far off from a distance:
she sparkles like the sun rising from morning mists;
press closer to examine:
she flames like the lotus flower topping the green wave.
She strikes a balance between plump and frail;
the tall and short of her are justly proportioned,
with shoulders shaped as if by carving,
waist narrow as though bound with white cords;
at her slim throat and curving neck
the pale flesh lies open to view,
no scented ointments overlaying it,
no coat of leaden powder applied.
Cloud-bank coiffure rising steeply,
long eyebrows delicately arched,
red lips that shed their light abroad,
white teeth gleaming within,
bright eyes skilled at glances,
a dimple to round off the base of the cheek —
her rare form wonderfully enchanting,
her manner quiet, her pose demure.
Gentle-hearted, broad of mind,
she entrances with every word she speaks;
her robes are of a strangeness seldom seen,
her face and figure live up to her paintings.
Wrapped in the soft rustle of silken garments,
she decks herself with flowery earrings of jasper and jade,
gold and kingfisher hairpins adorning her head,
strings of bright pearls to make her body shine.
She walks in figured slippers fashioned for distant wandering,
airy trains of mistlike gauze in tow,
dimmed by the odorous haze of unseen orchids,
pacing uncertainly beside the corner of the hill.
Then suddenly she puts on a freer air,

ready for rambling, for pleasant diversion.
To the left planting her colored pennants,
to the right spreading the shade of cassia flags,
she dips pale wrists into the holy river's brink,
plucks dark iris from the rippling shallows.
My fancy is charmed by her modest beauty,
but my heart, uneasy, stirs with distress:
without a skilled go-between to join us in bliss,
I must trust these little waves to bear my message.
Desiring that my sincerity first of all be known,
I undo a girdle-jade to offer as pledge.
Ah, the pure trust of the lovely lady,
trained in ritual, acquainted with the *Odes;*[2]
she holds up a garnet stone to match my gift,
pointing down into the depths to show where we should meet.
Clinging to a lover's passionate faith,
yet I fear that this spirit may deceive me;
warned by tales of how Chiao-fu was abandoned,[3]
I pause, uncertain and despairing;
then, stilling such thoughts, I turn a gentler face toward her,
signaling that for my part I abide by the rules of ritual.
The spirit of the Lo, moved by my action,
paces to and fro uncertainly,
the holy light deserting her, then reappearing,
now darkening, now shining again;
she lifts her light body in the posture of a crane,
as though about to fly but not yet taking wing.
She walks the heady perfume of pepper-scented roads,
strides through clumps of spikenard, scattering their fragrance,
wailing distractedly, a sign of endless longing,
her voice, sharp with sorrow, growing more prolonged.
Then a swarm of milling spirits appears,
calling companions, whistling to their mates,

2. The *Book of Odes,* where many exchanges of pledges between lovers are described.
3. Cheng Chiao-fu met two women beside the Yangtze and, unaware that they were goddesses of the river, asked them for their girdle stones. They obliged, but shortly after he had put the stones in the breast of his robe both the stones and the women vanished.

some sporting in the clear current,
some hovering over sacred isles,
some searching for bright pearls,
some collecting kingfisher plumes.
The goddess attends the two queens of Hsiang in the south,
joins hands with Wandering Girl from the banks of the Han,
sighs that the Gourd Star has no spouse,
laments that the Herdboy must live alone.[4]
Lifting the rare fabric of her thin jacket,
she makes a shield of her long sleeve, pausing in hesitation,
body nimbler than a winging duck,
swift, as befits the spirit she is;
traversing the waves in tiny steps,
her gauze slippers seem to stir a dust.
Her movements have no constant pattern,
now unsteady, now sedate;
hard to predict are her starts and pauses,
now advancing, now turning back.
Her roving glance flashes fire;
a radiant warmth shines in her jadelike face.
Her words, held back, remain unvoiced,
her breath scented as though with hidden orchids;
her fair face all loveliness —
she makes me forget my hunger!
Then the god Ping-i calls in his winds,
the River Lord stills the waves,
while P'ing-i beats a drum
and Nü-kua offers simple songs.
Speckled fish are sent aloft to clear the way for her carriage,
jade bells are jangled for accompaniment;
six dragon-steeds, solemn, pulling neck to neck,
she rides the swift passage of her cloudy chariot.

4. The two queens are O-huang and Nü-ying, wives of Emperor Shun, who after his death became goddesses of the Hsiang River in the south. Wandering Girl is identified as the goddess of the Han River. The legend pertaining to the Gourd Star is unknown. The Herdboy, another star, is separated from his love, the Weaving Maiden, by the Milky Way, and they are permitted to meet only one night a year.

Whales dance at the hubs on either side,
water birds fly in front to be her guard.
And when she has gone beyond the northern sandbars,
when she has crossed the southern ridges,
she bends her white neck,
clear eyes cast down,
moves her red lips,
speaking slowly;
discussing the great principles that govern friendship,
she complains that men and gods must follow separate ways,
voices anger that we cannot fulfill the hopes of youth,
holding up her gauze sleeve to hide her weeping,
torrents of teardrops drowning her lapels.
She laments that our happy meeting must end forever,
grieves that, once departed, we go to different lands.
"No way to express my unworthy love,
I give you this bright earring from south of the Yangtze.
Though I dwell in the Great Shadow down under the waters,
my heart will forever belong to you, my prince!"
Then suddenly I could not tell where she had gone;
to my sorrow the spirit vanished in darkness, veiling her light.
With this I turned my back on the lowland, climbed the height;
my feet went forward but my soul remained behind.
Thoughts taken up with the memory of her image,
I turned to look back, a heart full of despair.
Hoping that the spirit form might show itself again,
I embarked in a small boat to journey upstream,
drifting over the long river, forgetting to return,
wrapped in endless remembrances that made my longing greater.
Night found me fretful, unable to sleep;
heavy frosts soaked me until the break of day.
I ordered the groom to ready the carriage,
thinking to return to my eastern road,
but though I seized the reins and lifted up my whip,
I stayed lost in hesitation and could not break away.

CHAPTER FIVE

T'ao Yüan-ming

IWOULD like now to skip ahead a little in time to focus upon the writings of a man who is one of the most widely admired of the early Chinese poets, T'ao Yüan-ming (365-427) or T'ao Ch'ien. He lived in the period of disunity known as the Six Dynasties, when northern China was in the hands of non-Chinese leaders, and the south, where T'ao lived, was ruled by a succession of weak and short-lived dynasties that had their capital at the present-day city of Nanking. T'ao's poetry fully reflects the unease and anxiety that beset Chinese society at this time. At the same time, however, it strikes a rare and hardwon note of peace and contentment that, though only sporadic, seems to hold out some hope for escape from sorrow and suffering, a hope that is given poignant symbolic expression in his famous fable of the Peach Blossom Spring.

T'ao Yüan-ming was born near modern Kiukiang in Kiangsi province, within sight of the famous Mount Lu, the "southern mountain" that he mentions in his poetry. His father and grandfather had pursued official careers, and though it was against his inclination, he too in time took up a post as adviser to one of the military leaders of the time. He did not fare well in this and subsequent posts, however, and he longed for the quiet rural life of his birthplace. His last post, that of magistrate of P'eng-tse, he quit after only eighty days, retiring to the countryside to become a farmer for the remainder of his years.

His extant poems, some 130 works in *shih* form, seem to have been written mainly in his later years, when he was living in a small house on the outskirts of a village with his family (he had five sons). Many poems describe the quiet joys of country life, though others speak of famine, drought, and similar hardships. The Taoist side of the poet's nature no doubt told him he should be content with such a life of seclusion, but his dedication to Confucian ideals kept him longing for the less troubled times of the past when virtue prevailed and a scholar could in good conscience take an active part in affairs of state. There is an overall ambiguity in his poetry — exclamations upon the beauties of nature and the freedom and peace of rustic life, set uneasily alongside confessions of loneliness, frustration, and fear, particularly fear of death. He sought solace in his lute, his books, and above all in wine, about half of his poems mentioning his fondness for "the thing in the cup," though in one of the poems he wrote depicting his own funeral, he declares that he was never able to get enough of it.

At a time when Chinese poetry on the whole was marked by ornate diction and elaborate rhetorical devices, T'ao Yüan-ming chose to write in a relatively plain and simple style — in translation he may even sound rather flat on first reading. Probably because of this plainness of style, and the homey and personal nature of most of his poems, he was not highly esteemed by his contemporaries. It was some centuries before the true worth of his works was recognized, though few today would question that he is one of the finest of the pre-T'ang poets.

The first poem in my selection is in four-character form; all the others employ a five-character line.

Motionless Clouds

(4-ch.)

"Motionless Clouds" expresses thoughts of a close friend. The wine cask is newly filled to brimming, the garden's just coming into bloom, but I can't be with the one I want, and I grieve till tears fall on my collar.

Heavy and dull, the motionless clouds,
the seasonal rains drenching down;
all eight directions a single darkness,
all the level roads cut off.
Quietly I settle by the eastern eaves,
alone, fondling the milky spring wine.
My good friend is so far far away —
I scratch my head and go on waiting.

Motionless clouds dull and heavy,
these drenching seasonal rains;
all eight directions a single darkness,
all the flat land turned to rivers.
I have wine, I have wine,
idly drinking by the eastern window.
I think longingly of someone,
but no boat or carriage could get through.

Trees in the eastern garden,
branches beginning to flower,
outdoing each other in new beauty,
hoping to cheer my thoughts.
Just as people say,
the days and months hurry onward;
how can I seat you by my side
where we can talk of those times now past?

Flutter flutter, birds on the wing,
they light on the limbs in my garden,
fold their wings, rest peacefully,
blending their beautiful cries.
Not that there are no others,
but I think of you so very often.
With longings unfulfilled,
brooding on my sorrow, what shall I do?

Substance, Shadow, and Spirit

Exalted or lowly, wise or stupid, there is no one who does
not worry and fret in his anxiety to go on living. This seems to me
a grave error. Therefore I have allowed substance and shadow to
describe at length their hardships, and then have enlisted spirit to
discourse on the natural way in order to resolve the problem. I
trust that gentlemen who have a taste for such matters will perceive
my meaning.

Substance Addresses Shadow:

Heaven and earth go on forever, never ceasing,
mountains and rivers know no season of change.
Grass and trees hold to their constant rule,
dew and frost flowering and withering them.
Only man, called wisest, most divine,
alone is not like these.
By chance we see him here in this world,
then abruptly he departs, no hope of return.
And who will notice there's one man less?
Friends and kin, will they remember?
All that remains are the things he used in life,
things that, when we gaze at them, bring heartache and tears.
I've no arts to change myself, make myself immortal;

I must go like the rest — have no doubt.
So I ask you to heed my words —
faced with wine, never say no!

Shadow Replies to Substance:

Life eternal — useless to talk of that;
for one so clumsy, I've trial enough just living day to day.
Though we long to journey to Mount K'un-lun or Hua,[1]
they're too distant, and the way's cut off.
Since I first encountered you,
I've known no pains or joys but yours.
When you rest in the shade, I seem to leave you for a time,
but while you're in the sun, I never depart.
Yet such companionship can scarcely go on forever;
the two of us in time must vanish into the dark.
When the body perishes the name fades too —
thinking of it, my heart's on fire!
Let us do good and win the love of ages after;
why not bend all efforts toward that?
Wine they say can wash away care,
but surely it cannot compare to such a goal!

Spirit Expounds:

The Great Potter works no private favors,
the ten thousand principles are manifest in their variety.[2]
Man can form a triad with Heaven and earth
solely because I am present in him.[3]
But though I differ from you other two,
from birth we're bound together.
And since we must share the same good and ill,
should we not talk together?
The Three Sovereigns, the great sages of old,

1. Mountains where immortal spirits are said to dwell.
2. I.e., the Creator is impartial in his treatment of the things of creation and allows them to proceed according to their various principles.
3. The belief that man is worthy to form a triad with Heaven and earth is frequently expressed in early Confucianism.

where are they today?
P'eng Tsu loved longevity,
wanted to stay longer but it couldn't be.[4]
Old and young alike die a single death,
wise and foolish are not allotted different fates.
Your daily wine may help you to forget,
but I fear it's a pastime that shortens your years.
Doing good, you say, will be all your joy?
And who do you think will praise you?
Too much pondering may injure one's life;
better leave everything to fate.
Go along with the waves in the great process of change,
take no delight in it, have no fear.
When it's time to fade away, then fade away —
why should you alone be so full of care?

On Being Assigned as Military Adviser to the Garrison Army, Written when Passing Ch'ü-a

In younger years I stayed away from the world,
gave my whole heart to my lute and books.
Wearing coarse cloth, I was happy and at ease;
though often in want, I always took things calmly.
But a time came when I had to bend to circumstance,
to alter my course, go idling in streets and thoroughfares.[1]
I put aside my staff, ordered my baggage ready at dawn,
took leave for a time from my gardens and fields.
Farther, farther away the lone boat moved;
threads, threads entangling me — my dreams of return.

4. The Three Sovereigns are Fu Hsi, Shen Nung, and the Yellow Emperor, mythical rulers of high antiquity. P'eng Tsu was reputed to have lived 800 years.

1. I.e., he had to change the direction of his life and take up an official post.

The journey I made — how long it was,
climbing up and down a thousand li or more!
My eyes grew weary of the shifting rivers and roadways;
my mind thought always of my old hills and ponds.
Observing clouds, I envied the birds high up;
at water's edge I felt ashamed beside the carefree fish.
But with this longing for the true life that I treasure still,
who can say I'm bound by outward forms?
For the moment I'll let things shift as they may,
and in the end go back to Master Pan's hut.[2]

Returning to My Home in the Country, No.1

In youth I couldn't sing to the common tune;
it was my nature to love the mountains and hills.
By mistake I got caught in that dusty snare,
went away once and stayed thirteen years.[1]
The winging bird longs for its old woods,
the fish in the pond thinks of the deeps it once knew.
I've opened up some waste land by the southern fields;
stupid as ever, I've come home to the country.
My house plot measures ten *mou* or more,
a grass roof covering eight or nine spans.[2]
Elm and willow shade the back eaves,
peach and damson ranged in front of the hall.
Dim dim, a village of distant neighbors;

2. The historian Pan Ku (32-92), in a poem entitled *Yu-t'ung-fu*, wrote of his father Pan Piao: "To the end he guarded himself and left us a model,/ dwelling in the hut of the highest benevolence." *Wen-hsüan* 14.

---

1. The text says "thirty years." Various emendations have been suggested, but since T'ao's official career lasted exactly thirteen years, I adopt that emendation.

2. The *mou*, a land measure, differed at different times and places; T'ao's plot was probably about one and a half acres. A span is the distance between two pillars in a Chinese style house.

drifting drifting, the smoke from settlements.
A dog barks in the deep lanes,
chickens call from the tops of mulberry trees.
Around my door and courtyard, no dust or clutter;
in my empty rooms, leisure enough to spare.
After so long in that cage of mine,
I've come back to things as they are.

Returning to My Home in the Country, No. 2

Out here in the fields, few social affairs,
on backwoods lanes, rarely a horse or carriage;
bright daylight, but I shut my bramblewood door,
in empty rooms rid myself of dusty thoughts.
And then at times in the little village,
pushing through the grass, I come and go with the others,
but when we meet, no idle chatter,
only talk of how mulberry and hemp are growing.
My mulberry and hemp have daily grown taller,
my lands grown broader day by day,
but always I fear that frost or hail may come
and knock them all down like so many weeds.

Returning to My Home in the Country, No. 3

I planted beans at the foot of the southern mountain;
weeds flourished, but my bean shoots were few.
I get up at dawn, work to clear away the tangle;
wrapped in moonlight, I shoulder my hoe and come home.
The path is narrow, grass and trees tall;

the evening dew wets my clothes.
Wet clothes — they're not worth a worry,
just so my hopes aren't disappointed!

Returning to My Home in the Country, No. 4

So long since I've enjoyed the hills and ponds,
the boundless pleasures of woods and fields —
I take my sons and nephews in hand;
parting brushwood, we walk through the tangled site of a village,
strolling among the knolls and grave mounds,
lingering lingering where people lived long ago.
Here and there are traces of their wells and cooking ranges,
rotting stumps of mulberry and bamboo still remaining.
We asked someone gathering firewood,
"Where are all these people now?"
The wood gatherer turned to us and said,
"They're dead and gone, none of them left!"
In one generation both court and city change —
be assured, that's no idle saying.
Man's life is a phantom affair,
and he returns at last to the empty void.

Moving House, No. 1

A long time I've wanted to live in the southern village,
not because the houses seemed so right,
but I'd heard there were many simple-hearted people there
whose company I could enjoy of a morning or evening.
I've thought of this for quite some years;

today I put my plan into action.
Who would demand that a crude hut be spacious?
Enough if it keeps the rain off my bed and mat.
Neighbors now and then come around;
we exchange remarks, talking of times past.
Unusual writings we appreciate with one another,
working out the difficult passages together.

Moving House, No. 2

In spring and fall there are many fine days;
we climb the heights and compose new poems.[1]
Passing a gate, we call to one another,
and if there's wine, we ladle it out.
Busy with farm work, each goes to his own home,
but when times are slack we think of each other,
and thinking of each other, we put on our good clothes
and talk and laugh and never get tired.
This kind of pattern is best, is it not?
You won't find me leaving here in a hurry.
A man should provide his own food and clothing;
while I work the fields I am not false to myself.

Matching a Poem by Secretary Kuo, No. 1

Thick thick the woods in front of my house,
in midsummer storing up clear shade;
south winds come in season,

1. The poet is thinking in particular of the 9th day of the 9th month, when it was the custom to climb up to a high place to picnic and write poems.

gusts flapping open the breast of my robe.
Done with friends, I pass the time in idle studies,
out of bed, fondling books and lute;
garden vegetables with flavor to spare,
last year's grain that goes a little farther —
there's a limit to what you need;
more than enough would be no cause for joy.
I pound grain to make good wine,
ferment and ladle it myself.
The little boys play by my side,
learning words they can't pronounce —
true happiness lies in these things,
official hatpins all but forgotten.
Far far off I watch the white clouds,
my longing for the past deeper than words.

In the Year with the Cyclical Sign *Mou-shen* (408), in the Sixth Month We Had a Fire.

In a grass hut lodged at the end of the narrow lane,
I'm content to see no more of costly-decked carriages.
But in midsummer the steady winds blew so fiercely
my home in the woods suddenly burned down.
A whole house and not an eave left standing;
now we shelter in a two-hulled boat by the gate.
The endless expanse of an early fall evening,
high high up, the moon growing rounder;
fruit trees and plants are starting to come alive again,
though the frightened birds have yet to return.
I stand here in the night, my thoughts far away,
in one glance sweeping all the nine-tiered sky.
As a boy in braids, I held to my own odd ways;

then before I knew it I was over forty.
My body must go where the course of change takes it,
but the spirit within me will always be at peace.
Firm, unbending — such is my nature;
no stone or gem could be harder.
In imaginings I turn back to the age of Tung-hu,
when spare stores of food were left in the fields.[1]
People drummed on their bellies, had no cares,
rose up in the morning, came home at sundown to sleep.
But I haven't chanced on times like those,
so meanwhile let me water my garden.

Drinking Wine:
Twenty Poems with Introduction

(4 poems)

    I live quietly, with few amusements, and on top of that, the nights now have grown long. I happen to have some good wine, so every evening finds me drinking. Eyeing my shadow, I drink all alone, and before I know it I'm drunk. After I've gotten drunk, I proceed to compose a couple of lines of poetry for my own delight. The sheets of paper with writing on them in time make quite a pile, though there's no particular order or sequence to the poems. Now I've asked an old friend to write out a clean copy of them just so we'll have something to play with and laugh over.

Drinking Wine, No. 1.

Prosperity and decline have no fixed dwelling;
this man, that man confronts them in turn.

    1. A quotation attributed to Confucius' grandson Tzu-ssu says: "In the time of Tung-hu Chi-tzu, people walked single file along the road and didn't dare pick up lost articles. Extra supplies of food were left in the fields or by the roadside." The scrupulous honesty of the people in the golden ages of antiquity is a common theme in Confucian writings.

Master Shao in his melon patch —
hardly the same as when he was called Tung-ling.[1]
Cold weather and hot have their arriving and departing —
man's lot is ever the same sort of thing.
Enlightened people understand this point
and go on their way without further doubt.
Suddenly I find I have a cask of wine;
each day at evening I tip it with joy.

Drinking Wine, No. 3

The Way's been lost for a thousand years;
people are all too stingy with their feelings.
They have wine, but can't bring themselves to drink it —
all they think about is worldly fame.
Why do we value this body of ours?
Isn't it because we have just one life?
And this one lifetime — how long will it last?
It shoots by like a bolt of lightning!
With your hundred years slipping slipping away,
what do you hope to do with a thing like that?

Drinking Wine, No. 5

I built my hut in a place where people live,
and yet there's no clatter of carriage or horse.
You ask me how that could be?
With a mind remote, the region too grows distant.
I pick chrysanthemums by the eastern hedge,
see the southern mountain, calm and still.
The mountain air is beautiful at close of day,
birds on the wing coming home together.
In all this there's some principle of truth,
but try to define it and you forget the words.

---

1. Under the Ch'in dynasty, Shao P'ing held the title of Marquis of Tung-ling, but in the succeeding Han dynasty he lost his wealth and title and ended up raising melons.

Drinking Wine, No. 7

Fall chrysanthemums have beautiful colors:
dew still on them, I pick the blossoms,
float them on this drowner of care — [1]
it makes me feel farther than ever from the world.
Though I'm alone as I pour my wine,
when the cup's empty, somehow the jar tips itself.
The sun has set, all moving things stilled;
homing birds hurry to the woods, singing,
and I whistle jauntily by the eastern eaves —
another day I get to live this life.

Blaming Sons

White hair shrouds both my temples,
my skin and flesh have lost their fullness.
Though I have five male children,
not a one of them loves brush and paper.
A-shu's already twice times eight —
in laziness he's never been rivaled.
A-hsüan's going on fifteen
but cares nothing for letters or learning.
Yung and Tuan are thirteen
and can't tell a 6 from a 7!
T'ung-tzu's approaching age nine —
all he does is hunt for chestnuts and pears.
If this is the luck Heaven sends me,
then pour me the "thing in the cup"!

---

1. Literally, "the thing for forgetting care," one of T'ao's terms for wine. The chrysanthemum was believed to have medicinal properties.

Poem without a Category, No. 4

The brave man has ambitions wide as the four seas;
my desire is not to grow old,
to have parents and kin living all in one place,
children and grandchildren always healthy,
the cup and lute from sunup if I want them,
enough wine in the cask so it never runs dry,
to loosen my sash, try every kind of pleasure,
sleeping late mornings, early to bed each night.
Or should I be like the gentlemen of our time,
hearts filled with hopes that clash like ice and fire,
who, their hundred years ended, gone to tall graves,
find they've won themselves only empty names?

Poem without a Category, No. 7

Sun and moon refuse to slow their pace;
the four seasons press and hurry each other onward.
Cold wind shakes the bare branches,
fallen leaves blanket the long lane.
Weak by nature, I feel myself decay with time's passing,
the black hair at my temples already turned white.
Flecks of gray find their way into my head,
signs that the road ahead will grow more and more narrow.
What is a house but an inn on a journey,
and I a traveler who must keep moving on?
Move on, move on — and where will I go?
My old home is there on the southern mountain.[1]

1. In the memorial piece that T'ao wrote for his own funeral, he states: "Master T'ao is about to take leave of this inn where he's been staying and return for all time to his original home."

Reading *The Classic of Hills and Seas*[1]

(1st in a set of 13 poems)

Start of summer, grass and trees grown tall;
their leafy branches wrap around my roof.
Flocks of birds delight to find a place to rest,
and I in like manner love my hut.
I've finished plowing, done the planting too;
time now to return to my books.
A cramped lane far from the deep wheel tracks,
but once in a while an old friend turns his carriage here;
we talk together happily, dipping spring wine,
while I pick some greens from my garden.
A fine rain comes from the east,
pleasant breezes along with it.
I browse through the tale of the Chou king,[2]
let my eyes wander over pictures of hills and seas.
In the space of a nod I've toured the universe —
how could I be other than happy?

Imitating the Old Poems, No. 4

Tall tall, the hundred foot tower,
a clear view out over the land in four directions;
at twilight it serves as a haven for homing clouds,
mornings becomes a hall for birds on the wing.
Mountains and rivers fill the eye,
broad plains everywhere stretching on and on.

1. An early work on geography that contains many legends and accounts of strange
creatures. As we see later in the poem, T'ao's edition included illustrations.
2. The *Mu t'ien-tzu chuan,* an early work describing the fantastic travels of the ancient
King Mu of the Chou dynasty. The text was discovered in a tomb in 281.

Long ago, men in search of fame and honor
fought valiantly with each other over this ground,
but then their hundred years one morning ended
and together they went home to the northern hills.[1]
Now people have cut the pine and cypress on their graves;
only the tall mounds remain, dipping and rising side by side.
The graves wash away, no heirs to tend them;
and their wandering ghosts — where have they gone?
Wealth and glory — no doubt, worth prizing;
at the same time, a cause for sorrow and pain.

Stopping Wine

My home? I'm stopping near the town,
stopping in a peaceful way, free and easy.
My sitting stops with the shade of tall trees,
my strolling stops inside the brushwood gate.
Fine flavors? They stop with the mallows in my garden.
And my greatest joys stop with these boys of mine.
All my life I've never stopped wine;
stop wine and my heart would be robbed of delight.
Stop it at night and I couldn't sleep soundly,
stop it in the morning and I'd never get up.
Day after day I *wanted* to stop it,
but if I stopped my system wouldn't function right.
I only knew that stopping meant no more pleasure,
couldn't see how stopping would benefit me.
But now at last I realize that stopping is best.
This morning — mark me! — I've stopped for good!
From now on, I'm going to stay stopped,

1. Pei-mang, the graveyard in the hills north of Lo-yang; by extension, any graveyard.

and soon I'll be stopping by the Fu-sang shore,[1]
a bright and sober face stopping with me forever —
how could it stop in a thousand, ten thousand years?

Poem in the Form of a Coffin-Puller's Song, No. 1

What has a life must have a death;
an early end doesn't mean the lifespan's been shortened.
Last evening I was the same as other people;
this morning I'm listed in the roster of the dead.
When soul and breath scatter, where do they go,
when the wasted form's consigned to hollow wood?
My little boy, wailing, searches for his father;
my close friends caress me and mourn.
I know nothing now of gain or loss;
how could I distinguish right from wrong?
A thousand autumns, ten thousand years after,
who'll know if I lived in glory or disgrace?
I only regret that while I was in the world
I never got to drink enough wine!

Poem in the Form of a Coffin-Puller's Song, No. 2

In the old days I had no wine to drink;
this morning, when it's useless, the cup overflows,
spring brew making bubbles like floating ants,
but when can I ever taste it?

1. The Fu-sang is a fabulous tree that grows on the shore of the eastern sea at the place where the sun rises; see p. 60. The poet is jokingly suggesting that he will become an immortal spirit.

Trays with delicacies are heaped in front of me,
relatives and friends weep by my side.
I want to speak but my mouth won't make a sound,
I want to look but my pupils have lost their light.
Times past, I slept in a high hall;
now I lodge in a place of wild grasses.
One morning I went out the gate,
and there's no date set for my return.

Poem in the Form of a Coffin-Puller's Song, No. 3

A plain of wild grasses, broad and tangled,
white poplars that whisper and sigh;
biting frost of the mid-ninth month:
they are taking me far away from the city.
On four sides no human habitation,
only the ridge and rise of tall grave mounds.
For me the horses look skyward and neigh,
for me the wind takes on a mournful tone.
The dark chamber, once sealed,
for a thousand years will not see the dawn.
A thousand years it will not see the dawn;
neither worthy nor wise man can force its doors.
Those who just now saw me off
have all gone back, each to his home,
my kin perhaps with a lingering grief,
but the others have finished with their funeral songs.
And what of the one who has departed in death,
body left to merge with the round of the hill?

Preface to the Poem on the Peach Blossom Spring

(The following preface is one of the most famous and influential passages in all of early Chinese prose. The poem itself, which simply repeats the account given in the preface, is of secondary interest and has not been translated.)

During the T'ai-yüan era (376-397) of the Chin dynasty, there was a man of Wu-ling who caught fish for a living. Once he was making his way up a valley stream and had lost track of how far he had gone when he suddenly came upon a forest of peach trees in bloom. For several hundred paces on either bank of the stream there were no other trees to be seen, but fragrant grasses, fresh and beautiful, and falling petals whirling all around.

The fisherman, astonished at such a sight, pushed ahead, hoping to see what lay beyond the forest. Where the forest ended there was a spring that fed the stream, and beyond that a hill. The hill had a small opening in it, from which there seemed to come a gleam of light. Abandoning his boat, the fisherman went through the opening. At first it was very narrow, with barely room for a person to pass, but after he had gone twenty or thirty paces, it suddenly opened out and he could see clearly.

A plain stretched before him, broad and flat, with houses and sheds dotting it, and rich fields, pretty ponds, and mulberry and bamboo around them. Paths ran north and south, east and west across the fields, and chickens and dogs could be heard from farm to farm. The men and women who passed back and forth in the midst, sowing and tilling the fields, were all dressed just like any other people, and from white-haired elders to youngsters with their hair unbound, everyone seemed carefree and happy.

The people, seeing the fisherman, were greatly startled and asked where he had come from. When he had answered all their questions, they invited him to return with them to their home, where they set out wine and killed a chicken to prepare a meal.

As soon as the others in the village heard of his arrival, they all came to greet him. They told him that some generations in the past their people had fled from the troubled times of the Ch'in dynasty (221-207 B.C.) and had come with their wives and children and fellow villagers to this faraway place. They had never ventured out into the world again, and hence in time had come to be completely cut off from other people. They asked him what dynasty was ruling at present — they had not even heard of the Han dynasty, to say nothing of the Wei and Chin dynasties that succeeded it. The fisherman replied to each of their questions to the best of his knowledge, and everyone sighed with wonder.

The other villagers invited the fisherman to visit their homes as well, each setting out wine and food for him. Thus he remained for several days before taking his leave. One of the villagers said to him, "I trust you won't tell the people on the outside about this."

After the fisherman had made his way out of the place, he found his boat and followed the route he had taken earlier, taking care to note the places that he passed. When he reached the prefectural town, he went to call on the governor and reported what had happened. The governor immediately dispatched men to go with him to look for the place, but though he tried to locate the spots that he had taken note of earlier, in the end he became confused and could not find the way again.

Liu Tzu-chi of Nan-yang, a gentleman-recluse of lofty ideals, heard the story and began delightedly making plans to go there, but before he could carry them out, he fell sick and died. Since then there have been no more "seekers of the ford."[1]

---

1. An allusion to *Analects* XVIII, 6, in which Confucius sends one of his disciples to inquire about a fording place across a river. Here, of course, the phrase refers to seekers of the utopian land of the Peach Blossom Spring.

CHAPTER SIX

Chin, Six Dynasties, and Sui Poets

THE Wei dynasty, which had replaced the Han in 220, was unable to extend its rule over the entire nation, the south and west remaining in the hands of rival claimants to power. In 265 a dynasty known to history as the Western Chin reunited the empire, but soon fell victim to internal dissention and invasions from the north. In time, both the capital cities of Ch'ang-an and Lo-yang had fallen to non-Chinese armies, and in 317 the Chin emperor and his court fled south to safety in the area of the Yangtze, the dynasty thereafter being known as the Eastern Chin. For nearly three centuries, roughly the period known as the Six Dynasties, the north remained in the hands of non-Chinese states, while a succession of weak Chinese dynasties ruled the south. Unity was finally restored by the Sui (589-618), a short-lived dynasty that prepared the way for the more lasting T'ang.

The first figure in my selection, Juan Chi, was one of a group of distinguished poet-intellectuals noted for their eccentric behavior and aloofness from official life. His most famous work, a set of over eighty poems entitled *Yung-huai* or "Singing of Thoughts," is dominated — not surprisingly, in view of the temper of the times — by a mood of deep pessimism and sorrow. Cast largely in symbolic language, probably to avoid rousing the ire of the political leaders of the period, the poems dwell on the shortness of life, the stupidity and ill will of the poet's contemporaries, and his longing for a true friend to console him in his melancholy.

Other works in my selection touch on the same theme of friendship, often treating it in a more realistic and concrete manner, as in Hsieh Ling-yün's long poem-letter to his cousin. Still others deal with the life of the recluse, a subject important, as we have seen, in the poetry of T'ao Yüan-ming. One unusual poem by Wang K'angchü sharply attacks the eremitic ideal, chiding the artificiality and moral presumption of those who ostentatiously turn their back on human society.

Retirement from the world is likewise the theme of one of the four poems in *fu* or rhyme-prose form included in this chapter, P'an Yüeh's autobiographical "Rhyme-Prose on the Idle Life." The other three are impersonal descriptive pieces evoking, respectively, a city desolated by civil war, a snowy night, and the sea, the last a subject rare in traditional Chinese poetry.

We are fortunate in possessing many love poems from the period, thanks largely to an anthology of such poetry, the *Yü-t'ai hsin-yung* or *New Songs from the Jade Terrace*, compiled in the sixth century. Though military leaders exercised decisive power on the political scene, cultural life was dominated by the great aristocratic families such as the Hsieh clan, several of whose members are represented in my selection. They appear to have been less bound than families of earlier times by Confucian standards of decorum and unabashed in their pursuit of pleasure, and their women were better educated and accorded higher social status than was generally true of Chinese women in other periods. P'an Yüeh's tender poem to his wife when he was separated from her, and his laments on her death, give franker and more passionate expression to the love between husband and wife than most poets of either earlier or later periods were likely to venture. Other poems, less personal and more conventionalized in nature, deal with the shy mistress or the seductive courtesan, the depiction of feminine charm being one of the favorite topics of the poetry of this period.

Another important theme, which we have seen already in the poetry of T'ao Yüan-ming, is the beauty of the natural scene. The

Chinese, driven from their ancient homeland in the north, were apparently much struck by the lush scenery of the Yangtze valley, particularly its mists and other aerial effects. The result was a greatly intensified interest in the depiction of landscapes both in painting and in poetry. Hsieh Ling-yün in particular is noted for his rapt appreciation of the sights of nature and is often looked on as the father of "mountain-and-river" or landscape poetry.

Shen Yüeh (441-513), a poet represented in my selection by five poems on love, is credited with having laid down the principles for the kind of tonal regulation of poetry already described in the Introduction, in his "Eight Faults" defining various euphonic effects that are to be avoided. But many of his contemporaries declined to be bound by his dicta, and some of them claimed not even to understand what he was talking about. It was not until T'ang times that the tonally regulated verse forms reached full maturity.

In terms of style, even the best poetry of this period tends to be ornate in diction and much given to the use of rhetorical devices such as parallelism, allusion, and elegant variation. As time passed, the poetry of the southern dynasties (and almost all of my examples are from the south, there being little poetry of importance preserved from the northern states) became increasingly shallow and mannered, characteristics that carried over into the style of the Sui period. The great majority of extant works are either flattering pieces produced to commemorate some social occasion, or lifeless imitations of the old *yüeh-fu* ballads. This will explain the paucity of examples from these later centuries in my selection.

Very different in tone from these effete and flowery works are the anonymous songs with which my selection concludes, works of uncertain date and provenance. Among them are love songs, pert in tone, lively and colloquial in language, often employing puns to add an innuendo to the surface meaning. Many are associated with the name of Tzu-yeh, a professional singing girl of the time who was supposed to have originated the genre. Many, like Japanese haiku, contain references to a particular season of the year.

But love, one notes with regret, was not the only experience that moved the people of the time to song. Other songs, starker in expression, some of them from the north, depict the grimmer side of life in this era of continuing warfare and disunion. One, entitled *Ch'i-yü-ko* (meaning uncertain), though listed as southern in origin, was written to be sung to the semibarbarian music of the north. In it we sense something of the sweep and power that in time would characterize the works of the T'ang masters, the creators of the great age of poetry that was to follow:

Man — pitiful insect,
out the gate with fears of death in his breast,
a corpse fallen in narrow valleys,
white bones that no one gathers up.

JUAN CHI *(210-263)*

Singing of Thoughts

(5-ch.; 6 poems from a series)

I.

Beautiful trees make paths beneath themselves:
peach and plum in the eastern garden.
Autumn winds toss the drifting bean leaves;
now all things begin to wither and fall.
Brightest blossoms have their fading,
the high hall is grown over with brier and thorn.
Leave it — spur the horses and go,
climb the foot of Western Hill.[1]
Hard enough to keep one body whole;
harder when you long for wife and child.
Chill frost will clothe the grassy meadow,
the year will darken and then be gone.

2.

Years ago, when I was young,
heedless, rash, I loved strings and a song.
I wandered west to Hsien-yang,
passing time with the Chaos and Lis.[1]
Pleasures had not been fully tasted
when all at once the white sun slipped away.
I raced the horses, came home again,
turning my eyes over the three rivers.

1. The retreat of the ancient hermits Po Yi and Shu Ch'i.

1. Hsien-yang is the old name for Ch'ang-an, the capital of the Han dynasty. The Chao and Li families, related to the imperial family of the Former Han, represent the height of luxurious living.

My hundred taels of yellow gold gone,
every day I grumble at the cost of things.
Like the man who faced north when he meant to go south,
I've lost the road — where do I go now?

3.
Tung-ling melons — men say that long ago,[1]
close beyond the city's Green Gate,
they grew by field sides, rambling left and right,
mother vine and child linked and laced together,
five-colored fruit that shone in the morning sun,
rich buyers from four directions crowding round —
The grease-filled torch burns itself out,
abundant wealth will harm and harry you!
The body can get by in coarsest cloth;
lavish stipends — what use are they?

4.
Long ago, at fourteen or fifteen,
high in purpose, I loved the Classics,
dressed in coarse brown, a gem in my heart,
hoping some day to be like Yen and Min.[1]
I threw open the window, looked out on the four fields,
climbed the hills and let my hopeful eyes wander.
Grave mounds cover the heights,
ten thousand ages all brought to one!
A thousand autumns, ten thousand years from now,
what will be left of a "glorious name"?
At last I understand Master Hsien Mên;[2]
I can laugh out loud at what I used to be!

1. On the Tung-ling melons, see note p. 135 above.

1. Yen Yüan and Min Tzu-ch'ien, poor but eminently virtuous disciples of Confucius.
2. A *hsien* or immortal spirit of ancient times.

5.

This summer's burning heat,
in its last weeks now, beginning to fade;
green leaves drooping on fragrant trees,
cool clouds splayed across the sky —
the four seasons one by one take leave,
sun and moon trail each other in turn.
I wander weeping through empty halls;
there is no one who knows me!
I long for a friend to be glad with forever,
never to know the pain of parting.

6.

In North Ward they do many strange dances,
clandestine music on the banks of the P'u.[1]
The careless wanderer, bold and unwitting,
bobs and sinks, dips and follows with the age;
by shortcuts and byways he goes,
driving himself on to excess and ruin.
I may never see the immortal Prince Ch'iao
riding the clouds, flying up to Teng-lin;
but still I have his "art of long life";
with this let me console my heart.

1. References to the evil and licentious entertainments of lost dynasties of antiquity.

HSI K'ANG *(223-262)*

Sent to the *Hsiu-ts'ai* on His Entry into the Army

(Last of a series of five poems sent to his older brother Hsi Hsi, who had passed the civil service examination with the degree of *Hsiu-ts'ai* or Perfected Talent. 4-ch.)

The quiet night is solemn and still,
a bright moon lighting up the eaves.
Gentle breezes rustle my garments —
the corded blinds are looped up high.
Though fine wine brims in the casket,
I've no one to join me in delight.
The sounding lute rests beside me,
but for whom should I pluck its strings?
I look up, longing for one who shares my thoughts —
his fragrance is like the orchid.
My fine friend not by my side,
can I help endlessly sighing?

MU HUA *(c. A.D.300)*

Rhyme-Prose on the Sea

(The poem begins with a retelling of the ancient flood myth, when the hero Yü, serving under the sage rulers Yao and Shun, opened up the waterways and rescued the world from inundation by guiding the rivers so that they flowed harmlessly into the sea.)

Long ago, when Emperor Shun of Kuei was still minister to
      Yao of T'ang
the Heaven-appointed waterways swelled and overflowed,
causing blight, causing affliction;
giant billows, fiercely raging,
swept ten thousand li unbounded,
long waves that gather and build,
rolling abroad in eight directions.
      Then it was that Yü
sliced through the banks and ridges that loom along the waters,
pierced the ponds and reservoirs and let them drain;
broke open the cliffs and crags of Lung-men,
severing hills and ranges, hacking and chiseling through.
And when the crowded mountains had been subdued,
the hundred rivers drawn off in sunken channels,
then the massed waters in their depth and power
rose up, toppled, and sped on their way.
When he had guided the Yellow River and the Yangtze,
the myriad sluices so they flowed together,
then the Five Mountains plucked themselves up,
and the Nine Continents came forth as dry land.
Drops and driblets, the smallest ooze,
damp congestion of cloud and fog,
the least rivulet that trickles and trills —
there was none that failed to come draining down.
Ah, the vastness of the magic sea,
eternally receiving and taking them in,
its breadth and its strangeness
a fitting match for the gigantic size of it!
      This is its form:
a watery wasteland, tossing, heaving,
the sky afloat on it, no coast in sight;
fathomless, limitless,
bottomless, unending,
with waves like chains of mountains,
now linking, now shattering,

sucking in and spewing back the hundred rivers,
washing clear the Huai and the Han,
inundating the broad embankments,
immense and borderless, trackless and wild.
　　And when night's bright chariot
has turned rein toward the caves of Chin-shu,
when the winging fire of day starts up from Fu-sang fords,
and wind-driven sands, rustling and sighing,
scurry over the beaches of the islands,
then with a pounding fury
the giant combers lift and sway,
thumping and jarring one against another,
flinging foam, tossing their crests,
in form like wheels of heaven dizzily spinning,
or axles of the earth sticking up and turning round;
like jagged peaks that climb the air to fall back again,
or the Five Mountains drumming and dancing, hammering one
　　　　　another,
jostling, stumbling, piling up in heaps,
suddenly bulging into knolls and declivities,
whirling, sucking down to form hollows,
now shooting skyward in lonely pinnacles.
Schools of little waves dart off at an angle,
while hulking giants rear and crash together;
waves in panic flee with lightning quickness,
frightened waters huddle close together,
parting, closing, breaking, joining,
ceaselessly, restlessly,
troubled and turbulent,
hissing with spume.
And when the clouds of dust and darkness have settled and
　　　　　gone,
no longer racing, no longer scudding by,
when the lightest grain of sand no longer stirs,
and the vine's slimmest tendrils dangle unmoved,
still there is the gape and suck,

the solitary churning of the waves left over,
sloshing, pitching,
molding themselves into hummocks and hills
whose coves in turn are drowned by tides,
whose waters brim over to cut new beds,
turning their backs on barbarian lands,
rolling and tumbling ten thousand li.
     Should it happen that
sudden news comes from wild and distant regions,
the king's command to be speedily relayed,
then fleet horses set out, sculling oars are labored,
the former to cross the mountains, the latter to span the sea.
Then we watch for a vigorous wind,
step the hundred-foot mast,
rig the lengthy lines,
hoist the jibs and sails,
scan the surf, then take our long farewell,
gliding off, a bird in flight,
sudden as a wary duck parted from its mate,
swift, as though drawn by six dragons,
in one bound, three thousand li —
less than a morning and already we've reached our destination!
But should a man approach the deeps with guilt on his back,
a violater of oaths, a false invocator,
then the sea elves impede his progress,
horse monsters stand in his way,
the god T'ien-wu shows his dim semblance,
the demon Wang-hsiang of a sudden appears;
a host of wonders meet and confront him,
weird and freakish things he sees.
Tearing the sails, splitting the mast,
violent winds come to work mischief,
immense in magic transformations,
sudden as the pall of evening,
their breath like the mists of heaven,
banks of vapor rolling in like clouds.

Streaks of precipitate lightning
illumine a hundred unearthly colors,
abruptly flashing, abruptly gone,
blinding, dazzling the eye without measure.
Rushing waters clash together,
frenzied forces that collide,
like clouds that crumble, sheets of rain descending,
humming, moaning,
whooshing forward, reeling back,
bunching and straining apart,
roaring and reverberating,
dousing the cloud banks, washing the sun.
Then the sailors and fishermen
voyage south, explore the edges of the east,
some to end crushed in caves of loggerhead and sea lizard,
some caught and impaled on ragged mountain peaks,
some buffeted and blown to the country of naked men,
some floating far off to the Black Tooth land,
some drifting like duckweed, bobbing, circling,
some, wafted on homing winds, finding their way back,
knowing only that the wonders they've seen were many and
        fearsome,
witless whether the route they came by was near or far.
These are its dimensions:
south it batters the Vermilion Cliffs,
north washes the Waste of Heaven,
east extends as far as Split Tree,
west presses on Ch'ing and Hsü,
its expanse incalculable,
tens of thousands of li and more.
It breathes forth clouds and rainbows,
shelters dragons and fish,
conceals the scaly K'un,
hides spirit dwellings.
Is it only T'ai-tien's priceless shell,
the bright pearl of Marquis Sui that it holds in store?

These the world's collectors all have heard of,
but those others — the unnamed ones — they do not know exist.
Marvels rarely heard of in this world —
how should one know their names in full?
So I can only suggest their colors,
only dimly sketch their forms.
Within those watery treasure houses,
those courts unfathomably deep,
are tall islands, borne by the sea turtle,
reaching skyward, lofty and alone,
clearing the huge billows,
pointing toward the great pure air,
flaunting massive boulders,
home for a hundred immortal spirits.
When southern winds bluster, the islands march southward;
in the face of northern winds, they travel north.[1]
The sea's confines hold heavenly jewels, water wonders,
the halls of the shark-man,[2]
flawed gems that sparkle strangely,
scaled and armored beings of odd design.
Patterns like cloud brocade are flung
across the face of the sandy shore;
tints like those of shimmering damask
play about the lips of whorled shell and clam.
Multitudes of colors parade their brilliance,
ten thousand hues hold their freshness hidden,
sun-warmed ice that never melts,
shadowy fires that burn in secret,
smoldering charcoal flaring up again,
casting its glow over the earth's nine springs,
scarlet flames, green smoke,
leaping, spiraling upward and away.[3]

1. Because the monstrous turtle that bears the magic islands on its back always moves in the opposite direction to the wind.

2. A creature half fish, half man; his tears become pearls.

3. The passage on ice and smoldering fires may be taken to refer to the iridescent colors of the nacreous shells.

For fish there is the sea-straddling whale,
humped and lordly, swimming alone,
scraping the mountain's back,
pillowing on tall billows,
feeding on scaly and crustaceous creatures,
gobbling up even dragon-sized boats.
When he sucks in the waves then the tallest surfs come tumbling;
when he blows on the billows then the hundred streams flow
       backward.
And should he flounder where the waves run thin,
should he die stranded on salty flats,
his huge scales will pierce the clouds,
his dorsal fins stab the sky;
the bones of his skull will turn into a mountain,
the oils that exude from him collect in deep pools.
Meanwhile, in crevices of cliff and promontory,
by scarps carved of gravel and sand,
winged and feathered creatures rear their young,
pecking the eggs to let the chicks out,
ducklings, a ball of fuzz,
baby storks, their down still wet.
Winging in flocks, diving side by side,
they play about the open places, float on the deeps,
tagging and tailing after one another,
dipping and soaring;
their restless fluttering raises a thunder,
their milling flights become a forest,
screeching and shrilling back and forth,
rare in color, outlandish in sound.
     And then,
when the three lights, sun, moon, and stars shine clear
and heaven and earth are everywhere illumined,
then, without troubling Marquis Yang for passage,
one may mount on magic footsteps, break clean away,
to visit An-ch'i on the island of P'eng-lai,

to view the emperor's form as it was on Mount Ch'iao.[4]
In the distance faintly visible, troops of immortals
feast on jade by the clear-watered shore,
shod in sandals left behind at Fu-hsiang,
robed in drooping feathers and plumes.
They soar by the ponds of Heaven,
go sporting to the farthest darkness,
showing what it means to have a body but no desires,
to keep living on and on to the end of time.
These are the sea's capacities:
to enfold the heart of the *ch'ien* trigram,
encompass all the realms of the *k'un;*[5]
a house for spirits,
domicile of gods,
what rarity not found within it,
what wonder not in store?
Abundant the waters that gather there;
it accepts their forms, remaining empty within.
Far-flung, the virtue of the trigram *k'an,*
choosing the lowliest place to dwell!
It enhances what goes forth, receives what comes,
their ancestor, their metropolis;
of all things and creatures, all species alive,
what does it possess, what does it not?

4. Marquis Yang is the god of the waves. An-ch'i is an immortal spirit living on the magic island of P'eng-lai. A native of a place called Fu-hsiang, he left his sandals there when he went off to become an immortal, a fact referred to below. Mount Ch'iao is the place where the Yellow Emperor of ancient times left his hat and robe when he ascended into the sky to become an immortal.

5. *Ch'ien* and *k'un* are the trigrams representing Heaven and earth respectively in the *I Ching* or *Book of Changes; k'an,* referred to seven lines below, symbolizes water.

P'AN YÜEH *(d. A.D. 300)*

Thinking of My Wife

(5-ch.; 1st of 2 poems)

Alone in my sorrow, where do my thoughts go?
Man's life is like the morning dew.
Wandering in distant provinces,
fondly, tenderly I call up the past.
Your love follows me even here;
my heart too turns back in longing.
Though our bodies are parted and cannot touch,
our spirits join at journey's midpoint.
Have you never seen the hilltop pine,
how even in winter it keeps the same hue?
Have you never seen the knoll and valley cypresses,
in year-end cold, guarding their constant green?
Don't say it is my wish that parts us;
far away, my love grows stronger still.

Rhyme-Prose on the Idle Life

(The poem begins with a prose passage describing the thirty years of the
writer's career as a government official, a humorously stop-and-go affair of
complex advancements, transfers, and resignations. P'an Yüeh stresses the
words "inept" and "ineptness" in order to make clear why in the end he
thought it best to retire from politics and lead the life of a country squire and
filial son at his estate in the southern outskirts of Lo-yang.)

Whenever I read the "Biography of Chi An," noting that
Ssu-ma An four times advanced to the rank of the nine highest
ministers, and that the Good Historian characterizes him as
"clever at getting along in the official world," I never fail to

lay aside the book with a profound sigh.[1] Aha! I say to myself;
if even a clever man had such ups and downs, it's no wonder
that an inept one should!

It has always seemed to me that, when a man is born into
this world, if he is not fortunate enough to be a perfect and
matchless sage or a person of subtle and profound
understanding, then he must try to gain what merit and
achievement he can in the service of the times. If he does so
he may, by relying on loyal conduct and observing good faith,
go forward in virtue; and by minding his words and
establishing a name for sincerity, he may maintain a livelihood.
When I was young I enjoyed, undeservedly perhaps, the praise
of my fellow villagers, and with all due respect I heeded the
orders of the minister of works and grand commandant. The
master whom I served was none other than the high minister
Duke Wu of Lu.[2] I was chosen as a "man of outstanding talent"
and was made a "gentleman." Later, in the reign of Emperor
Wu, the Ancestor of Generations, I became magistrate of Ho-
yang and then of Huai. Next I became a palace secretary and
then an officer under the commandant of justice.[3] While the
present Son of Heaven was in mourning, I was appointed
secretary to the grand tutor, but when that official was
condemned to punishment, my name was stricken from the
roster and I was made a commoner.[4] Later I was suddenly
called back to office and made magistrate of Ch'ang-an. I was
transferred to the post of erudit, but before I could accept the
appointment one of my parents fell ill and I immediately
resigned and left my post. Thus, from the time of my capping
at the age of twenty until the age when I have learned to

---

1. The biography is found in chapter 120 of the *Shih chi* or *Records of the Historian;* the
"Good Historian" is Ssu-ma Ch'ien (145?-90? B.C.), author of the *Shih chi.*
2. Chia Ch'ung (217-282), who held the posts of minister of works and grand
commandant, was enfeoffed as duke of Lu, and granted the posthumous name of Wu.
P'an Yüeh served on his staff.
3. As his biography in *Chin shu* 55 makes clear, he resigned this last post. This is the
first of his two resignations.
4. The grand tutor Yang Chün was put to death in A.D. 291.

"understand fate" [i.e., fifty], I have changed office eight times. Once I rose a step in rank, twice I resigned, once my name was stricken from the roster, once I failed to accept an appointment, and three times I was transferred! Though all of this starting and stopping may to some extent be the work of fate, still I cannot help thinking that it was largely the result of my ineptness.

A man of great understanding, Ho Ch'ang-yü, once characterized me as being one who is "inept at using the many talents he possesses." The "many" part of the statement I would not dare lay claim to, but there is ample proof to support the charge of ineptness. At the present time, when "men of outstanding ability hold office" and "the hundred officials are all fitted for their jobs,"⁵ an inept person would do best to abandon any thought of winning favor or glory. I am still lucky enough to have my mother with me, though she suffers from the ills of age and infirmity. How could I neglect my duty — the duty to wait by her knee and observe what service may please her — merely to charge busily about in pursuance of some peck-and-bushel office?

And so I have turned my eyes toward that life that knows what is enough, that knows where to stop; I look on wealth and honor as mere drifting clouds. I have built rooms and planted trees where I may wander at will in perfect contentment. I possess ponds sufficient for all the fishing I will ever do, and the revenue from my grain-husking operations takes the place of farmlands. I water the garden and sell vegetables to provide something for our morning and evening meal; I raise sheep and peddle the milk products so I can put away a little extra for summer and winter festivals. Filial above all else, friendly to older and younger brother — this is the way the inept man may perform his "government service."⁶ And now I have written this *fu* on the idle life in

---

5. The phrases are quoted from the *Book of Documents, Kao-yao mo;* there is some doubt as to how P'an Yüeh and his contemporaries interpreted the second one.

6. Reference to *Analects* 11, 21: "Someone asked Confucius why he did not take part in government. The Master said,...'To be filial, to be friendly to elder and younger brother, these are qualities exercised in government. This then also constitutes a kind of government service.'"

order to describe my activities in song and give vent to my feelings.

I have strolled the long groves of the Classics and Canons,
walked the highroads of the wise men of old,
and though I put on a thick-skinned face,
within, I blush to think of Ning and Chü.[7]
The Way prevails, yet I do not take office;
it prevails no longer, yet I do not act the fool.
What is this but a lack of wit and wisdom,
a superabundance of ineptness and folly?
    So I have retired
to live the idle life on the banks of the Lo,
in body one with the hermit folk,
my name listed among the lower gentry.
The capital at my back, the Yi before me,
I face the suburbs, putting the market place behind.
The pontoon bridge, far-stretching, takes one straight across
      the river;
the Spirit Tower, lofty, lifts its tall form
where one may spy out hidden secrets of heavenly bodies,
trace the start and finish of human affairs.[8]
To the west lie the barracks of the palace guards,
black-curtained, pennanted in green;
cross-bows of the *hsi-tzu* and *chü-shu* style,
differing in their firing, in mechanism alike;
ballista stones, startling as thunder,
swift arrows like gadflies in flight,
leading off as the marchers set out,
lending glory to our Emperor's might.

---

7. *Analects* v, 20: "The Master said, 'When the Way prevailed in the state, Ning Wu acted like a wise man; when the Way did not prevail, he acted like a fool.'" *Ibid.* xv, 6: "The Master said,…'A superior man indeed is Chü Po-yü! When the Way prevails in the state, he takes office; when the Way does not prevail, he knows how to wrap up [his talents] and put them away in the folds of his robe.'"

8. The "floating" or pontoon bridge spanned the Lo River; the Spirit Tower was the imperial observatory.

To the east, the Bright Hall and the Hall of Learning,[9]
holy and majestic, spacious and still,
their encircling groves a belt of brightness,
the waters that ring them an orbit of deeps.
There filial remembrance pays careful tribute to the father,
honors noble forebears as the counterparts of Heaven,
illustrating obedience through respect for wise ancestral ways,
showing reverence for old age by cherishing the elders.
    And later,
winter behind us, strolling into spring,
as the yin bows out and the yang spreads abroad,
the Son of Heaven grows busy with his brushwood fires,
suburban sacrifice to progenitors, a display of duty,
performance of Vast Music, the Equalizer of Heaven,
replete with a thousand chariots, ten thousand riders,
vestments sober and solemn, one in blackness,
woodwinds tweet-tweeting, shrilling all around,
luminous, light-filled,
rich and resplendent,
the bravest aspect that ritual can wear;
of the king's institutions, the crowning beauty!
Nearby, the two schools are ranged side by side,[10]
their dual roofs identical,
the right one welcoming the sons of the state,
the left enrolling boys of promise and good report,
students earnest and well comported,
keen disciples of Confucian learning,
some "ascending the hall,"
others "entering the room."[11]
But learning has no constant master;

---

9. The *Ming-t'ang* and *Pi-yung*, semireligious and highly symbolic halls of state situated in the suburbs; in the former the ruler sacrificed to his ancestors, proclaimed the principles of his rule, honored elders and worthy men from among the common people, and performed similar ritual acts of virtue.

10. Two institutions of higher learning situated near the Hall of Learning, the Kuo-hsüeh for sons of the nobility, and the Ta-hsüeh for talented commoners.

11. Stages of advancement in learning.

where the Way resides, there it will be found.
And so distinguished statesmen doff their cords of office,
famous princes hide their seals;
for instruction is like a wind passing over —
men bow to it as the grasses nod.
This is why benevolence is called the adornment of the village,
why Mencius's mother moved three times.[12]

    And so I have made my home here,
building rooms, scooping out ponds.
Tall willows shine in their surfaces,
fragrant spiny orange planted for my hedge;
playful fish leap and lash the water,
lotus blossoms reach out and unfurl.
Bamboo thickets, dense and shady,
the rarest fruits crowding all around;
pears from Lord Chang's Great Valley orchard,
persimmons from Marquis Liang's *wu-pi* strain,
King Wen of Chou's supple-limbed jujubes,
Chu Chung's plums from the region of Fang-ling —
none are lacking in these well-stocked groves.
Peach with its twin cousins, walnut and cherry,
two shades of crabapple gleaming pink and white,
pomegranate and grape, exotic wonders,
rambling, luxuriating by their side;
prune, apricot, almond and cherry apple
adding lush and vivid beauty to the decoration,
flowers and fruit growing in such splendor
words cannot describe them all!

    For vegetables we have
onions, leeks, garlic and taro root,
blue-green shoots of bamboo, purple ginger,
wild parsley and shepherd's purse, sweet to the taste,

12. When Mencius was little, his mother moved to a house near a cemetery, but to her distress she found the little boy playing at being a grave digger. She then moved to a house near the market place, but this time found him playing shopkeeper. Finally she moved near a school, where he soon learned to imitate the ceremonies and acts of politeness that were taught there.

smartweed and coriander, pungent with perfume,
myoga ginger that hugs the shade,
legumes whose leaves turn toward the sun,
green mallows enfolding the dew,
white scallions with frost on their spines.
    And then,
in brisk autumn, when the heat has dispersed,
in shining spring, when the cold is gone,
when the gentle rains have newly lifted
and the six directions are bright and clear,
then my mother, mounting a plain board carriage,
climbing up into a light rig,
rides far off to view the royal environs,
or, closer, takes a turn around the house and gardens,
her body pleasantly fatigued by exercise,
the exertion aiding the effects of the medicine,
so that when her tray is brought, she eats all the better,
and her old ailment in time is cured.
Then we roll out the long mats
and line up the grandchildren;
where willows spread their shade we halt the carriages,
on hillsides gathering purple fruit,
over the waters angling for ruddy carp,
sometimes picnicking in the woods,
sometimes bathing on the riverbank.
My brothers and I, our heads flecked with gray,
our children still in infancy,
wish my mother long life, offer a toast,
on the one hand fearful, on the other full of joy;[13]
and as the cup of congratulation is lifted,
her gentle face beams with delight.
Floating winecups on the water, we drink merrily,
strings and woodwinds ranged all about;
stamping feet, we leap up to dance,

---

13. *Analects* IV, 21: "The Master said, 'One should always know the age of one's parents. On the one had it will inspire joy, on the other, fear.' "

raising voices in boisterous song.
When life offers such peace and joy,
who would take thought for anything further?
    So I have retired,
to search within in self-reflection,
for truly my accomplishments are paltry and my talents poor.
I have honored Chou Jen's excellent words;
would I dare exert my strength and step into the ranks?[14]
I can barely keep this poor body alive,
much less emulate enlightened men and sages!
So with eyes upon the "many wonders,"[15] other thoughts cut
        off,
cherishing my ineptness, I will live carefree to the end.

Lamenting the Dead

(5-ch.; 1st of 3 poems in memory of the poet's wife)

Before I know it, winter and spring depart,
cold and heat suddenly trading places,
and she has gone to the deepest springs;
heaped earth forever seals her apart.
My secret longings I cannot fulfill;[1]
what good would it do to linger there?
Swearing allegiance to the sovereign's command,
I turn my heart back to former tasks.
But seeing the house, I think of her;
entering its rooms, I recall the past.

---

14. *Analects* XVI, 1: "Chou Jen had a saying: 'He who can exert his strength steps into the ranks; he who cannot stays behind.'"

15. Epithet for the Way. (Lao Tzu, *Tao-te-ching* 1.)

---

1. The poet hints that he is tempted to join his wife by committing suicide at her grave.

Curtains and screens hold no shadow of her,
her writings the only trace that remains,
the drifting scent that never quite fades,
her things left forgotten, hung on the wall.
Dazed by longing, I think she is here,
then come to myself with a twinge of pain.
We were a pair of birds winging to the wood,
mated, then suddenly one morning alone;
a pair of fish swimming the stream,
eye to eye, then parted midway.
Spring wind filters in through the cracks,
morning rain drips down from the eaves;
lying at rest, when will I forget?
Each day I sink into deeper sorrow.
Perhaps a time will come when it will fade
and I, like Chuang Tzu, can pound the tub.[2]

FU HSIEN *(239-294)*

Ruinous Rains

(5-ch.)

Lift your feet and you sink deeper in the mud!
On market roads, no carts go by.
Orchids and cinnamon sell for the price of garbage,
firewood and grain more precious than bright pearls.

---

2. When the philosopher Chuang Tzu first lost his wife, he grieved for her like other men, but in time he became reconciled and spent his days singing and pounding on a tub. *Chuang Tzu,* sec. 18.

LU CHI *(261-303)*

Two Poems Presented to the Gentleman in the Office of Palace Writers Ku Yen-hsien

(5-ch., 2nd of 2 poems)

Off at dawn to service in the walled and storied palace;
rest at evening, back to the officials' lodge.
Shrill thunder blares at midnight,
Shafts of swift lightning streak the darkness.
Black clouds oppress the vermilion towers,
rough winds beat on lattice windows.
Streams gush and spill from the long roof gutters,
yellow puddles swallow up the terrace stairs.
Stolid skies mesh and will not break apart,
the broad thoroughfares turn into canals.
Crops are under water in Liang and Ying;
toward Ching and Hsü the homeless peasants drift.
And what, I wonder, of our old home?
There they'll be no better off than fish![1]

LU YÜN *(262-303)*

For Ku Yen-hsien, A Poem for Him to Give to His Wife

(5-ch.)

I on the sunny side of Three Rivers,
you in the gloom south of Five Lakes,

1. Both the poet and his fellow official Ku Yen-hsien were from Wu, the region of the Yangtze delta, where the rains presumably had the worst effect.

mountains and seas vast between us,
farther apart than bird and fish —
my eyes envision your lovely form,
my ears still ring with your soft sweet voice.
I lie down alone, full of far-off thoughts;
waking, I stroke the collar of my empty robe.
Beautiful one, sharer of my longing,
who but you will ever hold my heart?

KUO P'U *(276-324)*

Poem on the Wandering Immortal

(5-ch., from a series of 14 poems)

Kingfishers frolic among the orchid blossoms,
each form and hue lending freshness to the others.
Green creepers twine over the tall grove,
their leafy darkness shadowing the whole hill.
And in the midst, a man of quiet retirement
softly whistles, strokes the clear lute strings,
frees his thoughts to soar beyond the blue,
munches flower stamens, dips from a waterfall.
When Red Pine appears, roaming on high,
this man rides a stork, mounting the purple mists,
his left hand holding Floating Hill's sleeve,
his right hand patting Vast Cliff on the shoulder.[1]
Let me ask those short-lived mayflies,
what could they know of the years of the tortoise and the crane?

1. The Master of Red Pine has appeared earlier on p. 111; Floating Hill (Fu-ch'iu) and Vast Cliff (Hung-yai) are immortals of ancient times.

YANG FANG *(4th cen.)*

The Joy of Union

(5-ch.; 2nd of 5 poems)

The loadstone beckons to the long needle,
the burning glass calls down fire and smoke;
kung and *shang* blend their voices;[1]
hearts alike draw closer still.
My love binds me to you,
shadow in pursuit of form;
we sleep side by side beneath close-woven quilts,
stuffed with wadding from a concord of cocoons.
In heat our waving fans are two wings that touch,
in cold the felt mat seats us shoulder to shoulder.
You laugh and suddenly I am laughing too;
you grieve and all my joy has vanished.
Coming, I match my steps with yours;
going, we share the very same dust;
equals of the *ch'iung-ch'iung* beasts,[2]
in no act forsaking one another.
My only wish is that we never part,
that we unite our bodies in a single form,
in life partners of a common chamber,
in death two people in one coffin.
Lady Hsü proclaimed her love the truest;
our love surpasses words.[3]

1. *Kung* and *shang* are the first two notes of the musical scale.

2. The *ch'iung-ch'iung*, a fabulous beast, is an inseparable companion of the equally fabulous *chü-hsü* beast, hence a symbol of fidelity.

3. Hsü Shu was the wife of an official of the Eastern Han named Ch'in Chia; several love poems are attributed to the devoted couple.

HSIEH SHANG *(308-357)*

Song of the Thoroughfare

(5-ch.)

The second and third month of sunny spring,
willows green and peach trees red:
carriages, horses, hard to make out —
noises that fall through the yellow dust.

HSIEH LING-YÜN *(385-433)*

Written on the Lake, Returning from the Retreat at Stone Cliff

(5-ch.)

The weather changeable at dusk and dawn,
mountain waters shot through with clear light,
a clear light that makes men joyful:
the wanderer, lulled, forgets to go home.
Out of the valley, the sun still high;
boarding the boat, the light fading now,
forest and ravine clothed in sombering color,
clouds of sunset wrapped in evening mist;
lotus and caltrop, their leaves one by one shining;
reeds and cattails propped against each other —
push through, hurry down the trail to the south,
returning contented to bed behind the eastern door.
Thoughts at ease, outside things weigh lightly;
mind relaxed, nothing going wrong.
A word to you gentlemen "nourishers of life" —
try using this method for a while!

Replying to a Poem from My Cousin Hui-lien

(Written in 430 when the poet was living in retirement at K'uai-chi and had received news, in the form of a poem, that his cousin Hsieh Hui-lien was on his way to visit. 5-ch.)

Brought to bed by sickness, cut off from men,
I hid myself among cloudy peaks.
Cliffs and valleys filled the eye and ear;
the ones I loved — their faces, their voices far away;
gone the hope of finding a heart's companion,
long regretting I must always be alone,
near the end of the road, I met my honored cousin:
frowns faded, hearts were opened up.

After we had opened our hearts,
my sole contentment was in you.
Across the valleys you searched out my room;
I opened my books, told you all I knew.
At evening I thought how the dawn moon would pale;
mornings I fretted that the sun would set too soon.
We walked together, never tiring;
we met — and now we're parted again.

Parted, taking leave at the western river;
I turned my shadow back to hills of the east.
When we parted it was sorrowful enough;
since then the pain never seems to end.
One thought — to wait for joyful news;
then came your poem about a "river-crossing,"
about your trials with wind and wave,
of every aspect of the beaches and shoals.

Beaches and shoals where you linger so long,
wind and wave delaying your journey.
Wrapped in your memories of the bright capital far away,
how could I expect you to recall these empty valleys?
And though you favor me with this message,
it serves only to trouble my thoughts.

If — if you would come back as you said,
together we could enjoy the late spring.

Late spring — there would still be time!
more time for pleasure if you came the month before,
when the mountain peach unfurls its crimson petals
and meadow ferns are sheathed in purple.
Already the chatter of birds delights me,
but still there's gloom in my out-of-the-way home.
In dreams I wait your boat returning,
coming to free me from meanness and care.

An Exchange of Poems by Tung-yang Stream

(5-ch.)

I.
How fetching! somebody's wife,
washing her white feet beside the stream;
a bright moon among the clouds,
far away, too far away to reach!

2.
How fetching! somebody's husband,
riding a white skiff down the stream.
May I ask what your intentions are,
now that the moon has gone behind the clouds?

WANG K'ANG-CHÜ *(4th cen.)*

Refuting the "Invitation to Hiding"

(A type of poem called "Invitation to Hiding" which lauded the life of the recluse was popular at this time. The following poem is a rebuttal to such poems, ridiculing the eremetic ideal. Po Yi has already appeared on p. 149. Lao Tan is the philosopher Lao Tzu, who served as librarian at the Chou court with the title Clerk of the Pillar. The Nest-dwelling Man is Ch'ao-fu, a malcontent who lived in the golden age of the sage ruler Yao but insisted on retiring to the wilderness. (5-ch.)

Little hiders hide in the hills and groves,
big hiders hide in the city market.
Po Yi burrowed in on Shou-yang Mountain,
Lao Tan lay low as Clerk of the Pillar.
Long ago, that time of perfect peace —
it too had its Nest-dwelling Man.
Today in a bright and glorious age,
are we without our forest gentry?
You would free your soul beyond the blue clouds,
bury your traces in the deepest hills;
but partridges cry before the break of dawn,
mournful winds come with nightfall;
icy frost scars your ruddy face,
cold fountains hurt your jade-white feet.
All-round talent the mass of men trust;
one-sided wisdom has only itself to lean on.
Do with what's given you and gain heavenly harmony;
twist your nature and you lose the highest truth.
Come back! And what is there to hope for?
To live and die the same as other things!

HSIEH HUI-LIEN *(397-433)*

Fulling Cloth for Clothes

(It was customary in the autumn to pound cloth in the process known as fulling to make it suitable for use in winter clothes. (5-ch.)

The stars Heng and Chi never halt their courses,
the sun runs swiftly as though pursued.
White dew wets the garden chrysanthemums,
fall winds strip the ash tree in the court.
Whirr whirr go the wings of the grasshopper;
shrill shrill the cold crickets' cry.
Twilight dusk enfolds the empty curtains,
the night moon enters white into chambers
where lovely women put on their robes,
jeweled and powdered, calling to each other.
Hairpinned in jade, they come from northern rooms;
with a clinking of gold, they walk the southern stairs.
Where eaves are high comes the echo of fulling mallets,
where columns are tall, the sad sound of their pounding.
A faint fragrance rises from their sleeves,
light sweat stains each side of the brow.
"My cloth of glossy silk is done;
my lord is wandering and does not return.
I cut it with scissors drawn from this sheath,
sew it to make a robe you'll wear ten thousand miles.
With my own hands I lay it in the box,
fix the seal that waits for you to break.
Waist and belt I made to the old measure,
uncertain if they will fit you now or not."

Rhyme-Prose on the Snow

(The poem is in the form of a literary fiction, being set in what was looked on as one of the golden ages of *fu* writing, the time and court of the early Han nobleman King Hsiao of Liang. Three famous poets of the period are depicted as contributing to the composition of the poem, while the snow itself speaks the concluding words.)

The year was ending, the season in its twilight; cold winds piled up and cheerless clouds filled the sky. The king of Liang, dispirited, wandered in the Rabbit Garden; then he laid out choice wine and sent for his guests and companions, a summons to Master Tsou, an invitation to uncle Mei; Ssu-ma Hsiang-ju arrived last, taking the place of honor to the right of the other guests.[1] All at once a fine sleet began to fall, followed by heavy snow. The king proceeded to intone the "North Wind" from the songs of Wei, and to hum the "Southern Mountain" from the odes of Chou.[2] Then, offering a writing tablet to Lord Ssu-ma, he said, "Try delving into your secret thoughts, setting your sleekest words to galloping; match color for color, weigh your fine effects, and make me a *fu* on this scene!"

Ssu-ma Hsiang-ju moved politely off his mat, rose, retreated a few steps, and bowed. "I have heard," he said, "that the Snow Palace was constructed in an eastern country, that the Snow Mountain soars in a western borderland. Ch'ang of Ch'i poured out his lament of 'when we come back'; Man of the Chi clan fashioned his song on the yellow bamboo.[3] The Ts'ao air employs hemp robes as a simile for its color; Ch'u singers pair the Hidden

---

1. Liu Wu, posthumously known as King Hsiao of Liang, was a younger brother of Emperor Ching (reigned 157-141 B.C.) of the Former Han. The Rabbit Garden, where he and his guests took part in cultured pastimes, is famous in literary history. The poets referred to here are Tsou Yang (2nd cen. B.C.), Mei Sheng (d. 140 B.C.), and Ssu-ma Hsiang-ju (179-117 B.C.).

2. *Book of Odes*, no. 41 and no. 210, both songs having to do in part with snow.

3. Ch'ang, posthumously known as King Wen of Chou, is supposed to have written the song, no. 167 in the *Odes*, that contains this line; see p. 36. Man is the personal name of King Mu of Chou, who wrote the Yellow Bamboo song at a time of severe cold. In characteristic Chinese fashion, Ssu-ma Hsiang-ju begins with a barrage of classical allusions before settling down to the actual description.

Orchid with the song about it.[4] If it piles up a foot deep, it offers
fair omen for a rich year ahead; but more than ten feet, it signals
disharmony besetting the power of the yin. The snow has far-
reaching significance where the seasons are concerned. With your
permission, I'll speak of how it all begins:
When the dark months have run out
and harsh breaths are ascendant;
when Scorching Creek ices over,
and Hot Water Valley freezes,
the Well of Fire is quenched
and Warm Springs congeal,
their bubbling pools no longer churning,
their fiery winds having ceased to stir;
when north-facing doorways have been chinked with plaster
and the land of the naked swathes itself in cloth;
then rivers and seas bring forth clouds,
northern deserts send their sands flying,
wreathing vapor to vapor, piling up mists,
hiding the sun, engulfing its red rays.
Sleet is the first to come hissing down,
followed by thicker and thicker flurries of snow;
see them darting, scattering, mingling, turning,
blanketing, blinding, dense and dark,
softly seething, bobbing, gliding,
faster and faster falling now,
endless wings that beat and flutter,
swirling till they come to rest in drifts.
At first they light on roof tiles, crowning the ridgepole;
in the end they force the blinds apart, slither in through cracks;
where earlier they sidled nimbly over porch and veranda,
now they whirl and tumble by curtain and mat.
In square hollows they form jade pilasters,
in round holes they're transformed into circlets of jade.
Mark the lowlands — ten thousand acres of the same fabric;

---

4. *Odes* no. 150, one of the airs of the state of Ts'ao, compares the whiteness of snow
to that of hemp robes; Hidden Orchid and White Snow are two pieces often performed
by singers and lute players of the state of Ch'u.

look at the mountains — a thousand cliffs all white!
Now terraces become like stacked jade discs,
highways like ribbons of alabaster;
courtyards are fitted with flights of jasper steps,
forests ranged with chalcedony trees.
The snowy crane is robbed of distinction,
the silver pheasant bereft of hue;
silken sleeves find their beauty shamefully lacking,
jade faces hide their fairness from sight.
While the heaps of whiteness have not yet melted,
and the bright sun of morning shines clear,
they gleam like the Torch Dragon,
flame in mouth, that illumines the K'un-lun Mountains;
and when rivulets flow and drip down from icicles,
dangling from gutters, hanging at roof corners,
they sparkle as though P'ing-i, god of rivers,
had pried open mussels and hung out bright pearls.
Such is this show of tangled profusion,
this model of stainlessness, purity, white;
the force of this wheeling, staggering onrush,
the wonder of this dazzle and charge,
that its shifting forms seem never to end —
ah, who can hope to understand them all!
Before I finish, shall I describe our pastimes?
The night, dark and still, wakes many thoughts.
Wind buffets the columns, its echoes tumbling;
moonlight rests on curtains, its rays pouring through.
We dip rich wine brewed from Hsiang waters in Wu,
don double capes of fox and badger,
face the garden pheasants that dance in pairs,
watch the cloud-borne goose winging alone.
And as I walk the drifts of mingled sleet and snow,
I pity these leaves and branches forced apart;
distant thoughts race a thousand miles away,
I long to join hands and go home together."[5]

5. According to commentators, the leaves and branches remind the poet of his brothers
and kinsmen far away and he longs to join them.

Tsou Yang, hearing these words, was moved by pity and admiration and, thinking to add to the beautiful flow of sound, he respectfully asked if he might contribute a composition of his own. Then he rose to his feet and recited this "Song of the Drifted Snow":

> "Join hands, my lovely,
> lift the folded curtains,
> spread silken comforters,
> perfumed mats to sit on.
> We'll light up incense burners,
> make the torches glow,
> ladle cassia-scented wine
> to sing this pure refrain."

Continuing, he composed the "Song of the White Snow":

> "Songs have been sung,
> wine already drunk;
> red faces flushed now,
> thoughts must turn to love.
> I want to let down the curtains, push the pillows closer;
> I dream of untying sashes, of loosing girdle bands.
> I hate the year so quickly ended,
> grieve we have no means to meet again.
> Only see the white snow on the stairs —
> how little will be left to shine in the warmth of spring!"

When he had finished, the king tried singing the songs over to himself two or three times, getting the feel of them, waving his arm to keep time. Then, turning to Mei Sheng, he asked him to stand up and compose a Reprise. This is how it went:

White feathers too are white,
but lightness is their special nature;[6]

---

6. Lightness would also seem to be a characteristic of snow; but I think Hsieh has in mind the contrast between an accumulation of feathers, which is still relatively light, and an accumulation of snow, which is much heavier than one would anticipate from watching it fall.

white jade too is white,
but stubbornly it guards the chaste hardness of its form.
Neither can match this snow
that comes into being and melts away with the season.
When the dark yin freezes, its purity stays unsullied,
but when the warm sun shines, it no longer strives to guard its
      virtue:

"Virtue — when was that my fame?
Purity — what concern of mine?
Riding the clouds, I soar and descend,
tagging the wind, I tumble and fall,
taking on the form of things I encounter,
assuming the shape of the land where I lie.
I'm white when that which I touch is so,
grimy when surroundings stain me.
Free, my heart wanders far and wide;
what is there to fret over, what is there to plan?"

PAO CHAO *(414-466)*

Imitating the Old Poems

(5-ch.)

Many strange mountains in Shu and Han;
looking up, I see them level with the clouds,
shaded scarps piled with summer snow,
sunny ravines where autumn flowers fall.
Morning after morning I watch the clouds go home,
evening on evening, hear the monkeys wail,
a melancholy man, sorrow always with me,
a lonely traveler, easily cast down.
From my room I look out, wine jar by my side,
plying the dipper, thinking back on life —

It is the nature of the stone to be firm:
do not forsake the friendship we once had!

In Imitation of "The King of Huai-nan"

(Liu An [d. 123 B.C.], the king of Huai-nan, was a prince of the Han imperial
family whose name is associated in popular lore with the cult of the immortals.
Yüeh-fu style, 5-ch. & 7-ch.)

The King of Huai-nan,
craving long life,
tried elixirs and breath control, studied the Classic of the Immortals;
of lapis lazuli his bowls, of ivory his plates;
in golden caldrons with spoons of jade mixing magic cinnabar,
mixing magic cinnabar,
sporting in purple rooms,
purple rooms where bright-robed ladies toyed with earrings of pearl,
sang like the *luan* bird, danced like phoenixes — how they broke my
        lord's heart!
Nine gates to the vermilion city, each with nine small portals;
I want to chase the bright moon, to enter my lord's bosom,
enter my lord's bosom,
twine myself at his sash.
I hate my lord, I curse my lord, I wait for my lord's love.
May it be firm as a builded city, may it be keen as swords;
may I flourish with him, wane with him, and never be cut off!

Rhyme-Prose on the Desolate City

(The poem deals with the city of Kuang-ling, situated north of the Yangtze, not far from its mouth, in present-day Kiangsu. A canal, linking the Yangtze to the Huai River in the north, ran by its side. It saw its first great period of glory in Former Han times as capital of the state of Wu when Liu P'i, the king of Wu, grew rich by boiling sea water to extract salt and minting cash from the copper ore in its mountains. In 154 B.C. Liu P'i led six other feudal states in an abortive revolt against the supreme ruler, Emperor Ching, which quickly ended in disaster. Much later, in A.D. 459, another feudal lord with his base in Kuang-ling raised a rebellion against the Sung dynasty but was soon crushed, his city destroyed, and over three thousand of its inhabitants massacred. The poet-official Pao Chao, visiting the area shortly after, recalls the former wealth and grandeur of the city and laments its present sad state.)

Broad and far-reaching, the level plain,
hurrying south to Ts'ang-wu and the Sea of Chang,
racing north to Purple Barriers, the Wild Goose Gate,
its barge canal like a tow rope to haul it about,
its K'un-lun of hills to serve as an axle,
a fastness of double rivers, of many-fold passes,
a corridor where four roads meet, where five pass through.
Long ago, at the time of its greatest prospering,
carriages clashed axle heads,
men jostled shoulders,
house rows and alley gates crowded the earth,
songs and piping shrilled to the sky.
There was wealth to be wrung from fields of salt,
profit to be pared from copper mountains;
its talented and strong ones grew rich and mighty,
its horses and riders were handsome and well trained.
So it could flout the laws of Ch'in,
overstep the regulations of Chou,
troweling smooth its lofty battlements,
channeling out the deepest moats,
hoping to prolong its generations with the help of fair fortune.
    Thus
pounded earth was raised to form a forest of parapets,
an awesome file of turrets and beacon towers,

taller in measure than the Five Mountains,
broader across than the Three Dikes,
precipitous as a sheer escarpment,
rising straight up like a bank of long clouds.
They were fitted with magnets to guard against assault,[1]
daubed with russet clay to lend the fancy of design.
Gazing on the firmness of those gates and bastions,
you'd think one lord could hold them for ten thousand years;
yet now, when three dynasties have come and gone,[2]
five hundred years and more have passed,
they lie split like melons, like bean pods broken open.

Damp mosses cling to the well,
tangles of kudzu vine snare the path;
halls are laced with vipers and crawling things,
musk deer and flying squirrel quarrel by the stairs.
Tree goblin and mountain sprite,
field rat, fox in the wall
howl at the wind, whimper in the rain,
at dusk appearing, scampering off at dawn.
Hungry falcons whet their beaks,
cold hawks hiss at those who menace their chicks;
lurking tigers, crouching cats
suck blood and dine on flesh.
Thickets of fallen trees clog the road,
the old thoroughfare, deep and overgrown;
white poplars shed their leaves early,
bleak grasses already withered;
breath of frost, keen and biting;
soo-soo, the bullying of the wind:
a lone tumbleweed trembles by itself,
puffs of sand for no reason suddenly start up.
Dense copses murky and unending,
a jungle of weeds and brush leaning on each other;

1. The gates of ancient cities were said to have been fitted with loadstones to detect weapons concealed on those who entered.
2. The Han, Wei, and Chin.

the circling moat caved in long ago,
towering battlements — they too have tumbled:
one looks straight out a thousand li or more,
seeing only the whirls of yellow dust.
Dwell on it, listen in silence —
it wounds the heart, breaking it in two.
    And so
the painted doors, the gaily stitched hangings,
sites where once were halls of song, pavilions of the dance,
jasper pools, trees of jadeite,
lodges for those who hunt in woods, who fish the shores,
music of Wu, Ts'ai, Ch'i, Ch'in,
vessels in shapes of fish and dragon, sparrow and horse —
all have lost their incense, gone to ash,
their radiance engulfed, their echoes cut off.
Mysterious princess from the Eastern Capital,
beautiful lady from a southern land,
with heart of orchis, limbs of white lawn,
marble features, carmine lip —
none whose soul is not entombed in somber stone,
whose bones do not lie dwindling in the dust.
Do you recall now what joy it was to share your lord's carriage?
the pain of being banished to a palace apart?
Is it Heaven's way
to make so many taste sorrow?
Bring the lute — I will sing,
fashioning a song of the Desolate City.
    The song says:

Border winds hurrying
above the castle cold.
Well and pathway gone from sight,
hill and grave mound crumbling.
A thousand years,
    ten thousand ages,
all end thus —
    what is there to say?

WANG SENG-TA *(423-458)*

To Match the Prince of Lang-yeh's Poem in the Old Style

(5-ch.)

In youth I loved the adventurous race;
an official, I traveled riverbed and pass.
I have walked in the footprints of far-off times,
I can tell tales of glory and decay:
majestic Chou is now a thicket and a marsh,
stately Han — grave mounds with fences!
The very sites of summer palaces have vanished long ago;
mausoleum gardens — who can find them now?
Midautumn: north border winds are rising;
a lone tumbleweed rolls from its frost-bound roots.
The white sun grows lusterless,
yellow sands spread darkness ten thousand miles.
Down the bright lane, no carriage that does not follow the rut;
on the somber road, who but ghosts go there?
Sages, wise men — they too have departed —
Hold life close, have no regret!

SHEN YÜEH *(441-513)*

Six Poems on Remembering

(3-ch. & 5-ch.; 3 from the set of 6)

I.
I think of when she comes —
shining, shining, up the garden stairs,

impatient, impatient to end our parting.
Tireless, tireless, we talk of love,
gaze at each other but never get our fill,
look at one another till hunger is forgotten.

2.
I think of when she sits –
prim, prim before the gauze curtain,
sometimes singing four or five songs,
sometimes plucking two or three strings.
When she laughs, there's no one like her;
when she sulks, she's more lovely than before.

3.
I think of when she sleeps —
struggling to stay awake when others have retired,
undoing her sheer gown without waiting to be urged,
resting on the pillow till caresses find her.
Fearful that the one by her side is watching,
she blushes under the candle's glow.

Out Early One Morning, I Met an Old Acquaintance; I Composed This in the Carriage to Present to Her.

(5-ch.)

A touch of red left on your lip,
traces of powder clinging here and there:
where did you spend the night last night,
that at dawn you brush through the dew, returning?

Written for My Neighbor: He Waited for a Loved One Who Never Came.

(5-ch.)

Her shadow races with slanting moonbeams,
her fragrance is borne on the distant breeze.
She said yes when she really meant no —
you'd like to laugh but you cry instead.

HSIEH T'IAO (464-499)

In a Provincial Capital Sick in Bed: Presented to the *Shang-shu* Shen

(Written in 495 when the poet was serving in Hsüan-ch'eng in present-day Anhwei as governor of the province. It is addressed to his friend, the poet-official Shen Yüeh. 5-ch.)

The governor of Huai-yang, arm and leg to the ruler,
served his term from a bed of ease.[1]
And this post of mine, far in the southern hills?
Hardly different from a hermit's life!
Incessant rains — busy season for farmers:
straw hats gather in fallow fields to the east.
Daytime my state chambers are always closed,
few law suits to hear on the grass-grown terrace.
Soft mats refresh me in summer rooms,
light fans stir a cooling breeze.
Tasty bream I am urged to try,
helping myself to the best strained wine.

1. Chi An (d. 112 B.C.), an official of the Han who was highly regarded by the emperor, tried to decline the post of governor of Huai-yang on grounds of illness, but the emperor assured him that he could carry out his duties while resting in bed.

Summer plums — crimson fruit chilled in water;
autumn lotus root — tender threads to pluck;
but our happy days, when will they come?
Nightly I meet you in my dreams.
I sit whistling while time piles up,
a year already since I came here to govern;
I could never do it with strings and song —
patting the armrest, I chuckle to myself in scorn.[2]

WU CHÜN *(469-520)*

Song of Spring

(5-ch.)

Spring — where has it come from,
brushing the waters, surprising the plum?
Clouds bar the green-fretted gate,
wind sweeps the terrace that lies open to the dew.
A thousand miles keep me from my fair one,
her gauze curtains drawn and never parted.
No way to share a word with you,
in vain I face the cup that wakes these memories.

2. Reference to *Analects* XVII, 4, the story of how Confucius' disciple Tzu-yu governed a city by teaching the people to sing and play stringed instruments.

HSÜ CHÜN-CH'IEN *(6th cen.)*

Sitting Up with My Wife on New Year's Eve

(It was the custom at New Year's to place a daddy longlegs, whose name, *hsi-tzu*, is a homophone for "happiness," in the wine, and to hide wild plums in the dumplings. 5-ch.)

So many delights the excitement has no end,
so much joy the cup is never still:
pluck a daddy longlegs out of the wine,
find a wild plum inside the dumpling!
The blinds swing open and wind lifts the curtain;
the candle burns low, its wick turned to ash.
No wonder the pins weigh heavy in your hair —
we've waited up so long for dawn light to come!

Beginning of Spring — A Stroll with My Wife

(5-ch.)

Hairdo and ornaments all the latest fashion,
your outfit strictly in the newest style;
the grass still short enough to poke through sandals,
the plums so fragrant their perfume rubs off!
Trees slant down to pluck at your brocade shawl,
breezes sidle up and get under your crimson kerchief —
Fill the cups with orchid blossom wine![1]
These are sights to make the spirit sing.

1. Wine on which blossoms have been floated.

LIU LING-HSIEN *(6th cen.), the wife of Hsü Fei*

Inscribed on a Plantain Leaf To Show to a Certain Person

(5-ch.)

Tears at evening? — not infrequent;
crying out in dreams — much too often!
All this my nightly pillow is aware of;
other than it, there's none that knows.

CHIANG LU *(6th cen.)*

Wrecked Boat on the River Shore

(An allegory. 5-ch.)

So fine, the boards of magnolia;
splendid, the cinnamon woodwork!
You chased the waves, only to come to this;
rode the wind, yet brought on your own downfall.
Grasses are rank, your canopy was buried long ago;
the sands are monstrous, your hull would never budge.
How long it's been since you sank in the dry land,
never again to ride the rippling sun.

HO SUN *(d. 518)*

At Parting

(5-ch.)

The traveler's heart has a hundred thoughts already,
his lonely journey piling mile on endless mile.
The river darkens, rain about to fall;
waves turn white as the wind comes up.

YIN SHIH *(early 7th cen.)*

Parting from the Courtier Sung

(5-ch.)

I, a wanderer north of Tu-ling,
see you off, bound east of the Han River;
one remains, the other takes leave;
both alike are wind-driven weeds.
Autumn heads whitened with frost and snow,
aging faces that wait for wine to glow again —
parting is a time for thoughts,
when the raven's cry comes on the night wind.

ANONYMOUS SONGS

Ti-ch'ü Song Words

(A song from north China in 4-ch. form; all the other songs are in 5-ch. form unless otherwise indicated.)

Oh oh — ah ah —
thoughts of you will never end!
Your left arm I used for a pillow,
and when you turned on your side, I turned with you.

Tzu-yeh Songs

(Tzu-yeh was reputedly a professional singing girl of the 4th cen. and many songs of the period bear her name.)

1.
Hems gathered up, sash not yet tied,
eyebrows lightly sketched, I appear at the front window.
This flimsy skirt so easily blown about —
if it opens a little, I'll blame the spring wind.

2.
Cool breezes — I sleep by the open window
where the light of the setting moon shines in.
At midnight there are no voices,
but within my gauze curtains, a pair of smiles.

3.
[He]
Out the southern gate at sundown
I look and see you passing by,
your lovely face and intricate hairdo,
fragrant perfume that even now fills the road!

4.
[She]
The fragrance comes from the scent I wear,
a lovely face I wouldn't dare claim.
Heaven's not deaf to a body's pleas —
that's why it has brought you to me!

5.
In the hottest time, when all is still and windless
and summer clouds rise up at dusk,
under the dense leaves, take my hand
and we'll float melons on the water, dunk crimson plums.

6.
When ice on the pond is three feet thick
and white snow stretches a thousand miles,
my heart will still be like the pine and cypress,
but your heart — what will it be?

7.
Nights are long and I cannot sleep,
the clear moon so bright and shining.
I think I hear a voice fitfully calling,
and futilely I answer yes to the empty sky.

Ch'ing-yang Ford

Greenest jade for a clothes-pounding stone,
a golden lotus pestle set with seven jewels —
lift it high, slowly slowly bring it down,
gently pounding for you alone.

Stone Castle Music

They say my love is going far away;
I've come to see him off at Fang Hill Stop.
Wind blowing over the *huang-po* hedges—
How I hate to hear that bitter parting sound.[1]

The Goddess Chiao

Crowds of shuffling feet pass over the bridge
where river waters flow west to east;
above, the immortal goddess dwells;
below are fishes, westward swimming.
When they go, they never go alone,
but three by three or two by two.

Picking Rushes

At dawn setting out from a cassia and orchid shore,
noontime resting beneath mulberry and elm;
picking rushes along with you,
one whole day gets me less than an armful!

1. Like many of these songs, this involves a pun, here on the words *li,* "hedge," and *li,* "separation."

Ch'i-yü-ko

Man — pitiful insect,
out the gate with fears of death in his breast,
a corpse fallen in narrow valleys,
white bones that no one gathers up.

The Other Side of the Valley

(7-ch.)

1.

I am in the castle, my younger brother is beyond,
no string to my bow, no tips to my arrows;
rations all run out, how can I live?
Come and save me! Come and save me!

2.

I am taken captive to suffer hardship and shame,
bones bare, strength gone, food never enough!
My younger brother is an official, his horses eat grain —
why is he too stingy to come and ransom me?

Song of the Breaking of the Willow

(Written from the point of view of a non-Chinese prisoner in the north; the "River"
is the Yellow River, "Han man" is a term for the Chinese.)

Far off I see the River at Meng Ford,
willows thick and leafy there.
I am the son of a captive family
and cannot understand the Han man's song.

CHAPTER SEVEN

Major T'ang Poets I:
Wang Wei, Li Po, Tu Fu

WANG WEI (699?-761)

W ANG WEI, a painter and musician as well as writer, is one
of the leading poets of the period known as the High T'ang
(713-765), so-called by later critics because they believed that this
era represented the peak of poetic excellence in the T'ang. The period
corresponds roughly to the reign of Emperor Hsüan-tsung, a ruler
whose early years on the throne were marked by power and splendor
and his later years by disastrous rebellion.

The early decades of the T'ang saw a continuation of the dec-
orative and impersonal style that had held favor in late Six Dynasties
and Sui times. But it was not long before poets began to adopt a
more vigorous and robust manner and to strike a more personal
note, turning for their inspiration to the powerful works of the Han
and Wei period. This new trend, its potentialities deepened and
developed with the passing of time, led to the great flowering of
poetic talent that marked the High T'ang, particularly as seen in the
works of Wang Wei, Li Po, and Tu Fu, the three poets to be treated
in this chapter.

During the T'ang, the civil service examination system played a vital role in encouraging learning and enlisting men of promise for service in the bureaucracy. Wang Wei, like many of the T'ang poet-officials, was a product of the system, passing the examination at an early age and entering upon a long and distinguished career in government service, interspersed with periods of banishment or voluntary withdrawal to the countryside. He wrote a certain number of poems of a public nature related to court functions, but he is best remembered for his descriptions of the life he lived in his country retreats and the scenes that surrounded him there. As a celebrator of the quiet joys of rural life, he follows a line of development earlier explored by T'ao Yüan-ming, though he writes with greater calm and detachment than had T'ao.

Wang Wei was a devout Buddhist, a fact that no doubt deeply influenced the way in which he viewed the world and his place in it. Buddhism had been introduced to China as early as the first century A.D., but it was several centuries before its major scriptural writings had been satisfactorily translated into the Chinese language and its complex doctrines made fully intelligible to Chinese adherents, and even longer before its beliefs and practices became assimilated into Chinese life as a whole. A number of Six Dynasties poets, notably Hsieh Ling-yün, had been Buddhist followers and had even written a certain amount of doctrinal poetry. (T'ao Yüan-ming was said to have been associated with Buddhist circles on Mount Lu, though the facts are uncertain.) But on the whole their religious beliefs do not appear to be directly reflected in their secular writings. With Wang Wei, however, we come to a writer whose entire poetic output has been characterized as so many sermons on the Buddhist faith.

Mahayana Buddhism, the kind of Buddhism familiar to Wang Wei and his contemporaries, teaches that all the dharmas or things of existence are absolutely equal. This means that, though each thing may have its distinctive characteristics, all are to be equally acknowledged and accepted by the enlightened person. It is this attitude of calm affirmation that most strikes one in Wang Wei's poetry. He does not assiduously seek out the wild or picturesque elements in the natural landscape, as nature poets often do, nor does he avert his eyes from the evidences of human habitation or activity. He registers the scenes about him just as they appear to him, the human along with the non-human components, his very impartiality a gauge, one feels, of his level of enlightenment.

WANG WEI

Lady Hsi

(5-ch. *chüeh-chü*)

(When the king of Ch'u overthrew the state of Hsi, he seized Lady Hsi and took her home with him. She bore him two children but would never speak to him. Asked the reason, she replied, "One woman that I am, I have served two husbands. Though I could not bring myself to commit suicide [in order to avoid such a disgrace], how would I venture to speak?" *Tso chuan*, Duke Chuang 14th year.)

"Do not force me with present favor
to forget my love of days gone by!"
She stares at the flowers, eyes full of tears,
and will not speak to the king of Ch'u.

Twenty Views of Wang-ch'uan

(5-ch. *chüeh-chü*, the 1st, 5th, and 17th in the series)

Meng-ch'eng Hollow

A new home at the mouth of Meng-ch'eng;
old trees — last of a stand of dying willows:
years to come, who will be its owner,
vainly pitying the one who had it before?

Deer Fence

Empty hills, no one in sight,
only the sound of someone talking;
late sunlight enters the deep wood,
shining over the green moss again.

Bamboo Mile Lodge

Alone I sit in dark bamboo,
strumming the lute, whistling away;
deep woods that no one knows,
where a bright moon comes to shine on me.

Duckweed Pond

(5-ch. *chüeh-chü*)

By the spring pond, deep and wide,
you must be waiting for the light boat to return.
Supple and soft, the green duckweed meshes,
till dangling willows sweep it open again.

Joys of the Country:
Seven Poems

(6-ch. *chüeh-chü,* 4th in the series

Lush lush, fragrant grasses in autumn green;
tall tall, towering pines in summer cold;
cows and sheep come home by themselves to village lanes;
little boys know nothing of capped and robed officials.

Seeing Someone Off

(5-ch. old style)

We dismount; I give you wine
and ask, where are you off to?
You answer, nothing goes right! —
back home to lie down by Southern Mountain.
Go then — I'll ask no more —
there's no end to white clouds there.

At My Country Home in Chung-nan

(5-ch. regulated verse)

Middle age — I grow somewhat fond of the Way,
my evening home at the foot of the southern hills.
When moods come I follow them alone,
to no purpose learning fine things for myself,
going till I come to where the river ends,
sitting and watching when clouds rise up.
By chance I meet an old man of the woods;
we talk and laugh — we have no "going-home" time.

Visiting the Temple of Accumulated Fragrance

(5-ch. regulated verse)

I didn't know where the temple was,
pushing mile on mile among cloudy peaks;

old trees, peopleless paths,
deep mountains, somewhere a bell.
Brook voices choke over craggy boulders,
sun rays turn cold in the green pines.
At dusk by the bend of a deserted pond,
a monk in meditation, taming poison dragons.[1]

Weather Newly Cleared, the View at Evening

(5-ch. regulated verse)

Weather newly cleared, plains and meadows seem broader,
far as the eye can see, not a smudge of dust.
The hamlet gate overlooks the ferry landing,
village trees stretching down to the valley mouth.
White river shining beyond the paddies,
emerald peaks jutting up behind the hills —
these are the farming months, when no one's idle,
whole families out working in the southern fields.

---

1. The poison dragons are passions and illusions that impede enlightenment. They also recall the tale of a poison dragon that lived in a lake and killed passing merchants until it was subdued by a certain Prince P'an-t'o through the use of spells. The dragon changed into a man and apologized for its evil ways.

Weeping for Ying Yao

(Ying Yao, poet and official, was a close friend of Wang Wei and a fellow student of Buddhism. 7-ch. *chüeh-chü*.)

We send you home to a grave on Stone Tower Mountain;
through the green green of pine and cypress, mourners' carriages
     return.
Among white clouds we've laid your bones — it is ended forever;
only the mindless waters remain, flowing down to the world of men.

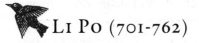# LI PO (701-762)

L I PO would probably be close to the top on almost anyone's
list of the greatest Chinese poets of premodern times. It is
generally agreed that he and Tu Fu raised poetry in the *shih* form to
its highest level of power and expressiveness; later poets at times
approached but never surpassed them. It was some centuries before
the true worth of Tu Fu's work was acknowledged, but Li Po's
poetry seems to have gained almost immediate recognition. This
may be due to the fact that, unlike Tu Fu, Li Po was no innovator.
For the most part he was content to employ the poetic forms inher-
ited from his predecessors and to devote himself to the conventional
themes of the past. Of the 1,000 poems attributed to him, about
one sixth are in *yüeh-fu* style, which means that they are reworkings
of themes drawn from the old folk song tradition, while another
group of his poems is entitled *ku-feng* or "in the old manner." Li
Po's distinction lies in the fact that he brought an unparalleled grace
and eloquence to his treatment of the traditional themes, a flow and
grandeur that lift his works far above the level of mere imitations of
the past.

Another characteristic of Li Po's poetry is the air of playfulness,
hyperbole and outright fantasy that infuses much of it. The last
poem in my selection is a good example, a work in irregular form
that in rhapsodic language describes a dream journey to T'ien-mu,
a mountain on the Chekiang coast associated with Taoist lore. After
the poet awakes, he resolves to leave the world of fawning and
hypocrisy and retire to the mountains, the carefree life of the recluse
being another important theme in his poetry. Other works stress
the poet's unique rapport with nature, or his love of wine, the last
a trait for which he is proverbial.

Though a wealth of legend has accrued about Li Po's name,

little is known of the facts of his life. He grew up in Szechwan in western China and later traveled extensively in the eastern and central regions. Just what kept him so constantly on the move is difficult to say, since his poetry, unlike that of Tu Fu and many other major Chinese poets, tends to be impersonal in tone and to reveal relatively little about the poet's own activities. Around 742 he gained recognition from Emperor Hsüan-tsung and was appointed to a post in the Hanlin Academy, a government office charged with literary activities, but a few years later he was exiled from the capital as a result of slanders. He fled south at the time of the An Lu-shan rebellion in 755 and in time entered the service of Prince Yung, a member of the imperial family who was later accused of treason. The prince's downfall involved Li Po in a second exile, though he was eventually pardoned and resumed his life of wandering.

In spite of such vicissitudes of fortune, Li Po is little given to expressions of unmitigated despair or bitterness, his poetry on the whole being unusually calm, even at times sunny in outlook. It appears to grow not so much out of the actual scenes and experiences of his lifetime as it does out of certain convictions that he held regarding life and art, out of a tireless search for spiritual freedom and communion with nature, a lively imagination and a deep sensitivity to the beauties of language.

LI PO

Tzu-yeh Song

(The poem deals with autumn, when cloth is fulled to make uniforms to send to the soldiers stationed at the frontier; Jade Pass is in Kansu far to the west. 5-ch. old style, *yüeh-fu*.)

Ch'ang-an — one slip of moon;
in ten thousand houses, the sound of fulling mallets.
Autumn winds keep on blowing,
all things make me think of Jade Pass!
When will they put down the barbarians
and my good man come home from his far campaign?

Bring the Wine!

(7-ch. old style, *yüeh-fu*)

Have you never seen
the Yellow River waters descending from the sky,
racing restless toward the ocean, never to return?
Have you never seen
bright mirrors in high halls, the white-haired ones lamenting,
their black silk of morning by evening turned to snow?
If life is to have meaning, seize every joy you can;
do not let the golden cask sit idle in the moonlight!
Heaven gave me talents and meant them to be used;
gold scattered by the thousand comes home to me again.
Boil the mutton, roast the ox — we will be merry,

at one bout no less than three hundred cups.
Master Ts'en!
Scholar Tan-ch'iu![1]
Bring wine and no delay!
For you I'll sing a song —
be pleased to bend your ears and hear.
Bells and drums, food rare as jade — these aren't worth prizing;
all I ask is to be drunk forever, never to sober up!
Sages and worthies from antiquity — all gone into silence;
only the great drinkers have left a name behind.
The Prince of Ch'en once feasted in the Hall of Calm Delight;
wine, ten thousand coins a cask, flowed for his revelers' joy.[2]
Why does my host tell me the money has run out?
Buy more wine at once — my friends have cups to be refilled!
My dappled mount,
my furs worth a thousand —
call the boy, have him take them and barter for fine wine!
Together we'll wash away ten thousand years of care.

At Su Terrace Viewing the Past

(Written when the post visited the site of Ku-su Terrace, built by Fu-ch'a, king of Wu, just south of the Yangtze; the king's infatuation for Hsi-shih, the "lady" of the poem, weakened his state and led to its overthrow in 472 B.C. by its rival, the state of Yüeh. 7-ch. *chüeh-chü*.)

Old gardens, a ruined terrace, willow trees new;
caltrop gatherers, clear chant of songs, a spring unbearable;
and now there is only the west river moon
that shone once on a lady in the palace of the king of Wu.

1. Master Ts'en has been tentatively identified as the poet Ts'en Ts'an (715-70); Scholar Tan-ch'iu is Yüan Tan-ch'iu, a Taoist friend.

• 2. Prince of Ch'en is the early poet Ts'ao Chih (see p. 111); Li Po echoes the following lines from Ts'ao Chih's poem "City of Fame":
  I return to feast in the Hall of Calm Delight,
  with fine wine, ten thousand coins a cask.

In Yüeh Viewing the Past

(Kou-chien was the ruler of Yüeh who overthrew King Fu-ch'a of Wu. 7-ch. *chüeh-chü*.)

Kou-chien, king of Yüeh, came back from the broken land of Wu;
his brave men returned to their homes, all in robes of brocade.
Ladies in waiting like flowers filled his spring palace
where now only the partridges fly.

Autumn Cove

(5-ch. *chüeh-chü*)

At Autumn Cove, so many white monkeys,
bounding, leaping up like snowflakes in flight!
They coax and pull their young ones down from the branches
to drink and frolic with the water-borne moon.

Viewing the Waterfall at Mount Lu

(Mt. Lu in Kiangsi has earlier appeared in the poetry of T'ao Yüan-ming; Incense Stone is one of its peaks. 5-ch. *chüeh-chü*.)

Sunlight streaming on Incense Stone kindles violet smoke;
far off I watch the waterfall plunge to the long river,
flying waters descending straight three thousand feet,
till I think the Milky Way has tumbled from the ninth height of
    Heaven.

Spring Night in Lo-yang — Hearing a Flute

(The willow-breaking song is sung at parting, when people break off willow wands
to use as gifts. 7-ch. *chüeh-chü*.)

In what house, the jade flute that sends these dark notes drifting,
scattering on the spring wind that fills Lo-yang?
Tonight if we should hear the willow-breaking song,
who could help but long for the gardens of home?

Still Night Thoughts

(5-ch. *chüeh-chü*)

Moonlight in front of my bed —
I took it for frost on the ground!
I lift my eyes to watch the mountain moon,
lower them and dream of home.

Summer Day in the Mountains

(5-ch. *chüeh-chü*)

Too lazy to wave the white plume fan,
stripped to the waist in the green wood's midst,
I loose my headcloth, hang it on a stony wall,
bare my topknot for the pine winds to riffle.

Presented to Wang Lun

(7-ch. *chüeh-chü*)

Li Po on board, ready to push off,
suddenly heard the tramping and singing on the bank.
Peach Flower Pool a thousand feet deep
is shallower than the love of Wang Lun who sees me off.

At Yellow Crane Tower Taking Leave of
Meng Hao-jan as He Sets off for Kuang-ling

(The poet Meng Hao-jan [689-740] parted from Li Po at Yellow Crane Tower,
overlooking the Yangtze at Wu-ch'ang in Hupei, to sail east down the river to
Yang-chou in Kiangsu. 7-ch. *chüeh-chü*.)

My old friend takes leave of the west at Yellow Crane Tower,
in misty third-month blossoms goes downstream to Yang-chou.
The far-off shape of his lone sail disappears in the blue-green void,
and all I see is the long river flowing to the edge of the sky.

Thinking of East Mountain

(East Mountain is in Shao-hsing in Chekiang. 5-ch. *chüeh-chü*.)

It's been so long since I headed for East Mountain —
how many times have the roses bloomed?
White clouds have scattered themselves away —
and this bright moon — whose house is it setting on?

Seeing a Friend Off

(5-ch. regulated verse)

Green hills sloping from the nothern wall,
white water rounding the eastern city:
once parted from this place
the lone weed tumbles ten thousand miles.
Drifting clouds — a traveler's thoughts;
setting sun — an old friend's heart.
Wave hands and let us take leave now,
hsiao-hsiao our hesitant horses neighing.

A Night with a Friend

(5-ch. old style)

Dousing clean a thousand old cares,
sticking it out through a hundred pots of wine,
a good night needing the best of conversation,
a brilliant moon that will not let us sleep —
drunk we lie down in empty hills,
heaven and earth our quilt and pillow.

Facing Wine with Memories of Lord Ho: Introduction and Two Poems

(5-ch. old style, the first of the two)

Lord Ho, a high official in the household of the Crown Prince, on our first meeting at the Tzu-chi Temple in Ch'ang-an at once dubbed me the "banished immortal."[1] Then he took off his golden tortoise badge and exchanged it for wine for our enjoyment. He is gone now, and I face the wine, wrapped in thought, and write these poems.

Wild man of Ssu-ming Mountain,[2]
incomparable Ho Chi-chen,
in Ch'ang-an when we first met,
calling me a "banished immortal" —
He used to love the "thing in the cup"
(now he's dust under the pine tree),
and traded the golden tortoise for wine —
my robe is wet with tears, remembering.

In Reply When Lesser Officials of Chung-tu Brought a Pot of Wine and Two Fish to My Inn as Gifts

(5-ch. and 7-ch. old style)

Lu wine like amber,
fish from the Wen, the purple damask of their scales;
and Shantung's fine officials, in expansive mood,
their hands bearing gifts for a man from far away.

1. Implying that Li Po was an immortal spirit of Heaven who, because of some offense, had been condemned to take on human form.
2. In Chekiang, where Ho lived after he left court and became a Taoist recluse.

We've taken to each other — we hit it off;
the pot of wine, the pair of fish convey this thought.
Wine comes — I drink it;
fish to be carved at parting,
twin gills that gape and pant, back and body taut-finned,
they twitch and twitter on a silver plate, all but taking wing.
I call the boy to clear the cuttingboard; frosty blades whirl —
red flesh and pale: fallen flowers, a gleam of whitest snow.[1]
With your leave I dip my chopsticks, eat my fill,
then climb into the golden saddle, still drunk, to set off home.

Poem No. 19 in the Old Manner

(Lotus Flower Mountain is the highest peak of Mt. Hua, one of the five sacred mountains of China, on the border between Shansi and Shensi. In a lake on its summit were said to grow lotuses that have the power to transform one into an immortal spirit. Bright Star is a spirit who lived on Mt. Hua. Wei Shu-ch'ing, a man of the Han dynasty who became an immortal by drinking an infusion of mica, lived on Cloud Terrace, another peak of Mt. Hua. 5-ch. old style.)

West ascending Lotus Flower Mountain,
far far away I saw the Bright Star maid;
with pale hands she plucked lotus blossoms,
with airy steps she walked the great clear void;
her rainbow skirts, their broad belt trailing,
dipped and fluttered as she strode up the sky.
She called me to climb with her to Cloud Terrace,
to lift hands in salutation to Wei Shu-ch'ing.
Dazed and enraptured, I went with her;
mounting a stork, we rode the purple gloom.
I looked down and saw the Lo-yang River,
barbarian troops marching in endless files;

1. The red and white portions of the fish; the Chinese in early times often ate their fish raw.

streams of blood that stained the meadow grasses,
wildcats and wolves wearing the hats of men![1]

Sent to My Two Little Children in the East of Lu

(Li Po seems to have married several times; as the following poem indicates, he had children by at least one marriage. At the time it was written, Li Po had left his family in Jen-ch'eng in Shantung [referred to in the poem as Lu], and was traveling in the south [Wu] on the way to the capital. Mt. Kuei and the Wen-yang River are in Shantung, near where his family was living. 5-ch. old style.)

Wu land mulberry leaves grow green,
already Wu silkworms have slept three times.[1]
I left my family in the east of Lu;
who sows our fields there on the dark side of Mt. Kuei?
Spring chores too long untended,
river journeys that leave me dazed —
south winds blow my homing heart;
it soars and comes to rest before the wine tower.
East of the tower a peach tree grows,
branches and leaves brushed with blue mist,
a tree I planted myself,
parted from it these three years.
The peach now is tall as the tower
and still my journey knows no return.
P'ing-yang, my darling girl,
picks blossoms, leaning by the peach,
picks blossoms and does not see me;
her tears flow like a welling fountain.
The little boy, named Po-ch'in,

1. The closing lines refer to the forces of the rebel An Lu-shan, who led a body of Chinese and foreign troops west to attack Ch'ang-an in 755.

---

1. The silkworms sleep and shed their skins four times before they weave their cocoons.

is shoulder high to his elder sister;
side by side they walk beneath the peach —
who will pat them with loving hands?
I lose myself in thoughts of them;
day by day care burns out my heart.
On this piece of cut silk I'll write my far-away thoughts
and send them floating down the river Wen-yang.

Song of a Dream Visit to T'ien-mu: Farewell to Those I Leave Behind

(T'ien-mu or Matron of Heaven is a mountain near the sea in Chekiang [here referred to as Yüeh], northwest of the more famous Mt. T'ien-t'ai. Irregular old style.)

Seafarers tell of the Isles of Ying,[1]
shadowy in spindrift and waves, truly hard to seek out;
Yüeh men describe T'ien-mu,
in clouds and rainbows clear or shrouded, there for eyes to glimpse;
T'ien-mu touching the sky, surging toward the sky,
lord above the Five Peaks, shadowing the Red Wall;
T'ien-t'ai's forty-eight thousand fathoms
beside it seem to topple and sprawl to south and east.
I longed, and my longing became a dream of Wu-Yüeh;
in the night I flew across the moon of Mirror Lake;
the lake moon, lighting my shadow,
saw me to the Valley of Shan,
Lord Hsieh's old home there today,
where green waters rush and roil and shrill monkeys cry.[2]
Feet thrust into Lord Hsieh's clogs,
body climbing ladders of blue cloud,

1. Fabled islands in the eastern sea where immortal spirits live.
2. Lord Hsieh is the Six Dynasties poet Hsieh Ling-yün (see p. 172). For mountain climbing he invented a special type of clogs with detachable teeth.

halfway up the scarps I see the ocean sun,
and in the air hear the cocks of heaven.[3]
A thousand cliffs, ten thousand clefts, trails uncertain,
I turn aside for flowers, rest on rocks — suddenly it's night;
bear growls, dragon purrs in the din of cliffside torrents
shake the deep forest, startle the piled-up peaks;
clouds blue-dark, threatening rain,
waters soft-seething, sending up mists:
a rent of lightning, crack of thunder,
and hilltops sunder and fall;
doors of stone at grotto mouths
swing inward with a grinding roar,
and from the blue darkness, bottomless, vast and wild,
sun and moon shine sparkling on terraces of silver and gold.
Rainbows for robes, wind for horses,
whirling whirling, the Lord of the Clouds comes down,[4]
tigers twanging zithers, *Juan* birds to turn his carriage,
and immortal men in files think as hemp —
Suddenly my soul shudders, my spirit leaps,
in terror I rise up with repeated sighs:
only the mat and pillow where now I woke —
lost are the mists of a moment ago!
All the joys of this world are like this,
the many-evented past a river flowing east.
I leave you now — when will I return? —
to loose the white deer among green bluffs,
in my wandering to ride them in search of famed hills.
How can I knit brows, bend back to serve influence and power,
never dare to wear an open-hearted face?

3. Another name for the golden pheasant.
4. A deity addressed in the shaman songs of the *Ch'u Tz'u*.

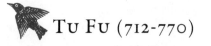# Tu Fu (712-770)

IF the poetry of Li Po conveys a feeling of spontaneity and effortless flow, that of his illustrious contemporary Tu Fu gives a quite different impression. Though Tu Fu wrote in a variety of styles, his most characteristic work is innovative in language and subject matter and densely packed with meaning. He seems to have labored over his compositions, employing parallelisms and other rhetorical and prosodic devices in novel and surprising ways, striving to open up new areas of expression, his professed aim being to startle with the creativeness of his work. This is undoubtedly one reason why his importance was not widely recognized by the readers of his time. As in the case of so many artists whose work is experimental and forward-looking, it remained for posterity to recognize the full extent of his genius.

Tu Fu was born in Honan in the region of Lo-yang. Though he came from a distinguished literary family and had influential contacts, his early efforts to secure a government position through the examination system or special appointment met with repeated failure. He was 43 when, in 755, he finally succeeded in obtaining an official post. It was anything but an auspicious time to enter the service of the dynasty.

Emperor Hsüan-tsung, a distinguished and able ruler in his earlier years, had in his sixties become infatuated with the beautiful Yang Kuei-fei, making her his concubine and showering favors on her relations, a move that Tu fu obliquely censures in one of the poems in my selection. With the emperor thus distracted from affairs of state, the court soon became plagued by factionalism and the military leaders in the outlying areas grew dangerously powerful. In 755, the year Tu Fu took office, one such leader with his base in the northeast, An Lu-shan, raised a revolt and began marching toward the T'ang capital area. In time Emperor Hsüan-tsung was forced to flee to the west and abdicate in favor of his son, who set up a new regime. Meanwhile, Tu Fu and his wife and children fled north to escape the rebel armies. He left his family there while he himself attempted to make his way to the headquarters of the new emperor, but was captured by the rebels and held prisoner in Ch'ang-an.

After a semblance of order had been restored, Tu Fu was once more given a post in the capital, but incurred the emperor's displeasure and was removed to a minor provincial position. In 759 he left this post and spent the remainder of his life in restless wanderings, broken by an interval of relative tranquility when he lived on the outskirts of Ch'eng-tu in Szechwan. In his last years, much troubled by illness, he journeyed by stages down the Yangtze, attempting to reach his old home in the east, but died along the way.

Since much of Tu Fu's poetry is intensely personal, we can follow in it the tortured course of his life as it was molded by the tumultuous events of the time. He was imbued with a strong Confucian sense of duty that kept him striving to serve the dynasty to which he professed such deep loyalty, hoping thereby to help assuage the ills of the nation. As a government official, he proved in his sporadic terms in office to be well-meaning but ineffectual. In a larger sense, however, he fulfilled his moral purpose through his art, in his poems describing in moving terms the griefs that famine, misrule, and civil unrest were inflicting upon his countrymen and himself. His greatest works are at once a lament upon the appalling sorrows that he saw around him, and a reproach to those who, through folly or ignorance, were to some degree responsible for the creation of so much misery. It is no doubt this deeply sincere and compassionate tone in his work that led later ages to bestow on him the epithet *shih-sheng*, the "Sage of Poetry," acknowledging him the artistic counterpart of Confucius himself.

Unlike Li Po, who preferred the relative freedom of the old style verse forms, Tu Fu welcomed the technical demands made by the "modern style" or tonally regulated forms, particularly the 8-line *lü-shih* or regulated verse. Of his approximately 1,450 extant poems, over 1,000 are in such forms. This fact, along with the great compression of language and thought that marks many of his works, makes his poetry particularly difficult to translate. One should keep in mind that many of the beauties of language that Chinese readers admire so greatly in his work inevitably are lost in translation. Because of the personal nature of his works and the fact that most of them can be dated, I have arranged my selection in chronological order.

TU FU

On the Border, First Series

(5-ch. old style; the 4th and 6th poems in the series)

1.
We recruits have our commanders to send us off,
but, bound for distant duty, we're people too!
From here we go out to face life or death —
no cause for the officers to scowl at us so!
Along the route we come on someone we know,
give him a letter to hand to close kin.
Sad as it is, we and they are parted now,
no longer to share the same troubles and pain.

2.
If you draw a bow, draw a strong one;
if you use an arrow, use one that's long.
If you want to shoot a man, shoot his horse first;
if you want to seize the enemy, seize their leader first.
But killing people has limits too,
and when you guard a state, there are boundaries to be observed.
Just so you manage to keep invaders out —
Seeing how many you can slaughter — that's not the point!

Song of the Beautiful Ladies

(A veiled attack on the Yang family, relatives of Emperor Hsüan-tsung's favorite, Yang Kuei-fei. The gathering centers on the two elder sisters of Yang Kuei-fei, enfeoffed as the Ladies of Kuo and Ch'in respectively; the gentleman who arrives later is Yang Kuei-fei's cousin, Yang Kuo-chung, a high minister. The scene is the spring outing held on the 3rd day of the 3rd lunar month at Ch'ü-chiang or Winding River, a park in Ch'ang-an. 7-ch. old style.)

Third month, third day, in the air a breath of newness;
by Ch'ang-an riverbanks the beautiful ladies crowd,
warm-bodied, modest-minded, mild and pure,
with clear sleek complexions, bone and flesh well matched,
in figured gauze robes that shine in the late spring,
worked with golden peacocks, silver unicorns.
On their heads what do they wear?
Kingfisher glinting from hairpins that dangle by sidelock borders.
On their back what do I see?
Pearls that weight the waistband and subtly set off the form.
Among them, kin of the lady of cloud screen and pepper-scented
        halls,
granted titles to the great fiefs of Kuo and Ch'in.
Humps of purple camel proffered from blue caldrons,
platters of crystal spread with slivers of raw fish;
but ivory chopsticks, sated, dip down no more,
and phoenix knives in vain hasten to cut and serve.
Yellow Gate horses ride swiftly, leaving the dust unstirred,
bearing from royal kitchens unending rare delights.
Plaintive notes of flute and drum, enough to move the gods;
throngs of guests and lackeys, all the highest rank;
and last, another rider, with slow and measured stride,
dismounts at the tent door, ascends the brocade carpet.
The snow of willow catkins blankets the white-flowered reeds;
a bluebird flies away, in its bill a crimson kerchief—[1]
Where power is all-surpassing, fingers may be burned;
take care and draw no closer to His Excellency's glare!

1. There were rumors that Yang Kuo-chung was carrying on an intrigue with the Lady of Kuo, and this probably explains the reference to the bluebird, the traditional bearer of love notes.

Song of P'eng-ya

(An account of the journey made by Tu Fu and his family in 756 when they fled
north from Ch'ang-an to avoid the rebel armies led by An Lu-shan. 5-ch. old style.)

I remember when we first fled the rebels,
hurrying north over dangerous trails;
night deepened on P'eng-ya Road,
the moon shone over White-water Hills.
A whole family endlessly trudging,
begging without shame from the people we met:
valley birds sang, a jangle of soft voices;
we didn't see a single traveler returning.
The baby girl in her hunger bit me;
fearful that tigers or wolves would hear her cries,
I hugged her to my chest, muffling her mouth,
but she squirmed and wailed louder than before.
The little boy pretended he knew what was happening;
importantly he searched for sour plums to eat.
Ten days, half in rain and thunder,
through mud and slime we pulled each other on.
There was no escaping from the rain,
trails slick, clothes wet and clammy;
getting past the hardest places,
a whole day advanced us no more than three or four li.
Mountain fruits served for rations,
low-hung branches were our rafter and roof.
Mornings we traveled by rock-bedded streams,
evenings camped in mists that closed in the sky.
We stopped a little while at the marsh of T'ung-chia,
thinking to go out by Lu-tzu Pass;
an old friend there, Sun Tsai,
ideals higher than the piled-up clouds;
he came out to meet us as dusk turned to darkness,
called for torches, opening gate after gate,
heated water to wash our feet,

cut strips of paper to call back our souls.[1]
Then his wife and children came;
seeing us, their tears fell in streams.
My little chicks had gone sound to sleep;
he called them to wake up and eat from his plate,
said he would make a vow with me,
the two of us to be brothers forever.
At last he cleared the room where we sat,
wished us goodnight, all he had at our command.
Who is willing, in the hard, bleak times,
to break open, lay bare his innermost heart?
Parting from you, a year of months has rounded,
Tartar tribes still plotting evil,
and I think how it would be to have strong wings
that would carry me away, set me down before you.

Moonlight Night

(Written in 756 when Tu Fu had been taken prisoner by the rebels and was held captive in Ch'ang-an. His wife and family were at Fu-chou to the north. 5-ch. regulated verse.)

From her room in Fu-chou tonight
all alone she watches the moon.
Far away, I grieve that her children
can't understand why she thinks of Ch'ang-an.
Fragrant mist in her cloud hair damp,
clear lucence on her jade arms cold —
when will we lean by chamber curtains
and let it light the two of us, our tear stains dried?

---

1. Reference to an ancient rite used to call back the souls of travelers, which have been dispersed by fright. Commentators disagree whether in this case the rite was actually performed, or whether the allusion to it here is merely figurative.

Spring Prospect

(Written early in 757 when the poet was still a captive in Ch'ang-an. 5-ch. regulated verse.)

The nation shattered, hills and streams remain.
The city in spring, grass and trees deep:
feeling the times, flowers draw tears;
hating separation, birds alarm the heart.
Beacon fires three months running,
a letter from home worth ten thousand in gold —
white hairs, fewer for the scratching,
soon too few to hold a hairpin up.[1]

Passing Chao-ling Again

(Chao-ling was the mausoleum of Emperor T'ai-tsung (r. 627-48), second ruler of the T'ang and the one who was largely responsible for the actual founding of the dynasty. The first eight lines describe his rise to power. The five-hued clouds of the last line are an auspicious omen appearing in response to T'ai-tsung's greatness. The poem was written in 757, when the dynasty's fortunes seemed anything but glorious. 5-ch. *p'ai-lü*.)

From rude darkness the heroes rose;
amid songs of praise, destiny chose him;
in wind and dust, his three-foot sword,
armor donned for the altars of the land;
wings to his father, pure in civil virtue;
heir of the great charge, wielder of war's might;
his holy vision wide and huge as heaven,
in service of ancestors more radiant than the sun.
The mound-side chamber lies wrapped in empty slopes;
warriors, bearlike, to guard the blue-green hill.
Once more I gaze up the pine and cypress road,
watching five-hued clouds drift by.

1. Men wore hairpins to keep their caps in place.

Lovely Lady

(A description of a woman whose family had been wiped out in the rebellion and whose husband had deserted her. 5-ch. old style.)

Lovely lady, fairest of the time,
hiding away in an empty valley;
daughter of a good house, she said,
fallen now among grasses of the wood.
"There was tumult and death within the passes then;
my brothers, old and young, were killed.
Office, position — what help were they?
I couldn't even gather up my brothers' bones!
The world despises you when your luck is down;
all I had went with the turn of the flame.
My husband was a fickle fellow,
his new girl as fair as jade.
Blossoms that close at dusk keep faith with the hour,
mandarin ducks will not rest apart;
but he could only see the new one laughing,
never hear the former one's tears —"
Within the mountain the stream runs clear;
out of the mountain it turns to mud.
Her maid returns from selling a pearl,
braids vines to mend their roof of thatch.
The lady picks a flower but does not put it in her hair,
gathers juniper berries, sometimes a handful.
When the sky is cold, in thin azure sleeves,
at dusk she stands leaning by the tall bamboo.

Presented to Wei Pa,
Gentleman in Retirement

(5-ch. old style)

Life is not made for meetings;
like stars at opposite ends of the sky we move.
What night is it, then, tonight,
when we can share the light of this lamp?
Youth — how long did it last?
The two of us grayheaded now,
we ask about old friends — half are ghosts;
cries of unbelief stab the heart.
Who would have thought? — twenty years
and once again I enter your house.
You weren't married when I left you;
now suddenly a whole row of boys and girls!
merrily greeting their father's friend,
asking me what places I've been.
Before I finish answering,
you send the boys to set out wine and a meal,
spring scallions cut in night rain,
new cooked rice mixed with yellow millet.
Meetings are rare enough, you say;
pour the wine till we've downed ten cups!
But ten cups do not make me drunk;
your steadfast love is what moves me now.
Tomorrow hills and ranges will part us,
the wide world coming between us again.

The Man with No Family
To Take Leave Of

(T'ien-pao in the first line refers to the outbreak of the An Lu-shan rebellion in the
14th year of the T'ien-pao era, 755. 5-ch. old style.)

Ever since T'ien-pao, this silence and desolation,
fields and sheds mere masses of pigweed and bramble;
my village of a hundred households or more,
in these troubled times scattered, some east, some west;
not a word from those still living,
the dead ones all gone to dust and mire.
I was on the side that lost the battle,[1]
so I came home, looking for the old paths,
so long on the road, to find empty lanes,
the sun grown feeble, pain and sorrow in the air.
All I meet are foxes and raccoon dogs,
their fur on end, snarling at me in anger.
And for neighbors on four sides, who do I have?
One or two aging widows.
But the roosting bird loves his old branch;
how could he reject it, narrow perch though it is?
Now that spring's here I shoulder the hoe alone,
in the evening sun once more pour water on the fields.
The local officials know I'm back;
the call me in, order me to practice the big drum.[2]
Maybe they'll assign me to duty in my own province —
but still I've no wife, no one to take by hand.
Traveling to a post nearby, I'm one man all alone;
sent to a far-off assignment, I'll be more lost than ever.
But, since my house and village are a wilderness now,
near or far, it's all the same to me.
And always I grieve for my mother, sick so long;
five years I've left her buried in a mere ditch of a grave.

1. The defeat of the T'ang forces at Hsiang-chou in 759.
2. The drum used in battle to signal troop movements.

She bore me, but I hadn't the strength to help her;
to the end, both of us breathed bitter sighs.
A living man, but with no family to take leave of —
how can I be called a proper human being?

Seven Songs Written During the Ch'ien-yüan Era While Staying at T'ung-ku-hsien

(Poems recording Tu Fu's experiences in 759 when, fleeing from famine, he led his family west to T'ung-ku in Kansu. Tzu-mei is Tu Fu's courtesy name. 7-ch. old style, the 1st, 2nd, 3rd, 4th, and 6th of the series.)

1.
A traveler, a traveler, Tzu-mei his name,
white hair tousled, dangling below the ears,
through the years gathering acorns in the wake of the monkey pack:
cold skies at dusk within a mountain valley.
No word from the middle plain, no hope of going home;
hands and feet chilled and chapped, skin and flesh grown numb,
Ah-ah, song the first, a song already sad;
mournful winds for my sake come down from the sky.

2.
Long hoe, long hoe, handle of white wood,
I trust my life to you — you must save me now!
No shoots of wild taro where mountain snows drift high;[1]
robe so short, pull as I may it will not hide my shins.
And so with you I go empty-handed home;
the boy grumbles, the girls whine, my four walls are still.
Ah-ah, song the second, the song at last breaks free;
village lanes for my sake put on the face of pity.

1. Or, following another text, "shoots of wild lily," used in medicine.

3.
(Tu Fu had four brothers, the youngest with him in T'ung-ku; the others were living in the east.)

I have brothers, younger brothers in a place far away,
three of them sickly, not one of them strong;
parted in life, to veer and turn, never to meet;
barbarian dust blackens the sky, the road is long.
Wild geese flying east, behind them the cranes —
if they could only carry me to your side!
Ah-ah, song the third, the singer's third refrain;
if I should die here, how would you find my bones?

4.
(Chung-li is in Anhwei south of the Huai River.)

I have a sister, little sister, living in Chung-li,
husband dead these many years, her orphan ones still young.
On the long Huai the waves leap up, dragons and serpents rage;
we haven't met for ten years — when will you come?
I want to go in a little boat but arrows fill my eyes;
far away in that southern land, banners of war abound.
Ah-ah, song the fourth, four times I've sung;
forest monkeys for my sake wail even at noon.

6.
(Clearly a political allegory, though commentators do not agree on exactly what the dragon and the vipers stand for.)

To the south there is a dragon living in a mountain pool,
where old trees, dark and lush, touch limb to bending limb.
When tree leaves yellow and fall, he goes to his winter sleep,
and from the east come vipers to play on the waters there.
Passing by, I marveled that they would dare come forth;
I drew a sword to slash them, but put it up again.
Ah-ah, song the sixth, its purpose long denied;
stream-cut valley, for my sake put on spring clothes again!

Dreaming of Li Po

(Written in 759, when Tu Fu was in the far west and Li Po was in exile in the south. The two men had known each other since their young days. 5-ch. old style; 1st of 2 poems.)

Parting from the dead, I've stifled my sobs,
but this parting from the living brings me constant pain.
South of the Yangtze is a land of plague and fever;
no word comes from the exile.
Yet my old friend has entered my dreams,
proof of how long I've pined for him.
He didn't look the way he used to,
the road so far — farther than I can guess.
His spirit came from where the maple groves are green,
then went back, leaving me in borderland blackness.
Now you're caught in the meshes of the law —
how could you have wings to fly with?
The sinking moon floods the rafters of my room
and still I seem to see it lighting your face.
Where you go, waters are deep, the waves so wide —
don't let the dragons, the horned dragons harm you!

A Guest Arrives

(Written in 760 when Tu Fu was living on the outskirts of Ch'eng-tu. 7-ch. regulated verse.)

North of my lodge, south of my lodge, spring rivers all;
day by day I see only flocks of gulls convening.
Flower paths have not been swept for any guest;
my thatch gate for the first time opens to you.
For food — the market's far — no wealth of flavors;
for wine — my house is poor — only old muddy brew.
If you don't mind drinking with the old man next door,
I'll call across the hedge and we can finish off what's left.

On the Spur of the Moment

(7-ch. regulated verse)

River slopes, already into the midmonth of spring;
under the blossoms, bright mornings again:
I look up, eager to watch the birds;
turn my head, answering what I took for a call.
Reading books, I skip the difficult parts;
faced with wine, I keep my cup filled.
These days I've gotten to know the old man of O-mei;[1]
he understands this idleness that is my true nature.

Restless Night

(5-ch. regulated verse)

The cool of bamboo invades my room;
moonlight from the fields fills the corners of the court;
dew gathers till it falls in drops;
a scattering of stars, now there, now gone.
A firefly threading the darkness makes his own light;
birds at rest on the water call to each other;
all these lie within the shadow of the sword —
Powerless I grieve as the clear night passes.

Chüeh-chü

(5-ch. *chüeh-chü*; written in 764)

In late sun, the beauty of river and hill;
on, spring wind, fragrance of grass and flower:
where mud is soft the swallows fly;
where sands are warm the mandarin ducks doze.

1. O-mei is a famous mountain southwest of Ch'eng-tu.

They Say You're Staying in a Mountain Temple

(Written in 766, when Tu Fu was in K'uei-chou on the upper Yangtze, the Chiang-han region mentioned in the poem; his brother was in the seacoast area south of the Yangtze delta. 5-ch. regulated verse, the 2nd of the two poems.)

My younger brother Feng is alone in the region east of the
Yangtze and for three or four years I have had no word from him;
I am looking for someone to take him these two poems.

They say you're staying in a mountain temple,
In Hang-chou — or is it Yüeh-chou?
In the wind and grime of war, how long since we parted!
At Chiang-han, bright autumns waste away.
While my shadow rests by monkey-loud trees,
my soul whirls off to where shell-born towers rise.[1]
Next year on floods of spring I'll go downriver,
to the white clouds at the end of the east I'll look for you!

A Traveler at Night Writes His Thoughts

(5-ch. regulated verse)

Delicate grasses, faint wind on the bank;
stark mast, a lone night boat:
stars hang down, over broad fields sweeping;
the moon boils up, on the great river flowing.
Fame — how can my writings win me that?
Office — age and sickness have brought it to an end.
Fluttering, fluttering — where is my likeness?
Sky and earth and one sandy gull.

1. Towerlike mirages at sea, believed to be formed by the breath of mollusks.

On the River

(Written around 766 on the upper Yangtze; Ching-ch'u is the old name for the region. 5-ch. regulated verse.)

On the river, every day these heavy rains —
bleak, bleak, autumn in Ching-ch'u!
High winds strip the leaves from the trees;
through the long night I hug my fur robe.
I recall my official record, keep looking in the mirror,
recall my comings and goings, leaning alone in an upper room.
In these perilous times I long to serve my sovereign —
old and feeble as I am, I can't stop thinking of it!

CHAPTER EIGHT

Major T'ang Poets II:
Han Yü, Po Chü-i, Han-shan

HAN YÜ (768-824)

THE sufferings which the upheaval of the An Lu-shan rebellion inflicted on the High T'ang poets such as Tu Fu undoubtedly led them to write some of their finest and most poignant poetry. The effect of the revolt on the economic and political life of the T'ang, however, was little short of disastrous. Though the dynasty continued in power until its final demise in 907, it never recovered its former stability, and the country was repeatedly torn by social and political strife. In keeping with the changed nature of the times, poetry in the later years of the dynasty takes on an increasingly autumnal air. Gone are the ingenuous celebrations of imperial splendor, the tone of exuberance that had marked the earlier decades. As the dynasty passes into decline, poetry sheds some of its opulence, its heroic scale, and assumes a more muted and even somber hue.

The surprising weaknesses and faults in the political structure that were revealed by the An Lu-shan uprising seemed to indicate a need for redirection and reform. In the field of literature and thought, a pioneer in such efforts at reform was the Confucian thinker and litterateur Han Yü (768-824). The son of a literary family, he entered government service through the examination system and held a number of official posts, as well as serving as a teacher at the Imperial University in Ch'ang-an. He was twice exiled, the second time because of the famous memorial he submitted to the emperor in which he reprimanded the ruler for his devotion to Buddhism.

Han Yü is best known as a leader of the *ku-wen* or old prose movement, which urged the rejection of the stilted and elaborately rhetorical prose style then in vogue in favor of a return to the simplicity and naturalness that had characterized the prose style of ancient times. In the realm of poetry, likewise, he strove for reform, working to do away with stale diction and to encourage greater freedom of form and expression. At the same time he attempted to broaden the subject matter of poetry and to introduce a more openly philosophical note.

His innovations in style and diction, important though they are, can hardly be illustrated in translation. I hope that the first poem in the selection that follows, however, will show something of his vigorous narrative style, as well as exhibiting his celebrated animosity toward Buddhism and Taoism. The poem begins by describing the immense popularity enjoyed by the Buddhist preachers of the capital, who have drawn listeners away from their Taoist rivals. The situation is dramatically reversed, however, with the appearance of the "girl of Mt. Hua," a beautiful young Taoist priestess who had attracted the attention even of the emperor himself (the "Jade Countenance" of line 23). The last section chides the rich young men of the capital who have flocked about the priestess for other than religious reasons, hinting that her favors are reserved for more exalted personages.

HAN YÜ

The Girl of Mt. Hua

(7-ch. old style)

In streets east, streets west, they expound the Buddhist canon,
clanging bells, sounding conches, till the din invades the palace;
"sin," "blessing," wildly inflated, give force to threats and decep-
       tions;
throngs of listeners elbow and shove as though through duckweed
       seas.
Yellow-robed Taoist priests preach their sermons too,
but beneath their lecterns, ranks grow thinner than stars in the flush
       of dawn.
The girl of Mount Hua, child of a Taoist home,
longed to expel the foreign faith, win men back to the Immortals;
she washed off her powder, wiped her face, put on cap and shawl.
With white throat, crimson cheeks, long eyebrows of gray,
she came at last to ascend the chair, unfolding the secrets of Truth.
For anyone else the Taoist halls would hardly have opened their
       doors;
I do not know who first whispered the word abroad,
but all at once the very earth rocked with the roar of thunder.
Buddhist temples were swept clean, no trace of a believer,
while elegant teams jammed the lanes and ladies' coaches piled up;
Taoist halls were packed with people, many sat outside;
for latecomers there was no room, no way to get within hearing.
Hairpins, bracelets, girdle stones were doffed, undone, snatched off,
till the heaped-up gold, the mounds of jade glinted and glowed in
       the sunlight.
Eminent eunuchs from the heavenly court came with a summons to
       audience;

ladies of the six palaces longed to see the Master's face.
The Jade Countenance nodded approval, granting her return;
dragon-drawn, mounting a crane, she came through blue-dark skies.
These youths of the great families — what do they know of the Tao,
milling about her a hundred deep, shifting from foot to foot?
Beyond cloud-barred windows, in misty towers, who knows what
      happens there
where kingfisher curtains hang tier on tier and golden screens are
      deep?
The immortal's ladder is hard to climb, your bonds with this world
      weighty;
vainly you call on the bluebird to deliver your passionate pleas!

Autumn Thoughts

(5-ch. old style; the 2nd, 6th, and 8th from a set of 11 poems)

I.

When white dew descends on the hundred grasses,
mugwort and orchid alike wither and die;
then, green green by my four walls,
they come alive again, spreading over the ground.
The summer cicada has hardly gone silent
when autumn crickets sound their willful cries.
The rounding cycle never ends,
yet each thing differs in the nature it bears.
Each has its season, its own proper time;
why should pine and cypress alone be prized?

2.

This morning I can't seem to get out of bed,
instead sit bolt upright through the daylight hours.
Insects chirp, the room grows darker;
a moon pops up, shining in the window.

My mind dazed, as though I'd lost my bearings,
idle thoughts welling up to prick me like thorns —
I'm sick of paying court to the dusty world;
writing — my concerns race solely in that direction.
Yet I must try to curb this perversity —
I have duties in the service of the king.

3.
Leaves fall turning turning to the ground,
by the front eaves racing, following the wind;
murmuring voices seem to speak to me
as they whirl and toss in headlong flight.
An empty hall in the yellow dusk of evening:
I sit here silent, unspeaking.
The young boy comes in from outdoors,
trims the lamp, sets it before me,
asks me questions I do not answer,
brings me a supper I do not eat.
He goes and sits down by the west wall,
reading me poetry — three or four poems;
the poet is not a man of today —
already a thousand years divide us —
but something in his words strikes my heart,
fills it again with an acid grief.
I turn and call to the boy:
Put down the book and go to bed now —
a man has times when he must think,
and work to do that never ends.

Written on My Way into Exile When I Reached the Lan-t'ien Pass and Shown to My Brother's Grandson Hsiang

(Written in 819 when the poet was on his way into exile after incurring the imperial wrath because of his attack on Buddhism expressed in his famous "Memorial on the Buddha Bone." Hsiang had accompanied the poet as far as the Lan-t'ien Pass south of Ch'ang-an. 7-ch. regulated verse.)

One document at dawn, submitted to the nine-tiered palace;
by evening, banished to Ch'ao-chou eight thousand li away.
For the sake of our holy ruler I longed to drive away the evil;
what thought for this old body, for the few years remaining?
Clouds blanket the Ch'in Range — which way is home?
Snow blocks the Lan Pass — my horse will not go on.
You must have some purpose, coming so far with me;
be kind and gather up my bones from the shores of the fetid river.

A Pond in a Jardiniere

(7-ch. *chüeh-chü;* 1st, 3rd, and 5th from a set of 5)

1.

Old men are like little boys:
I draw water, fill the jardiniere to make a tiny pond.
All night green frogs gabble till dawn,
just like the time I went fishing at Fang-k'ou.

2.

My ceramic lake in dawn, water settled clear,
numberless tiny bugs — I don't know what you call them;
suddenly they dart and scatter, not a shadow left;
only a squadron of baby fish advancing.

3.
Pond shine and sky glow, blue matching blue;
a few bucketfuls of water poured is all that laps these shores.
I'll wait until the night is cold, the bright moon set,
then count how many stars come swimming here.

Po Chü-i (772-846)

PO CHÜ-I or Po Lo-t'ien had a long and checkered career as a government official, at times holding high office in Ch'ang-an or Lo-yang, at other times languishing in exile in minor provincial posts because of his outspoken criticisms of government policy. He was one of the most prolific of the major T'ang poets and took care to insure the preservation of his works by personally compiling and arranging them in an edition in 75 chapters. It contains some 2,800 poems, as well as various types of prose writings. He himself placed the highest value on his poems of social criticism such as the *Hsin Yüeh-fu* or "New Music Bureau Ballads," though he is probably best known for the narrative poems "Song of Everlasting Regret" and "Song of the Lute," the latter translated here. He is also noted for the exchanges of poems he carried out with his lifetime friend Yüan Chen, his depictions of the quiet pleasures of old age, and his treatment of Buddhist themes. In many of his poems he employed a style marked by deliberate simplicity, even blandness, and some critics have found him rather too facile for their taste. But this very simplicity won him wide popularity among the public at large, and made him a favorite with readers in Korea and Japan as well.

As Arthur Waley discovered some decades ago, Po Chü-i, for reasons I find it difficult to define, seems to come over into English more effectively than almost any other of the major Chinese poets, and I have accordingly included a rather large number of his poems. They are arranged roughly in chronological order.

PO CHÜ-I

A Quiet House in Ch'ang-lo Ward

(Written in 803, when the poet was living in Ch'ang-lo ward in Ch'ang-an and working as a Collater of Texts in the government archives. 5-ch. old style.)

The emperor's city, a place of fame and profit:
from cockcrow on, no one relaxes.
I alone play the idler,
the sun high, my hair as yet uncombed.
The clever and the clumsy differ in nature;
advancers and laggards go separate ways.
Luckily I've happened on a time of great peace
when the Son of Heaven loves scholars and learning.
With small talent it's hard to perform great services:
I collate texts in the palace archives.
Out of thirty days I spend twenty at the office,
and so get to nurture my perversity and sloth.
A thatched roof, four or five rooms,
one horse, two hired men,
a salary that runs to 16,000 cash —
it gets me through the month with some to spare.
So I'm not pressed for clothing and food,
likewise little bothered with social affairs.
Thus I can follow my youthful inclinations,
passing day after day in constant quietude.
But don't suppose I'm lacking in friends;
the bustler and the quiet one each has his own crowd.
There're seven or eight men of the Orchid Terrace[1]
                    for the government archives.

who do the same sort of work I do.
But on my days off, I'm robbed of their talk and laughter,
morning and night I long to see a caller's carriage.
Who can find time from chores of collating,
loosen his belt and stretch out in my hut?
In front of the window there's bamboo for diversion,
outside the gate, a shop that sells wine.
And what do I have to entertain you?
A few stalks in the background, one pot of brew.

Pine Sounds

(In Ch'ang-an, 806. 5-ch. old style.)

The moonlight is good, good for solitary sitting;
there's a pair of pine trees in front of my roof.
From the southwest a faint breeze comes,
stealing in among the branches and leaves,
making a sad and sighing sound,
at midnight here in the bright moon's presence,
like the rustle, rustle of rain on cold hills,
or the clear clean note of autumn lute strings.
One hearing and the fierce heat is washed away,
a second hearing wipes out worry and gloom.
I stay up all evening, never sleeping,
till mind and body are both wiped clean.
On the avenue to the south, horses and carriages pass;
from neighbors to the west, frequent songs and flutes —
who'd suppose that here under the eaves
the sounds that fill my ears are in no way noisy.

Feelings Wakened by a Mirror

(5-ch. old style)

My beautiful one gave it to me when we parted,
but I leave the mirror stored in its box.
Since her flowering face left my sight,
autumn waters have no more lotus blooms.
For years I've never opened the box;
red dust coats the mirror's green bronze.
This morning I took it out and wiped it off,
peered into it at my haggard face,
and, done peering, went on to ponder sadly
the pair of twined dragons carved on its back.

Liao-ling

(One of the "New *Yüeh-fu*," a series of 50 poems attacking social evils of the time.
Liao-ling is a kind of fine silk. 7-ch. old style.)

Liao-ling, sheer patterned silk - what is it like?
Not like poorer silks, *lo, shao, wan* or *chi*,
but the forty-five-foot waterfall
that leaps in the moonlight of Mount T'ien-t'ai;
woven with wonderful designs:
on a ground clothed in white mist, clustered snowflake flowers.
Who does the weaving, who wears the robe?
A poor woman in the glens of Yüeh, a lady in the palace of Han.
Last year eunuch envoys relayed the royal wish:
patterns from heaven to be woven by human hands;
woven with flights of autumn geese clearing the clouds,
dyed with hue of spring rivers south of the Yangtze,
cut broad for making cloak sleeves, long for sweeping skirts,
hot irons to smooth the wrinkles, scissors to trim the seams,

rare colors, strange designs that shine and recede again,
patterns to be seen from every angle, patterns never in repose.
For dancing girls of Chao-yang, token of profoundest favor,
one set of spring robes worth a thousand in gold —
to be stained in sweat, rouge-soiled, never worn again,
dragged on the ground, trampled in mud — who is there to care?
The *liao-ling* weave takes time and toil,
not to be compared to common *tseng* or *po;*
thin threads endlessly plied, till the weaver's fingers ache;
clack-clack the loom cries a thousand times but less than a foot is
      done.
You singers and dancers of the Chao-yang Palace,
could you see her weaving, you'd pity her too!

Light Furs, Fat Horses

(5-ch. old style)

A show of arrogant spirit fills the road;
a glitter of saddles and horses lights up the dust.
I ask who these people are —
trusted servants of the ruler, I'm told.
The vermilion sashes are all high-ranking courtiers;
the purple ribbons are probably generals.
Proudly they repair to the regimental feast,
their galloping horses passing like clouds.
Tankards and wine cups brim with nine kinds of spirits;
from water and land, an array of eight delicacies.
For fruit they break open Tung-t'ing oranges,
for fish salad, carve up scaly bounty from T'ien-ch'ih.
Stuffed with food, they rest content in heart;
livened by wine, their mood grows merrier than ever.
This year there's a drought south of the Yangtze.
In Ch'ü-chou, people are eating people.

The Traveler's Moon

(5-ch. old style)

A traveler has come from south of the Yangtze;
when he set out, the moon was a mere crescent.
During the long long stages of his journey
three times he saw its clear light rounded.
At dawn he followed after a setting moon,
evenings lodged with a moon newly risen.
Who says the moon has no heart?
A thousand long miles it has followed me.
This morning I set out from Wei River Bridge;
by evening I had entered the streets of Ch'ang-an.
And now I wonder about the moon —
whose house will that traveler put up at tonight?

Pouring Out My Feelings after Parting from Yüan Chen

(Written in 810, when the poet's close friend Yüan Chen was banished from Ch'ang-an for political reasons. 5-ch. old style.)

Drip drip, the rain on paulownia leaves;
softly sighing, the wind in the mallow flowers.
Sad sad the early autumn thoughts
that come to me in my dark solitude.
How much more so when I part from an old friend —
no delight then in my musings.
Don't say I didn't see you off —
in heart I went as far as the Green Gate and beyond.[1]
With friends, it's not how many you have

1. A gate in the southeast part of Ch'ang-an. Yüan Chen was being banished to Chiang-ling in Hupei and hence left the city in that direction.

but only whether they share your heart or not.
One who shares my heart has gone away
and I learn how empty Ch'ang-an can be.

Village Night

(Written in 811 when the poet was living in the country in mourning for his
mother. 7-ch. *chüeh-chü.*)

Gray gray of frosty grasses, insects chirp-chirping;
south of the village, north of the village, no sign of travelers.
Alone I go out in front of the gate, gazing over the fields;
in the bright moonlight, buckwheat blossoms are like snow.

Aboard a Boat, Reading Yüan Chen's Poems

(7-ch. *chüeh-chü*)

I pick up your scroll of poems, read in front of the lamp;
the poems are ended, the lamp gutters, the sky not yet light.
My eyes hurt, I put out the lamp, go on sitting in the dark;
a sound of waves blown up by head winds, sloshing against the
          boat.

Night Snow

(5-ch. *chüeh-chü*)

I wondered why the covers felt so cold,
and then I saw how bright my window was.
Night far gone, I know the snow must be deep —
from time to time I hear the bamboos cracking.

Song of the Lute: Preface and Poem

(7-ch. old style)

In the tenth year of the Yüan-ho era (815), I was exiled to the district of Chiu-chiang (Chiang-chou) with the post of marshal. In the autumn of the following year, I was seeing a visitor off at the P'en River landing when I heard someone on one of the boats playing a *p'i-p'a* lute in the night. Listening to its tone, I could detect a note of the capital in its clear twanging. When I inquired who the player was, I found it was a former singing girl of Ch'ang-an who had once studied the lute under two masters named Mu and Ts'ao. Later, when she grew older and her beauty faded, she had entrusted herself to a traveling merchant and became his wife.

I proceeded to order wine and lost no time in requesting her to play a few selections. After the selections were over, she fell into a moody silence, and then told us of the happy times of her youth and of her present life of drifting and deprivation, moving about here and there in the region of the Yangtze and the lakes.

Two years had passed since I was assigned to this post, and I had been feeling rather contented and at ease. But this evening, moved by her words, I realized for the first time just what it means to be an exile. Therefore I have written this long song to present to her. It contains a total of 612 characters and is entitled "Song of the Lute."

Hsün-yang on the Yangtze, seeing off a guest at night;
maple leaves, reed flowers, autumn somber and sad:
the host had dismounted, the guest already aboard the boat,
we raised our wine, prepared to drink, though we lacked flutes and
     strings.
But drunkenness brought no pleasure, we grieved at the imminent
     parting;
at parting time, vague and vast, the river lay drenched in moonlight.
Suddenly we heard the sound of a lute out on the water;
the host forgot about going home, the guest failed to start on his
     way.

We traced the sound, discreetly inquired who the player might be.
The lute sounds ceased, but words were slow in coming.
We edged our boat closer, inviting the player to join us,
poured more wine, turned the lamps around, began our revels again.
A thousand pleas, ten thousand calls, and at last she appeared,
but even then she held the lute so it half hid her face.

She turned the pegs, brushed the strings, sounding two or three
      notes —
before they had formed a melody, already the feeling came through.
Each string seemed tense with it, each sound to hold a thought,
as though she were protesting a lifetime of wishes unfulfilled.
Eyebrows lowered, hand moving freely, she played on and on,
speaking of all the numberless things that were in her heart.
Lightly she pressed the strings, slowly plucked, pulled and snapped
      them,
first performing "Rainbow Skirts," then "Waists of Green."
The big strings plang-planged like swift-falling rain;
the little strings went buzz-buzz like secret conversations;
plang-plang, buzz-buzz mixed and mingled in her playing
like big pearls and little pearls falling on a plate of jade,
or the soft call of warbler voices resonant under the blossoms,
the hidden sobbing of springs and rills barely moving beneath the
      ice.
Then the icy springs congealed with cold, the strings seemed to
      freeze,
freeze till the notes no longer could pass, the sound for a while cut
      off;
now something different, hidden anguish, dark reproaches taking
      form —
at such times the silence was finer than any sound.
Then a silver vase would abruptly break, water come splashing forth,
iron-clad horsemen would suddenly charge, swords and halberds
      clanging.
As the piece ended, she swept the plectrum in an arc before her
      breast,
and all four strings made a single sound, like the sound of rending
      silk.

In the boat to the east, the boat to the west, stillness, not a word;
all we could see was the autumn moon white in the heart of the
      river.

Lost in thought, she put down the plectrum, tucked it among the
      strings,
straightened her robes, rose, put on a grave expression,
told us she had once been a daughter of the capital,
living in a house at the foot of Toad Barrow.
By the age of thirteen she had mastered the lute,
was famed as a member of the finest troupe of players.
Whenever a piece was over, her teachers were enthralled;
each time she donned full makeup, the other girls were filled with
      envy.
Young men from the five tomb towns vied to give her presents;[1]
one selection won her she knew not how many red silks.
Silver hairpins set with inlay — she beat time with them till they
      broke;
blood-colored gauze skirts—she stained them with overturned wine.
This year brought joy and laughter, next year would be the same;
autumn moons, spring breezes — how casually she let them pass!
"Then my younger brother ran off to the army, the woman I called
      'mother' died;
and as evenings went and mornings came, my looks began to fade.
My gate became still and lonely, few horses or riders there;
getting on in years, I gave myself as wife to a traveling merchant.
But merchants think much of profit and little of separation;
last month he went off to Fou-liang to buy tea.
Since coming here to the river mouth, I've guarded my boat alone;
in the bright moonlight that encircles the boat, the river waters are
      cold.
And when night deepens, suddenly I dream of those days of youth,
and my dream-wept tears, mixed with rouge, come down in streams
      of crimson."

Earlier, when I heard her lute, already I felt sad;

1. The tomb towns, sites of imperial graves, were suburbs of the capital where wealthy families lived.

listening to her story, I doubled my sighs of pity.
Both of us hapless outcasts at the farther end of the sky;
meeting like this, why must we be old friends to understand one
            another?
Since last year when I left the capital,
I've lived in exile, sick in bed, in Hsün-yang town.
Hsün-yang is a far-off region — there's no music here;
all year long I never hear the sound of strings or woodwinds.
I live near the P'en River, an area low and damp,
with yellow reeds and bitter bamboo growing all around my house.
And there, morning and evening, what do I hear?
The cuckoo singing his heart out, the mournful cry of monkeys.
Blossom-filled mornings by the spring river, nights with an autumn
            moon,
sometimes I fetch wine and tip the cup alone.
To be sure, there's no lack of mountain songs and village pipes,
but their wails and bawls, squeaks and squawks are a trial to
            listen to.
Tonight, though, I've heard the words of your lute,
like hearing immortal music — for a moment my ears are clear.
Do not refuse me, sit and play one more piece,
and I'll fashion these things into a lute song for you.

Moved by these words of mine, she stood a long while,
then returned to her seat, tightened the strings, strings sounding
            swifter than ever,
crying, crying in pain, not like the earlier sound;
the whole company, listening again, forced back their tears.
And who among the company cried the most?
This marshal of Chiu-chiang, wetting his blue coat.

Sentimental Poem

(5-ch. old style)

Airing clothes and belongings in the courtyard,
suddenly I spy some shoes from my old home.
Who was it gave them to me long ago?
The pretty daughter of our neighbor to the east.
I remember the words she spoke when she gave them to me:
"With these let's promise to be true forever.
Our vows will be as lasting as these shoestrings;
we'll go as a pair, rest as a pair."
Since I was exiled to Chiang-chou
I've wandered like a drifter three thousand miles.
And because I was moved by her lasting love,
I've carried the shoes with me all the way.
This morning I'm filled with sad thoughts,
turning them over, examining them without end.
I am single, but the shoes are still a pair —
how little we resemble each other!
I sigh, thinking how pitiful they are,
with their brocade tops, their embroidered lining,
particularly now when they've come through the rainy season,
their colors darkened, their flower and leaf patterns withered.

After Eating

(Written around 816, in exile in Chiang-chou. 5-ch. old style.)

My meal finished, one short nap,
then get up for two bowls of tea.
I raise my head, look at the sun,
already declining in the southwest.

The happy man regrets the swiftness of the days,
the sad man hates the year for dragging.
But the man who is neither happy nor sad
accepts the life given him, long or short.

A Question Addressed to Liu Shih-chiu

(5-ch. *chüeh-chü*)

Green bubbles — new brewed wine;
lumps of red — a small stove for heating;
evening comes and the sky threatens snow —
Could you drink a cup, I wonder?

A New Thatched Hall

(Written in 817, when the poet was still in exile in Chiang-chou and had built a
home for himself on Mt. Lu; 7-ch. regulated verse.)

    Below Incense Burner Peak I built a new mountain dwelling.
When my thatched hall was first completed, I had occasion to
inscribe this on the eastern wall.

A new thatched hall, five spans by three;[1]
stone steps, cassia pillars, fence of plaited bamboo.
The south eaves catch the sun, warm on winter days;
a door to the north lets in the breeze, cool in summer moonlight.
The racing stream that flows over the eave stones splatters them a
      little;
the slanting bamboo that brushes the window isn't planted in rows.

1. A *chien* or span is the distance between two pillars.

Next spring I'll thatch the side room to the east,
fit it with paper panels and reed blinds for my Meng Kuang.[2]

Writing Again on the Same Theme

(7-ch. regulated verse)

The sun's high, I've slept enough, still too lazy to get up;
in a little room, quilts piled on, I'm not afraid of the cold.
The bell of the Temple of Bequeathed Love — I prop up my pillow
    to listen;
snow on Incense Burner Peak — rolling up the blind, I look at it.
K'uang's Mt. Lu, a place for running away from fame;
marshal — a fitting post to spend old age in.[1]
Mind peaceful, body at rest, this is where I belong.
Why should I always think of Ch'ang-an as home?

The Temple of Bequeathed Love

(5-ch. *chüeh-chü*)

Amusing myself with rocks, I sit peering into the valley;
searching for blossoms, I wander round and round the temple.
Again and again I hear the birds talking,
and everywhere there's a sound of fountains.

2. Meng Kuang was the wife of Liang Hung, a recluse of the Later Han; the couple
are symbols of conjugal happiness.

1. Mt. Lu was called K'uang's Lu because a recluse with the surname K'uang was said
to have lived there in Chou times. Ssu-ma or marshal was the post assigned to the poet
when he was exiled to Chiang-chou in the region of Mt. Lu.

Drunk, Facing Crimson Leaves

(5-ch. *chüeh-chü*)

Confronting the wind, late autumn trees;
facing wine, a man of some years,
his drunken face like the frosty leaves,
red enough, but not from a springtime glow.

Idle Droning

(7-ch. *chüeh-chü*)

Since earnestly studying the Buddhist doctrine of emptiness,
I've learned to still all the common states of mind.
Only the devil of poetry I have yet to conquer —
let me come on a bit of scenery and I start my idle droning.

Better Come Drink Wine with Me

(5-ch. regulated verse, 4 from a series of 14 poems entitled "Recommending Wine")

I.
Don't go hide in the deep mountains —
you'll only come to hate it.
Your teeth will ache with the chill of dawn water,
your face smart from the bite of the night frost.
Go off fishing and winds will blow up from the cove;
return from gathering firewood to find snow all over the cliffs.
Better come drink wine with me;
face to face we'll get mellowly, mellowly drunk.

2.
Don't go off and be a farmer —
you'll only make yourself miserable.
Come spring and you'll be plowing the lean soil,
twilight and it's time to feed the skinny ox.
Again and again you'll be hit for government taxes,
but seldom will you meet up with a year of good crops.
Better come drink wine with me;
together we'll get quietly, quietly drunk.

3.
Don't go climbing up to the blue clouds — [1]
the blue clouds are rife with passion and hate,
everyone a wise man, bragging of knowledge and vision,
flattening each other in the scramble for merit and power.
Fish get chowdered because they swallow the bait;
moths burn up when they bumble into the lamp.
Better come drink wine with me;
let yourself go, get roaring, roaring drunk.

4.
Don't go into the realm of red dust — [2]
it wears out a person's spirit and strength.
You war with each other like the two horns of a snail,[3]
end up with one ox-hair worth of gain.
Put out the fire that burns in your rage,
stop whetting the knife that hides in a smile.
Better come drink wine with me;
we'll lie down peacefully, merrily, merrily drunk.

1. The world of high government office.

2. The marketplace.

3. Reference to the parable in *Chuang Tzu* ch. 25 that tells of two kingdoms situated on the right and left horns of a snail that were continually at war.

Spring River

(Written around 820 when the poet was governor of Chung-chou on the upper Yangtze. 7-ch. regulated verse.)

Heat and cold, twilight and dawn succeed each other so swiftly,
before I know it, already two years in Chung-chou!
Shut up in my room, all I listen for are morning and evening drums;[1]
climbing the tower, I gaze absently down on boats that come and
       go.
Enticed by oriole voices, I've come here under the blossoms;
spellbound by the color of the grasses, I sit by the water's edge.
Nothing but spring river, and I never tire of watching it —
rounding the sand spits, circling rocks, a rippling, murmuring green.

Half in the Family, Half Out

(Written around 840, when the poet was nearing 70. To be "in the family" means to be a lay Buddhist believer; to be "out of the family" means to be a monk. 7-ch. regulated verse.)

Comfortably fixed for clothing and food, children married off,
from now on family affairs are no concern of mine.
In nightly rest, I'm a bird who's found his way to the forest;
at morning meals, I'm one in heart with the monk who begs his
       food.
Clear cries, several voices — cranes under the pines;
one spot of cold light — the lamp among the bamboo.
Late at night I practice meditation, sitting in lotus position.
My daughters call, my wife hoots — I don't answer any of them.

---

1. Drums that signal the time.

HAN-SHAN OR THE MASTER OF COLD MOUNTAIN

IT may strike readers as odd to find the poems of Han-shan included in a chapter entitled Major T'ang Poets. Some would no doubt question whether he is in fact to be regarded as a major poet of the period, while others might object to his being treated as "a poet" at all.

From at least Sung times, there has existed a collection of some three hundred poems associated with his name; most of the poems are attributed to Han-shan himself, with about fifty attributed to his alleged companion Shih-te or The Foundling, and a few to a Buddhist monk named Feng-kan. From the internal evidence of the poems attributed to Han-shan, it would appear that he was a scholar-farmer who later in life retired to a place called Cold Mountain (Han-shan, from which he takes his name), in the T'ien-t'ai Mountains, a range stretching along the seacoast in northeastern Chekiang Province. Some of the poems are highly personal in tone and of great literary appeal. But others are little more than conventional satires on the follies of the world or Buddhist sermons on the sin of meat-eating or other doctrinal matters, closely resembling the kind of didactic verse common in the popular Buddhism of the period. It has been conjectured, therefore, that the poems attributed to Han-shan may actually be from a number of different hands, which is why I have suggested that it is difficult to treat his works as though they were by a single poet. Some scholars even claim, on the basis of a study of the rhymes, that the poems attributed to him range in date over a period of several centuries, though this assertion has been contested. In any event, no way has so far been discovered to ascertain the exact date of the poems, though the late eighth and early ninth centuries is suggested as the most likely possibility.

A preface of unknown date that has been attached to the collection of poems pictures Han-shan and Shih-te as laughing and thoroughly enlightened eccentrics who were associated with a Buddhist temple on Mt. T'ien-t'ai, and they have become favorite figures in Chinese and Japanese Buddhist art and legend, particularly that associated with the Ch'an or Zen sect, in that carefree guise. The poems themselves, however, are by no means uniformly jolly in tone. Rather they reveal a man at times deeply contented, even rapturous with the delights of his mountain retreat, at other times troubled by privation and nagging loneliness. Underlying them throughout is the Zen—or more correctly, the Mahayana Buddhist — conviction that these very experiences of daily life, painful or peaceful, harsh or serene, are the stuff that enlightenment is made of. There is, in other words, no Way outside of the way of everyday life.

None of the poems have titles. All those in my selection are attributed to Han-shan and use a 5-character line, some in old style, some in regulated verse form. The latter can be readily identified by the verbal parallelisms employed in the middle couplets.

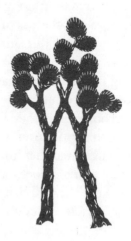

HAN-SHAN

1.
My father and mother left me a good living,
I needn't envy the fields of other men.
Clack — clack — my wife works her loom;
jabber jabber goes my son at play.
I clap hands, urging on the swirling petals;
chin in hand, I listen to singing birds.
Who comes to commend me on my way of life?
Well, a woodcutter sometimes passes by.

2.
As long as I was living in the village
they said I was the finest man around.
But yesterday I went to the city
and even the dogs eyed me askance.
Some people jeered at my skimpy trousers,
others said my jacket was too long.
If someone would poke out the eyes of the hawks
we sparrows could dance wherever we please!

3.
In the house east of here lives an old woman.
Three or four years ago, she got rich.
In the old days she was poorer than I;
now she laughs at me for not having a penny.
She laughs at me for being behind;
I laugh at her for getting ahead.
We laugh as though we'd never stop,
she from the east and I from the west!

4.

A certain scholar named Mr. Wang
was laughing at my poems for being so clumsy.
"Didn't you notice the wasp's waist here?
Don't you even know what stork's knees are?[1]
You don't seem to understand tones at all
but toss in any word that comes to mind!"
I laugh too, Mr. Wang, when *you* make a poem,
like a blind man trying to sing of the sun.

5.

Why am I always so depressed?
Man's life is like the morning mushroom.
Who can bear in a few dozen years
to see new friends and old all gone away?
Thinking of this I'm filled with sadness,
a sadness I can hardly endure.
What shall I do? What shall I do?
Take this old body home and hide it in the mountains!

6.

I think of all the places I've been,
chasing from one famous spot to another.
Delighting in mountains, I scaled the mile-high peaks;
loving the water, I sailed a thousand rivers.
I held farewell parties with my friends in Lute Valley,
brought my zither and played on Parrot Shoals.
Who would guess I'd end up under a pine tree,
clasping my knees in the whispering cold?

7.

The birds and their chatter overwhelm me with feeling;
at times like this I lie down in my thatched hut.
Cherries shine with crimson fire,
willows trail their slender boughs.
The morning sun pops from the jaws of blue peaks;

---

1. "Wasp's waist" and "stork's knees" are technical terms for certain undesirable tonal
effects in prosody.

bright clouds are washed in the green pond.
Who ever thought I'd leave the dusty world
and come bounding up the southern slope of Cold Mountain?

8.
I climb the road to Cold Mountain,
the road to Cold Mountain that never ends.
The valleys are long and strewn with stones,
the streams broad and banked with thick grass.
Moss is slippery, though no rain has fallen;
pines sigh but it isn't the wind.
Who can break from the snares of the world
and sit with me among the white clouds?

9.
Cold Mountain is full of weird sights;
people who try to climb it always get scared.
When the moon shines the water glints and sparkles;
when the wind blows the grasses rustle and sigh.
Snowflakes make blossoms for the bare plum,
clouds in place of leaves for the naked trees.
At a touch of rain the whole mountain shimmers —
but only in good weather can you make the climb.

10.
The place where I spend my days
is farther away than I can tell.
Without a wind the wild vines stir;
no fog, yet the bamboos are always dark.
Who do the valley streams sob for?
Why do the mists huddle together?
At noon, sitting in my hut,
I realize for the first time that the sun has risen.

11.
Wonderful, this road to Cold Mountain —
yet there's no sign of horse or carriage.
In winding valleys too tortuous to trace,
on crags piled who knows how high,

a thousand different grasses weep with dew
and pines hum all together in the wind.
Now it is that, straying from the path,
you ask your shadow, What way from here?

12.

As for me, I delight in the everyday Way,
among mist-wrapped vines and rocky caves.
Here in the wilderness I'm completely free,
with my friends, the white clouds, idling forever.
There are roads but they do not reach the world.
Since I'm mindless, who can rouse my thoughts?
On a bed of stone I sit, alone in the night,
while the round moon climbs up Cold Mountain.

13.

Last year in the spring when the birds were calling
I thought of my brothers and kin.
This year when fall chrysanthemums bloom
I remember the time of my youth,
when green waters murmured in a thousand streams
and yellow clouds filled the sky.
Ah, all the hundred years of my life
must I remember with such heartache those days in the capital?

14.

When people see the man of Cold Mountain
they all say, "There's a crackpot!
Hardly a face to make one look twice,
his body wrapped in nothing but rags...
The things we say he doesn't understand;
the things he says we wouldn't utter!"
A word to those of you passing by —
try coming to Cold Mountain sometime!

15.

I look far off at T'ien-t'ai's summit,
alone and high above the crowding peaks.
Pines and bamboos sing in the wind that sways them,

sea tides wash beneath the shining moon.
I gaze at the mountain's green borders below
and discuss philosophy with the white clouds.
In the wilderness mountains and seas are all right,
but I wish I had a companion in my search for the Way.

16.
Last night in a dream I returned to my old home
and saw my wife weaving at her loom.
She held her shuttle poised, as though lost in thought,
as though she had no strength to lift it further.
I called. She turned her head to look
but her eyes were blank — she didn't know me.
So many years we've been parted
the hair at my temples has lost its old color.

17.
Wise men, you have cast me aside.
Fools, I do the same to you.
I would be neither wise man nor fool;
from now on let's hear no more from each other.
When night comes I sing to the bright moon;
at dawn I dance with white clouds.
How could I still my voice and my hands
and sit stiff as a stick with my gray hair rumpled?

18.
Men these days search for a way through the clouds,
but the cloud way is dark and without sign.
The mountains are high and often steep and rocky;
in the broadest valleys the sun seldom shines.
Green crests before you and behind,
white clouds to east and west —
do you want to know where the cloud way lies?
There it is, in the midst of Nothing!

19.
I wanted to go off to the eastern cliff —
how many years now I've planned the trip?

Yesterday I pulled myself up by the vines,
but wind and fog forced me to stop halfway.
The path was narrow and my clothes kept catching,
the moss so spongy I couldn't move my feet.
So I stopped under this red cinnamon tree —
I guess I'll lay my head on a cloud and sleep.

20.

Yes, there are stingy people,
but I'm not one of the stingy kind.
The robe I wear is flimsy? The better to dance in.
Wine gone? It went with a toast and a song.
Just so you keep your belly full —
never let those two legs go weary.
When the weeds are poking through your skull,
that's the day you'll have regrets!

21.

I came once to sit on Cold Mountain
and lingered here for thirty years.
Yesterday I went to see relatives and friends —
over half had gone to the Yellow Springs.
Bit by bit life fades like a guttering lamp,
passes on like a river that never rests.
This morning I face my lonely shadow
and before I know it tears stream down.

22.

Today I sat before the cliff,
sat a long time till mists had cleared.
A single thread, the clear stream runs cold;
a thousand yards the green peaks lift their heads.
White clouds — the morning light is still.
Moonrise — the lamp of night drifts upward.
Body free from dust and stain,
what cares could trouble my mind?

23.
Have I a body or have I none?
Am I who I am or am I not?
Pondering these questions,
I sit leaning against the cliff while the years go by,
till the green grass grows between my feet
and the red dust settles on my head,
and the men of the world, thinking me dead,
come with offerings of wine and fruit to lay by my corpse.

24.
So Han-shan writes you these words,
these words that no one will believe.
Honey is sweet — men love the taste;
medicine is bitter and hard to swallow.
What soothes the feelings brings contentment;
what opposes the will calls forth anger.
But I ask you to look at the wooden puppets,
worn out by their moment of play on stage!

25.
Do you have the poems of Han-shan in your house?
They're better for you than sutra-reading!
Write them out and paste them on a screen
where you can glance them over from time to time.

CHAPTER NINE

Other T'ang Poets

THE early decades of the T'ang, as we have noted before, saw a continuation of the shallow and decorative poetic style that had characterized late Six Dynasties and Sui times. In the period that followed, known as the High T'ang, poets such as Wang Wei, Li Po, Tu Fu, and their contemporaries succeeded in infusing new vitality into the tradition by returning to the spirit of Han and Wei poetry and adapting its vigor, realism, and seriousness of tone to the treatment of contemporary themes. This forceful new style was carried on and developed by the poets of the succeeding age, notably Han Yü and Po Chü-i, who expanded its narrative possibilities and widened its range of subjects, though at times losing something of the grandeur that had marked the work of their immediate predecessors. The closing years of the dynasty were characterized by a diversity of styles, some poets concentrating upon skillful but rather bland descriptions of the natural scene, others dealing in complex imagery, often of a private nature.

The selection of 48 poems that follows is intended not so much to illustrate these stylistic developments as to present to the reader some of the best known works of the period and to suggest something of the range and tenor of T'ang poetry as a whole. If it seems to be weighted heavily on the side of short poems, that is because such works, with their air of suggesting much more than they actually say, have come to be regarded as particularly representative of the T'ang poetic genius.

As will be seen, the *yüeh-fu* or ballad type poem, so popular in preceding centuries, continued in favor, the T'ang poets frequently adopting the persona of a young girl to comment on the themes of love and separation, or of a soldier in the field to bewail the hardships of war. Another theme carried over from earlier times is that of the palace lady languishing in perfumed neglect, partly because she served as a symbol of the poet himself, similarly pining away for want of just recognition of his talents. Other poems in a more realistic vein deal with the examination system that so often constituted the poet's main hope for recognition and advancement, or with the troubled conditions of the times.

Two poets of particular importance, Li Ho and Li Shang-yin, are represented by five poems each and could equally well have been treated in the chapters on major T'ang poets. Li Ho (791-817), as his dates indicate, died so early that it is impossible to say what artistic stature he might have achieved had fate been kinder. Aside from the fact of his youthful genius, he is remembered chiefly for his works in old style that seek to recapture some of the mystery of the shaman songs of the *Ch'u Tz'u*, and for the general aura of eeriness that informs much of his imagery. Li Shang-yin (813?-858) worked in a variety of styles, as my sample shows, but is best known for the poems on clandestine love, many with the title "Untitled," that have so long intrigued commentators with their veiled and suggestive language.

In terms of poetic form, the T'ang poets showed great fondness for the "modern style" or tonally regulated forms. The 4-line *chüeh-chü* was a special favorite, as a glance at the selection below will show, while the 8-line *lü-shih* or regulated verse form, looked on in earlier times as mainly an occasion for clever wordplay, was in the hands of men like Tu Fu and Li Shang-yin transformed into a vehicle for serious poetic utterance. Poets at the same time continued to write in the "old poetry" forms, reveling, it would appear, in the comparative freedom from exacting prosodic demands that such forms offered. Toward the close of the dynasty, a new poetic form, the *tz'u* or "lyric meter," came to prominence. It will be discussed in chapter 12.

Few people would challenge the often-made assertion that Chinese poetry in the *shih* form reached its peak of excellence in the T'ang dynasty. Just why that should have been so, however, is not easy to say. The dynasty, in its early years at least, was powerful enough to insure stability within its borders and to extend its influence abroad, thereby inspiring a resurgence of national and cultural pride. The arts, encouraged by the patronage of the court and aristocracy and enriched by foreign influences, flourished. In addition, the examination system, which played an important role in recruiting men for government service, did much to foster devotion to literature and learning.

One notes immediately, however, that most of the best poetry of the T'ang was the product not of these bright initial decades, but of the dynasty's later and more troubled times. And though the examination system offered an opportunity for entrance into the bureaucracy, the exams were frequently maddeningly difficult to pass, and those men who were lucky enough to find themselves launched on a government career more often than not had to face bleak periods of disfavor or exile to the provinces because of shifts in the political scene.

It is perhaps this very combination of material and cultural wealth coupled with a precarious social and political situation, of bright possibilities with sudden reverses of fortune, that engendered in T'ang poetry its air of being simultaneously engaged with and yet distanced from reality. The poet seems to be acutely conscious of the joys of life, but conscious also of how suddenly and inexplicably those joys can be snatched away. Thus, at the same time that he seeks in his poetry to capture the scenes and experiences of everyday life, he invests them with a kind of timelessness that places them in a larger and more transcendent frame of reference. His work, even as it registers pity and despair at the passing of the particular moment, never ceases to be aware of the forces of time and change that make that passing inevitable.

CH'EN TZU-ANG *(661-702)*

Song on Climbing Yu-chou Gate Tower

(irregular old style)

Behind me I do not see the ancient men,
before me I do not see the ones to come.
Thinking of the endlessness of heaven and earth,
alone in despair, my tears fall down.

CHANG YÜEH *(667-730)*

Written When Drunk

(5-ch. *chüeh-chü*)

Once drunk, my delight knows no limits,
so much better than before I'm drunk.
My movements all are shaped like dances,
and everything I say comes out a poem!

CHANG CHIU-LING *(673-740)*

Watching the Moon with Thoughts of Far Away

(5-ch. regulated verse)

Bright moon born of the sea,
at sky's farthest edges we share it now.
A man of heart, hating the long night,
till the end of evening wakeful, remembering,
I put out the lamp, marvel at the moonlight's fullness,
don a cloak, aware of the dampness of dew.
No way to send my gift, this handful of moonbeams,
I go back to bed, dreaming of good times.

CH'IU WEI *(694-789?)*

Visiting a Recluse on West Mountain and Not Finding Him In

(5-ch. old style)

At the topmost peak, one thatch hut,
straight up for thirty li:
knock on the gate — there is no houseboy;
peer into the room — nothing but a desk;
if he hasn't rigged an awning on the shabby cart,
then he must be fishing in the autumn stream.
One this way, one that — we missed each other,
my admiration for you left untold.
But the color of the grasses under new rain,

the voice of the pines in an evening window —
these are the promised hidden wonders,
enough to open wide the ear and heart.
Though my plan for host and guest came to nothing,
somehow I've grasped the meaning of purity.
And now the mood is over, I'm off down the mountain —
what need to wait around for you?

WANG CH'ANG-LING *(698-757)*

Castleside Song

(5- and 7-ch. old style, *yüeh-fu*)

Fall winds wail in mulberry branches;
grasses whiten, the fox and rabbit frisk.
In Han-tan he's been drinking — before the wine wears off,
over broad plains north of the castle he flies his black falcon,
in the empty camp site shoots two pouncing tigers dead,
then turns home by crescent moon, bowcase slung at his belt.

TS'UI HAO *(704-754)*

Songs of Ch'ang-kan

(Ch'ang-kan is on the Yangtze near Nanking; 5-ch. *chüeh-chü, yüeh-fu*.)

SHE:
Tell me, where is your home?
I live at Sloping Banks myself —

Stop the boat, let me ask a minute —
who knows but maybe we're from the same town!
HE:
My home looks over the Nine River waters;
up and down the Nine Rivers I go.
True, I came from Ch'ang-kan like you,
but I was a boy then — we never met.

CH'U KUANG-HSI *(707-759)*

The Streets of Ch'ang-an

(5-ch. *chüeh-chü, yüeh-fu*)

Cracking whips, off to the wine shop,
in flashy clothes heading for the whorehouse door;
a million cash spent in an hour —
expressionless, they never speak a word.

A Farmer's Thoughts

(5-ch. old style; 1st in a series of 8 poems entitled "Varied Pleasures of a Farm Family")

Spring came, with orioles singing,
and I turned to the fields;
lacking strength to work them alone,
I begged for the hand of the girl next door.
Our first thoughts were of bearing sons,
then we planned how to broaden our acres.
Quiet times, we looked at each other and smiled,

gloating over a fine crop of grain.
Now each night I climb up Whistling Mound,
gazing south to the shore of Lake Tung-t'ing,
the hundred grasses mantled in frost and dew,
autumn hills echoing to the fulling mallets' sound,
and I long for those bygone days —
now my heart can find nothing to care for.

LIU CH'ANG-CH'ING *(710?-785?)*

Rejoicing that the Zen Master Pao Has Arrived from Dragon Mountain

(5-ch. regulated verse)

What day did you come down from that former place,
spring grasses ready to turn green and fair?
Still it faces the mountain moon,
but who listens now to its rock-bound stream?
Monkey cries tell you night is fading;
blossoms that open show you the flowing years.
With metal staff you quietly come and go,
mindless — for everywhere is Zen.

THE BUDDHIST PRIEST CHIAO-JAN *(730-799)*

Looking for Lu Hung-chien but Failing To Find Him

(5-ch. regulated verse)[1]

You've moved to a house backing the outer wall;
I reach it by wild paths through mulberry and hemp.
Along the fence chrysanthemums newly set out
have yet to bloom, though autumn's here.
I pound the gate but no dog barks.
About to go, I ask at the house next door;
they tell me you're up in the hills,
never come home till the sun is low.

WEI YING-WU *(b. 736)*

To Send to Li Tan and Yüan Hsi

(7-ch. regulated verse)

Last year among the flowers I saw you off;
today the buds unfolding make it a year.
The world's ways — dim and distant, hard to foretell;
spring griefs — dull and dark; I sleep alone,
body full of aches and ills, remembering fields of home.
Vagrants in the city — I'm ashamed to draw my pay.[1]
I hear you may be coming to visit —
from west tower, how many rounding moons must I wait?

1. The poem is unusual because, although it observes the tonal regulations required for a regulated verse, it ignores the rule demanding verbal parallelism in the two middle couplets.

1. The poet held an official post and hence felt responsible for the welfare of the people.

Sent to the Taoist Holy Man of Ch'üan-chiao

(5-ch. old style)

This morning it was cold in my office study
and suddenly I thought of you, living in the mountains,
in valley bottoms bundling thorns for kindling,
coming home to cook white stones.[1]
I wanted to take a gourdful of wine
to cheer you far off in evening wind and rain,
but falling leaves have filled the empty hills —
where could I find a trace of you?

West Creek at Ch'u-chou

(7-ch. *chüeh-chü*)

These I love: hidden plants that grow by the river's edge;
above, yellow warblers in the deep trees singing;
spring tides robed in rain, swifter by evening;
the ferry landing deserted where a boat swings by itself.

SSU-K'UNG SHU *(740-790?)*

The Rebellion Over, I See Off a Friend Who Is Returning North

(5-ch. regulated verse)

A world in turmoil — we came south together;
clear times — you return north alone.

1. Said to be the food of recluses.

In a strange country your hair turned white;
in your old land you'll see the blue hills,
by dawn moon passing ruined forts,
under crowding stars to rest by old frontiers,
cold birds and withered grasses
everywhere companion to your grieving eyes.

In Illness, Dismissing My Singing Girl

(7-ch. *chüeh-chü*)

Ten thousand things wound my heart when you're before my eyes,
I, lean and withered, to sleep facing such a flower!
I've used up all my yellow gold teaching you songs and dances —
go stay with someone else now, make a young man happy.

YÜ HU *(b. 745)*

Thoughts South of the Yangtze

(7-ch. *chüeh-chü, yüeh-fu*)

By the riverbank idly I pick white-budded reeds;
with the other girls, make offering to the river god.
So many people around I don't dare speak out loud;
in my heart I ask news of my wanderer, toss a questioning coin.

MENG CHIAO *(751-814)*

On Failing the Examination

The dawn moon struggles to shine its light,
the man of sorrows struggles with his feelings.
Who says in spring things are bound to flourish?
All I see is frost on the leaves.
The eagle sickens, his power vanishes,
while little wrens soar on borrowed wings.
But leave them, leave them be! —
these thoughts like wounds from a knife!

CHANG CHI *(768-830)*

Tying Up for the Night at Maple River Bridge

(7-ch. *chüeh-chü*)

Moon setting, crows cawing, frost filling the sky,
through river maples, fishermen's flares confront my uneasy eyes.
Outside Ku-su city,[1] Cold Mountain Temple —
late at night the sound of its bell reaches a traveler's boat.

1. An old name for Suchow.

WANG CHIEN *(768?-833?)*

Words of the Newly Wed Wife

(5-ch. *chüeh-chü*)

The third day I went into the kitchen,
washed my hands and made the soup.
Not yet sure of my mother-in-law's tastes,
I sent some first for sister-in-law to try.

Palace Song

(A neglected lady of the palace likens her plight to that of the scattered peach blossoms; 7-ch. *chüeh-chü*.)

I search the treetops, low-hung branches, for a trace of pink:
one petal drifting west, one petal east.
Peach blossoms thought only of fruit to come;
it would be wrong to rail at the dawn-watch wind.

LI SHEN *(772-846)*

Pitying the Farmer

(5-ch. *chüeh-chü*)

He hoes the grain under a midday sun,
sweat dripping down on the soil beneath the grain.
Who realizes that the food in the food bowl,
every last morsel of it, is bought with such toil?

LIU TSUNG-YÜAN *(773-819)*

River Snow

(5-ch. *chüeh-chü*)

From a thousand hills, bird flights have vanished;
on ten thousand paths, human traces wiped out:
lone boat, an old man in straw cape and hat,
fishing alone in the cold river snow.

A Poem to Send to Friends in the Capital

(Written when in exile in Kwangsi in the far south; 7-ch. *chüeh-chü*.)

Mountains by the seaside — sharp pointed swords:
when autumn comes, wherever I look, they stab my grieving heart.
If I could change into a million selves
I'd send one to climb each peak and gaze far off toward home.

YÜAN CHEN *(779-831)*

Airing Painful Memories

(Thoughts of the poet's dead wife. Tao-yün, daughter of the rich and powerful
Hsieh family in Six Dynasties times, was noted for her wit and intelligence. Ch'ien
Lou was a worthy but impoverished scholar of antiquity; 7-ch. regulated verse.)

Lord Hsieh's youngest, his favorite child,
married to Ch'ien Lou and a hundred cares!
She saw I had no clothes and went digging through her wicker
trunks;

I wheedled her into buying wine — off came her golden hairpins!
Garden greens filled our tray — we were thankful for lanky bean-
   stalks;
fallen leaves eked out the firewood — how we eyed the old ash tree!
Today my pay comes to more than a hundred thousand —
and all I can offer are fasts and services for your soul!

LI HO *(791-817)*

For the Examination at Ho-nan-fu: Songs of the Twelve Months (with Intercalary Month)

(One of a set of 13 poems written for a government examination taken and passed
in 810 at Lo-yang; 5-ch. old style.)

Stars rest cold by shoals of cloud;
dew spatters round into the plate.
From tree tips fair flowers unfold;
in deserted gardens fading orchids grieve.
The evening sky seems flagged with jade;
on the pool, lotus leaves, huge coins of green bronze.
With annoyance one finds the single dancing cloak too thin,
gradually grows aware of a chill on flowered mats.
Dawn winds — how they sough and sigh!
Blazoned in brightness, the Little Dipper gleams.

Song of the Sacred Strings

(7-ch. old style, *yüeh-fu*)

On western hills the sun dies, eastern hills are dusking;
whirlwinds buffet the horses, horses that prance on cloud.

Patterned strings and plain white flute — a shallow, dinning sound;
flowered skirts that rush and rustle, pacing the autumn dust.
Cassia leaves torn in the wind — the cassias drop their fruit;
blue raccoon dogs wail in blood, cold foxes die.
Painted dragons on the wall, tails glued with gold;
the Rain God rides them, down into the waters of an autumn pool.
The hundred-year-old owl puts on a tree sprite's form,
the voice of laughter, jade-green fire from the midst of his nest
     ascending.

The Northland in Cold

(7-ch. old style)

The blackness of one quarter lights up the mauve of three:
the Yellow River in a weld of ice, its fish and dragons die.
Bark of the three-foot trees splits into scar and crackle;
carts, strong beneath a hundred-weight, ascend the river's flow.
Blossoms of frost upon the grass, huge as copper coins;
brandished swords could not pierce these meshed and low-slung
     skies.
Ocean's wrest and tumble grows loud with hurtling ice;
mountain cascades are voiceless, dependent rainbows of jade.

At Ch'ang-ku, Reading: To Show to My Man Pa

(5-ch. *chüeh-chü*)

Echo of insects where the lamplight thins;
the cold night heavy with medicine fumes:
because you pity a broken-winged wanderer,
through bitterest toil you follow me still.

My Man Pa Replies

(5-ch. *chüeh-chü*)

Big-nose looks best in mountain-coarse clothes;
bushy-brows should stick to his poetry toils!
Were it not for the songs you sing,
who would know the depths of autumn sorrow?

CHIA TAO *(779-843)*

Looking for a Recluse but Failing to Find Him

(5-ch. *chüeh-chü*)

Under the pines I questioned the boy.
"My master's off gathering herbs.
All I know is he's here on the mountain—
clouds are so deep, I don't know where..."

The Last Night of the Third Month

(7-ch. *chüeh-chü*)

Third month, the thirtieth day:
the season takes leave of a hard-working poet.
You and I must not sleep tonight—
till we hear the bells of dawn, it is still spring!

TU MU *(803-853)*

Sent in Parting

(7-ch. *chüeh-chü*)

Great love may seem like none at all:
wine before us, we only know that smiles won't come.
The tallow candle has a heart — it grieves at parting,
in our place drips tears until the break of day.

LI SHANG-YIN *(812-858)*

Spring Rain

(7-ch. regulated verse)

Lying disconsolate in new spring white wadded robes,
by white gates lost and lonely, my wish too much denied:
a red pavilion beyond the rain — we watch each other coldly;
pearl blinds, a torch that flickers — she comes home alone.
A long road is grief enough in spring dusk and evening;
what's left of the night still offers me phantoms of a dream.
Jade earrings, a sealed letter — how to get them through?
Ten thousand miles of cloud gauze, a wild goose winging.

Thoughts in the Cold

(5-ch. regulated verse)

When he left, the waves were flush with the railing;
now cicadas are silent and branches full of dew,

and I keep on remembering at a time like this,
leaning here while seasons pass.
For the North Star too, spring is far away;
too late to send couriers to your southern hill.
At the sky's edge, over and over I question my dreams,
wondering if you haven't found someone new.

Untitled

(7-ch. regulated verse)

Last night's planets and stars, last night's wind,
by the painted tower's west side, east of Cassia Hall—
for us no nearness of phoenixes winging side by side,
yet our hearts became as one, like the rhino's one-thread horn.
From opposing seats we played pass-the-hook, spring wine was
    warm.
On rival teams we played what's-under-it?—wax candles shone red.
When I heard the drums that called me back to work,
I raced my horse to Orchid Terrace like tumbleweed torn loose.[1]

Untitled

(5-ch. old style)

At eight stealing a mirror glance,
already she knew how to paint long eyebrows.
At ten off to roam the green,
lotus flowers made skirts for her.
At twelve learning to play the lute,
never would she put the silver pick down.
At fourteen she hid from her six relations,
knowing their thoughts, though not yet a bride.
At fifteen in the spring wind she cried,
under the swing, her face turned away.

1. Orchid Terrace was the government archives, where the young man was an official.

Poem for My Little Boy

(5-ch. old style)

My little boy Kun-shih,
no finer, no handsomer lad;
in bellyband, less than one year old,
already he knew six from seven;
at three he could tell you his name,
had eyes for more than chestnuts and pears.[1]
My friends come to look him over,
call him the phoenix of Cinnabar Cave;
at former courts where looks were prized,
he'd have rated first, they say;
but no, he has the style of an immortal spirit,
the swallow-throat, the crane-walk of a nobleman!
Why do they praise him so?
His father poor and talentless, they hope to comfort me thus.
In green spring, the warm and gentle months,
cousins all, his companions in play,
he runs round the hall, threads the wood:
a rush of bronze caldrons bubbling over.
Elderly gentlemen come to the gate;
at once he dashes out to greet them;
in front of the guests, asked what he would like,
he mumbles shyly and won't speak up.
Guests gone, he mimics their faces,
bursting through the door, snatching his father's staff,
now aping Chang Fei's outlandish countenance,
now making fun of Teng Ai's stutter.[2]
A brave hawk on high wings soaring,
a noble horse with fierce snorting breath,
he cuts stout green bamboo for a pony,

1. An allusion to T'ao Yüan-ming's sons; see p. 136.
2. Historical figures of the second and third centuries, noted respectively for a swarthy bearded face and a stutter.

gallops wildly, banging into things.
Suddenly he is the General in a play,
in stage voice summoning his groom;
now beside the gauze-veiled lamp
he bows his head in evening obeisance to Buddha.
Whip upraised, he bats at spider webs;
head bent down, he sucks nectar from the flower,
so nimble he outruns the swallowtail butterfly,
so swift he hardly lags behind the flying willow catkins.
By the terrace stairs he comes on Elder Sister,
rolls dice with her, loses all he has;
sneaks in to play with her vanity case,
prying at the golden clasp till he breaks it off.
Try to hold him — he wiggles and squirms;
threaten and scold — he will not be ruled.
Crouching down, he drags on the window netting;
with globs of spit he polishes the lacquer lute.
Sometimes he watches while I practice calligraphy,
standing bolt upright, knees never moving;
old brocade book cover — can he cut it up for clothes?
the scroll's jade spindle — he begs for that too;
pleads with me to make him a spring garland,[3]
spring garland fit for spring days,
when plantain leaves angle up — furls of letter paper;
and magnolia buds droop — writing brushes proffered.
Your father once was fond of reading books;
sweating, slaving, he wrote some of his own;
going on forty now, worn and tired,
no meat for his meals, cringing from fleas and lice —
Take care, my son — do not copy your father,
studying, hoping for first or second on the exam!
Jang-chü's *Rules of the Marshal,*
Chang Liang's *Yellow Stone Strategy,*[4]
these will make you a teacher of kings;

3. A neck ornament of figured silk worn by boys and girls at the festivities celebrating the beginning of spring.

4. Works on military science of the late Chou and early Han respectively.

waste no time on trash and trifles!
Much less now when west and north,
barbarian tribes rise in defiance,
when neither force nor bribes will bring them to heel
and the burden of them saps us like an old disease.
My son, grow to manhood quickly,
seek out the cubs in the tiger's cave;
make yourself lord of ten thousand households —
don't huddle forever over some old book!

P'I JIH-HSIU *(c. 833-883)*

Impromptu on a Hangover

(7-ch. *chüeh-chü*)

I block out the midday brightness with a screen depicting dark
    woods,
burn a stick of heavy incense, nursing my hangover.
What's this? As evening comes I'm ready for a drink again!
Beyond the wall I hear the cry of someone selling clams.

WEI CHUANG *(836-910)*

Late Rising on Spring Days

(7-ch. *chüeh-chü*)

Too much to drink these days, late getting up each morning.
I lie and watch the southern hills, revising old poems;
open doors and the sun is high, spring hushed and lonely.
Singing birds — three or four voices — fly up to the blossoming
    bough.

TU HSÜN-HO *(846-907)*

Traveler's Thoughts

(7-ch. *chüeh-chü*)

Ring of the moon, starshine, swept away as I watch;
hue of the hilltops, river sounds, wrap me in unseen sorrow.
Midnight by lampglow — ten years of memory
join with the sudden rain to pelt my heart.

WANG CHIA *(9th cen.)*

Shrine Festival

(The festival, held at the village shrine around the beginning of autumn, celebrated
the harvest; 7-ch. *chüeh-chü*.)

By Goose Lake Mountain, rice and millet grown fat;
half the pig pens and chicken coops shut for the night.
Mulberry, paper mulberry shadows slanting, the autumn festival
        dispersed,
family after family holding up, helping their drunken ones home.

HSIANG SSU *(9th cen.)*

The Ailing Japanese Monk

(5-ch. regulated verse)

"Clouds and water block the way home,
though when I came, winds blew the ship along —"

He says nothing of what to do if he should die,
but, sick as he is, still sits in meditation.
Deep walls swallow up the light of the lamp,
open windows air out the moxa smoke.[1]
"Dreams of home are ended now —
make my grave by the temple gate."

CH'EN TAO *(9th cen.)*

Song of Lung-hsi

(Lung-hsi was a western outpost in Kansu; 7-ch. *chüeh-chü.*)

They swore to wipe out the nomads, no thought for themselves,
five thousand in sable and brocade, gone to barbarian dust.
Pity them — these bones by the shores of the Uncertain River —
to those who dream in spring chambers, they are still men!

---

1. The monk is taking moxa treatment for his illness.

LI TUNG *(9th cen.)*

For the Monk San-tsang on His Return to the Western Regions

(7-ch. *chüeh-chü*)

A hundred thousand li of journey, how many dangers?
Desert dragons, when you wag your tongue, will hear and be
      humbled.
The day you reach India's five lands, your hair will be white —
The moon sets on Ch'ang-an and its midnight bells.

YÜ WU-LING *(9th cen.)*

Offering Wine

(5-ch. *chüeh-chü*)

I offer you the golden flagon;
do not disdain its brimming gift.
Wind and rain await the opening flower,
and partings make up too much of our life.

CHIN CH'ANG-HSÜ *(10th cen.)*

Spring Grievance

(Liao-hsi is an outpost on the northeast border where the singer's lover is stationed; 5-ch. *chüeh-chü.*)

Shoo the orioles, drive them away,
don't let them sing in the branches!
When they sing they scare off my dreams
and I will never get to Liao-hsi!

THE RECLUSE T'AI-SHANG *(T'ang)*

In Reply to Questions

(5-ch. *chüeh-chü*)

I happened to come to the foot of a pine tree,
lay down and slept soundly on pillows of stone.
There are no calendars here in the mountain;
the cold passes but I don't know what year it is.

CHAPTER TEN

Two Major Sung Poets

 SU TUNG-P'O (1037-1101)

THE Sung dynasty, though it succeeded in uniting all of China under its rule, was never able to equal the T'ang in terms of military prestige and might. Within the borders of the empire a strong central government and a reasonably efficient bureaucracy permitted social and economic life to flourish and learning and the arts to reach new heights of achievement. But abroad the Sung faced menacing neighbors to the north and west. Powerless to overthrow them, it had to keep them at bay with strong border defenses or buy them off with tribute. The expenditures required by such a situation in time fatally weakened the dynasty. In 1125 the Jurchen or Jurched people of Manchuria, who had established a state called the Chin on the Sung's northern border, marched south into China, eventually seizing control of all of northern China and forcing the Sung to move its capital to Hangchow south of the Yangtze. The earlier period, when the Sung had its capital at Pien-ching (present-day K'ai-feng), is known as the Northern Sung (960-1125), the later as the Southern Sung (1127-1279).

The first figure to be treated in this chapter, Su Shih (1037-1101), often referred to by his literary name Su Tung-p'o, is generally acknowledged to be the greatest poet of the Northern Sung period. He was born and raised in Szechwan in western China and, after passing the civil service examinations in 1056 and 1057, embarked on a lengthy career in the bureaucracy. But because of his sharp criticisms of government policy, some of them expressed in his poems, and the shifts of power at court, he found himself in frequent disfavor. Twice he was condemned to exile, the first time to Huang-chou on the Yangtze in Hupei, the second time to the region of Canton in the south and later to the remote island of Hainan. He died while on his way back from the second period of exile.

As a government official, Su upheld the Confucian ideals of public service and concern for the welfare of the people, employing poetry, as the great T'ang poets had before him, to speak out against evils in government. At the same time, however, he was thoroughly versed in Taoist and Buddhist thought, particularly the teachings and practices of the Ch'an or Zen sect of Buddhism, and this fact seems to have lent a kind of equanimity and breadth of outlook to his character. In spite of all the reverses of fortune he suffered, he never, at least in his poetry, sinks into the sort of helpless despair that at times overtook the T'ang poets.

He left a large number of poetic works in both the *shih* and *tz'u* forms (for examples of the latter, see chapter 12), and was also well known as a prose writer, calligrapher, and literati-style painter. His poetry is characterized by a remarkable variety of subject matter and minute attention to detail. Many of his works have a light, almost playful tone, while others, particularly those addressed to his younger brother Su Ch'e or Su Tzu-yu, from whom he was so often separated by the exigencies of official life, are marked by great warmth and tenderness. Still other works are noteworthy for their narrative skill or carefully observed descriptive passages. He drew freely on the themes and conventions of the past, but at the same time expanded them and shaped them in novel ways, helping to create a new type of poetry that, though perhaps lacking the intensity of T'ang poetry at its best, is broader in scope and possessed of a complexity of tone and philosophical depth all its own.

SU TUNG-P'O

Rhyming with Tzu-yu's "Treading the Green"

("Treading the Green" refers to a day of picnics held in early spring. Su's younger brother Tzu-yu had written a poem describing the festival, and Su here adopts the same theme and rhymes for his own poem. The "priest" in line 9 may be either a Buddhist or Taoist priest. 7-ch. old style.)

East wind stirs fine dust on the roads,
fine chance for strollers to enjoy the new spring.
Slack season — just right for roadside drinking,
grain still too short to be crushed by carriage wheels.
City people sick of walls around them
clatter out at dawn and leave the whole town empty.
Songs and drums jar the hills, grass and trees shake;
picnic baskets strew the fields where crows pick them over.
Who draws a crowd there? A priest, he says,
blocking the way, selling charms and scowling:
"Good for silkworms — give you cocoons like water jugs!
Good for livestock — make your sheep big as deer!"
Passers-by aren't sure they believe his words —
buy charms anyway to consecrate the spring.
The priest grabs their money, heads for a wine shop.
Dead drunk, he mutters, "My charms really work!"

Spring Night

(7-ch. *chüeh-chü*)

Spring night — one hour worth a thousand gold coins;
clear scent of flowers, shadowy moon.
Songs and flutes upstairs — threads of sound;
in the garden, a swing, where night is deep and still.

I Travel Day and Night

(Written in 1071 when the poet was en route by water from the capital to
Hangchow. 7-ch. regulated verse.)

Passed the place where the Ying River enters the Huai, and
for the first time saw the mountains along the Huai. Today we
reached Shou-chou.

I travel day and night toward the Yangtze and the sea.
Maple leaves, reed flowers — fall has endless sights.
On the broad Huai I can't tell if the sky is near or far;
green hills keep rising and falling with the boat.
Shou-chou — already I see the white stone pagoda,
though short oars haven't brought us around Yellow Grass Hill.
Waves calm, wind mild — I look for the landing.
My friends have stood a long time in twilight mist.

New Year's Eve

(Written in 1071 when Su was vice-governor of Hangchow. By custom, criminal cases involving the death penalty had to be settled before New Year's. 5-ch. old style.)

New Year's Eve — you'd think I could go home early
but official business keeps me.
I hold the brush and face them with tears:
pitiful convicts in chains,
little men who tried to fill their bellies,
fell into the law's net, don't understand disgrace.
And I? In love with a meager stipend
I hold on to my job and miss the chance to retire.
Don't ask who is foolish or wise;
all of us alike scheme for a meal.
The ancients would have freed them a while at New Year's —
would I dare do likewise? I am silent with shame.

Lament of the Farm Wife of Wu

(7-ch. old style, *yüeh-fu*)

Rice this year ripens so late!
We watch, but when will frost winds come?
They come — with rain in bucketfuls;
the harrow sprouts mold, the sickle rusts.
My tears are all cried out, but rain never ends;
it hurts to see yellow stalks flattened in the mud.
We camped in a grass shelter a month by the fields;
then it cleared and we reaped the grain, followed the wagon home,
sweaty, shoulders sore, carting it to town —
the price it fetched, you'd think we came with chaff.
We sold the ox to pay taxes, broke up the roof for kindling;

we'll get by for the time, but what of next year's hunger?
Officials demand cash now — they won't take grain;
the long northwest border tempts invaders.
Wise men fill the court — why do things get worse?
I'd be better off bride to the River Lord![1]

On the Road to Hsin-ch'eng

(Written in 1073, when the poet made a tour of the districts under his jurisdiction, Hsin-ch'eng, southwest of Hangchow, being one of them. 7-ch. regulated verse.)

The east wind, knowing I plan to walk through the hills,
hushed the sound of endless rain between the eaves.
On peaks, fair-weather clouds — cloth caps pulled down;
early sun in treetops — a copper gong suspended.
Wild peach smiles over low bamboo hedges;
by clear sandy streams, valley willows sway.
These west hill families must be happiest of all,
boiling cress and roasting shoots to feed spring planters.

Children

(5-ch. old style)

Children don't know what worry means!
Stand up to go and they hang on my clothes.
I'm about to scold them

1. "Wise men" is literally Kung (Sui) and Huang (Pa), two officials of Han times who worked for the welfare of the peasants. The last line refers to the ancient custom of sacrificing a young girl each year as a "bride" to the River Lord, the god of the Yellow River; see p. 51.

but my wife eggs them on in their silliness.
"The children are silly but you're much worse!
What good does all this worrying do?"
Stung by her words, I go back to my seat.
She rinses a wine cup to put before me.
How much better than Liu Ling's wife,
grumbling at the cost of her husband's drinking![1]

The New Year's Eve Blizzard

(Written in 1077 when the poet was on his way from Mi-chou to the capital before proceeding to his next post as governor of Hsü-chou. 5-ch. old style.)

I was detained by a heavy snow at Wei-chou on New Year's Eve, but on the morning of the first day it cleared and I resumed my journey. Along the way, it started to snow again.

The New Year's Eve blizzard kept me from leaving;
on the first, clear skies see me off.
The east wind blows away last night's drunk;
on a lean horse, I nod in the remains of a dream.
Dim and hazy, the dawn light breaks through;
fluttering and turning, the last flakes fall.

1. Liu Ling was a poet of the Chin dynasty, one of the Seven Sages of the Bamboo Grove. When his wife begged him to give up drinking for the sake of his health, he protested he was too weak-willed to give it up alone, and could do so only if she would prepare offerings of wine and meat so he could take a temperance vow before the gods. When she had done so, he delivered this prayer:

Heaven gave birth to Liu Ling,
gave him the name of Wine.
One gallon at a gulp,
five quarts for a hangover.
The words of a woman —
take care not to heed them!

Then he helped himself to the offerings and was soon as drunk as ever. *Shih-shuo hsin-yü, Jen-tan* chapter.

I dismount and pour myself a drink in the field —
delicious — but who to share it with?
All at once evening clouds close down,
tumbling flurries that show no break.
Flakes big as goose feathers hang from the horse's mane
till I think I'm riding a great white bird.
Three years' drought plagues the east;
roofs sag on house rows, their owners fled.
The old farmer lays aside his plow and sighs,
gulps tears that burn his starving guts.
Spring snow falls late this year
but spring wheat can still be planted.
Do I grumble at the trials of official travel?
To help you I'll sing a song of good harvest.

Mid-Autumn Moon

(Second of three poems with this title addressed to the poet's younger brother Tzu-yu. Mid-autumn, the fifteenth day of the eighth month, was a time for moon viewing. Tzu-yu had visited the poet the previous year, their first meeting in a number of years, and they had enjoyed the moonlight together. At that time Tzu-yu composed a poem in *tz'u* form, the "farewell song" referred to. 5-ch. old style.)

Six years the moon shone at mid-autumn;
five years it saw us parted.
I sing your farewell song;
sobs from those who sit with me.
The southern capital must be busy,[1]
but you won't let the occasion pass:
hundred-league lake of melted silver,
thousand-foot towers in the pendant mirror —
at third watch, when songs and flutes are stilled

1. Nanking, where Tzu-yu was serving as a member of the prefect's staff. "Pendant mirror" in line 8 is a poetic term for the moon.

and figures blur in the clear shade of trees,
you return to your north hall rooms,
cold light glinting on the dew of leaves;
calling for wine, you drink with your wife
and tell the children stories, thinking of me.
You have no way of knowing I've been sick,
that I face the pears and chestnuts, cup empty,
and stare east of the old riverbed
where buckwheat blossoms spread their snow.
I wanted to write a verse to your last year's song
but I was afraid my heart would break.

Lotus Viewing

(Written at Hu-chou in 1079, the second of four poems. 5-ch. old style.)

The clear wind — what is it?
Something to be loved, not to be named.
Moving like a prince wherever it goes;
the grass and trees whisper its praise.
This outing of ours never had a purpose;
let the lone boat swing about as it will.
In the middle of the current, lying face up,
I greet the breeze that happens along
and lift a cup to offer to the vastness:
how pleasant — that we have no thought for each other!
Coming back through two river valleys,
clouds and water shine in the night.

Under the Heaven of Our Holy Ruler

(In 1079, the poet was arrested on charges of "slandering the emperor," i.e., criticizing government policy. This is the first of the two poems. 7-ch. regulated verse.)

Because of what has happened, I have been confined to the imperial censorate prison. The prison officials treat me with increasing harshness, and I doubt that I can stand it much longer. If I die in prison, I will have no chance to say good-bye to Tzu-yu, and therefore I wrote these two poems and gave them to the warden, Liang Hsü, to deliver to him.

Under the heaven of our holy ruler, all things turn to spring,
but I in dark ignorance have destroyed myself.
Before my hundred years are past, I'm called to settle up;
my leaderless family, ten mouths, must be your worry now.
Bury me anywhere on the green hills
and another year in night rain grieve for me alone.
Let us be brothers in lives and lives to come,
mending then the bonds that this world breaks.

Eastern Slope

(Three poems from a series of eight describing a small farm at a place called Eastern Slope [Tung-p'o] in Huang-chou, Hupei, where the poet lived in exile after his release from prison. The land was formerly the site of an army camp. 5-ch. old style.)

I.
Abandoned earthworks nobody tends,
collapsed wall tangled in vines —
who'd waste strength on land like this?
Work all year for no return.
But here's a stranger, alone,

Heaven against him, nowhere to go,
pitching in to clear the rubble and wrack.
Weather too dry, soil lean;
pushing through brambles and weeds,
wondering can I scrape out a handful of produce,
I sigh and let go the plow —
my barn — when will I fill it up?

2.

A little stream used to cross my land,
came from the mountain pass back there,
under city walls, through villages —
the current sluggish and choked with grass —
feeding finally into K'o Clan Pond,
ten *mou* stocked with fish and shrimp.
Drought this year dried it up,
its cracked bed plastered with brown duckweed.
Last night clouds came from hills to the south;
rain soaked the ground a plowshare deep.
Rivulets found the channel again,
knowing I'd chopped back the weeds.
In the mud a few old roots of cress
still alive from a year ago.
If white buds will open again,
when spring doves come I'll make a stew!

3.

I planted rice before Spring Festival
and already I'm counting joys!
Rainy skies darken the spring pond;
by green-bladed paddies I chat with friends.
Transplanting takes till the first of summer,
delight growing with wind-blown stalks.
The moon looks down on dew-wet leaves
strung one by one with hanging pearls.
Fall comes and frosty ears grow heavy,
topple, and lean propped on each other.

From banks and dikes I hear only
the sound of locusts like wind and rain.
Rice, newly hulled, goes to the steamer,
grains of jade that light up the basket.
A long time I've eaten only government fare,
old rusty rice no better than mud.
Now to taste something new —
I've already promised my mouth and belly.

Beginning of Autumn: A Poem to Send to Tzu-yu

(The poet recalls when he and his brother were studying for the examination that launched them on their careers as government officials and brought about their long separation. 5-ch. old style.)

The hundred rivers day and night flow on,
we and all things following;
only the heart remains unmoved,
clutching the past.
I recall when we stayed at Huai-yüan Stop,
door shut against fall heat,
eating boiled greens, studying,
wiping away the sweat, you and I.
The west wind suddenly turned cold;
dried leaves blew in the window.
You got up for a heavier coat
and took hold of my hand:
"We won't be young for long —
I needn't tell you.
Probably we'll have to part,
hard to tell when success may come — "
Even then I felt a chill of sorrow,
and now when both of us are old —

Too late to look for a lost road,
too late, I'm afraid, to study the Way.
This fall I began talks to buy some land;
if I build a house, it should be done by spring.
Nights at Snow Hall, in wind and rain,
already I hear you talking to me.

Written on a Painting Entitled "Misty Yangtze and Folded Hills" in the Collection of Wang Ting-kuo

(7-ch. old style)

Above the river, heavy on the heart, thousandfold hills:
layers of green floating in the sky like mist.
Mountains? clouds? too far away to tell
till clouds part, mist scatters, on mountains that remain.
Then I see, in gorge cliffs, black-green clefts
where a hundred waterfalls leap from the sky,
threading woods, tangling rocks, lost and seen again,
falling to valley mouths to feed swift streams.
Where the river broadens, mountains part, foothill forests end,
a small bridge, a country store set against the slope:
now and then travelers pass beyond tall trees;
a fishing boat — one speck where the river swallows the sky.
Tell me, where did you get this painting
sketched with these clean and certain strokes?
I didn't know the world had such places —
I'll go at once and buy some land!
But perhaps you've never seen those hidden spots
near Wu-ch'ang and Fan-k'ou, where I lived five years — [1]

1. Places south of the Yangtze opposite Huang-chou, where the poet lived in exile. In the four lines that follow, he recalls these places during the four seasons of the year.

Spring wind shook the river and sky was everywhere;
evening clouds rolled back the rain on gentle mountains;
from scarlet maples, crows flapped down to keep the boatman com-
         pany;
from tall pines, snow tumbled, startling his drunken sleep.
The peach flowers, the stream are in the world of men!
Wu-ling is not for immortals only.[2]
Rivers, hills, clean and empty: I live in city dust,
and though roads go there, they're not for me.
I give back your picture and sigh three sighs;
my hill friends will soon be sending poems to call me home.

Presented to Liu Ching-wen

(7-ch. *chüeh-chü*)

Lotuses have withered, they put up no umbrellas to the rain;
one branch of chrysanthemum holds out against frost.
Good sights of all the year I'd have you remember,
but especially now, with citrons yellow and tangerines still green.

Long Ago I Lived in the Country

(Written at the end of a Painting of the "Restoration of the Herdsmen" by Ch'ao
Yüeh-chih. 5-ch. and 7-ch. old style.)

Long ago I lived in the country,
knew only sheep and cows.

2. This is Su's answer to a poem by Li Po entitled "Dialogue in the Mountains":

You ask why I live in these jade-green mountains —
I smile and do not answer — my mind is still.
Peach flowers on the stream flow far away;
this is another world, not that of men.

The peach flowers refer to the peach forest at Wu-ling described by T'ao Yüan-ming
in the piece translated on p. 142.

Down smooth riverbeds on the cow's back,
steady as a hundred-weight barge,
a boat that needs no steering — while banks slipped by,
I stretched out and read a book — she didn't care.
Before us we drove a hundred sheep,
heeding my whip as soldiers heed a drum;
I didn't lay it on too often —
only stragglers I gave a lash to.
In lowlands, grass grows tall,
but tall grass is bad for cows and sheep;
so we headed for the hills, leaping sags and gullies
(climbing up and down made my muscles strong),
through long woods where mist wet my straw coat and hat...
But those days are gone — I see them only in a painting.
No one believes me when I say I regret
not staying a herdsman all my life.

Days of Rain; the Rivers Have Overflowed

(Written in 1095 at Hui-chou, near present-day Canton, where the poet was living
in exile. 7-ch. regulated verse.)

Drenching rain hisses down, cooling the evening;
I lie and listen to banyan noise echo on the porch.
By feeble lamp shine, I shake off a dream;
curtains and blinds, half soaked, breathe old incense.
High waves shake the bed, spray blows from the cistern;
dark wind rocks the trees — they clink like jade.
Even if it clears I have no place to go —
let it keep on all night pelting the empty stairs.

White Crane Hill

(Written in 1097 at a place called White Crane Hill overlooking the Tung River in Hui-chou. 5-ch. old style.)

At my new place at White Crane Hill we dug a well forty feet
deep. We struck a layer of rock partway down, but finally broke
through and got to water.

Seacoast wears you out with damp and heat;
my new place is better — high and cool.
In return for the sweat of hiking up and down
I've a dry spot to sleep and sit.
But paths to the river are a rocky hell;
I wince at the water bearer's aching back.
I hired four men, put them to work
hacking through layers of obdurate rock.
Ten days and they'd gone only eight or ten feet;
below was a stratum of solid blue stone.
Drills all day struck futile sparks —
when would we ever see springs bubble up?
I'll keep you filled with rice and wine,
you keep your drills and hammers flying!
Mountain rock must end some time —
stubborn as I am, I won't give up.
This morning the houseboy told me with joy
they're into dirt soft enough to knead!
At dawn the pitcher brought up milky water;
by evening, it was clearer than an icy stream.
All my life has been like this —
what way to turn and not run into blocks?
But Heaven has sent me a dipper of water;
arm for a pillow, my happiness overflows.[1]

1. An allusion to *Analects* VII,15: "The Master said, 'With coarse grain to eat, water
to drink, and my bended arm for a pillow — I still have joy in the midst of these. Riches
and honor unrighteously acquired are to me as a floating cloud.' "

Black Muzzle

(Written in 1100 at Ho-p'u on the mainland opposite Hainan. 5-ch. old style.)

When I came to Tan-chou, I acquired a watchdog named
Black Muzzle. He was very fierce, but soon got used to people. He
went with me to Ho-p'u, and when we passed Ch'eng-mai, he
startled everyone on the road by swimming across the river. So as
a joke I wrote this poem for him.

Black Muzzle, south sea dog,
how lucky I am to be your master!
On scraps growing plump as a gourd,
never grumbling for fancier food.
Gentle by day, you learn to tell my friends;
ferocious by night, you guard the gate.
When I told you I was going back north,
you wagged your tail and danced with delight,
bounced along after the boy,
tongue out, dripping a shower of sweat.
You wouldn't go by the long bridge
but took a short cut across the clear deep bay,
bobbing along like a water bird,
scrambling up the bank fiercer than a tiger.
You steal meat — a fault, though a minor one,
but I'll spare you the whip this time.
You nod your head by way of thanks,
Heaven having given you no words.
Someday I'll get you to take a letter home —
Yellow Ears was your ancestor, I'm sure.[1]

1. Pet dog of the poet Lu Chi (261-303). When Lu Chi was in the capital of Lo-
yang, he became worried because he had had no news from his family in Wu, near the
mouth of the Yangtze. So he wrote a letter and, putting it in a bamboo container, tied it
to Yellow Ears's neck and sent it home by way of the dog.

Following the Rhymes of Chiang Hui-shu

(Written in the summer of 1101 as the poet was traveling to his home. He died shortly after. 5-ch. regulated verse.)

Bell and drum on the south river bank —
home! I wake startled from a dream.
Drifting clouds — so the world shifts;
lone moon — such is the light of my mind.
Rain drenches down as from a tilted basin;
poems flow out like water spilled.
The two rivers vie to send me off;
beyond treetops I see the slant of a bridge.

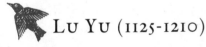

LU YU (1125-1210)

S U TUNG-P'O lived at a time when the Sung dynasty, though facing hostile neighbors abroad and troubled internally by fiscal difficulties, exercised control over all the lands that had traditionally belonged to the realm of China. By the time Lu Yu (1125-1210), the second great Sung poet to be treated here, grew to maturity, however, this situation had changed drastically. The Jurchen invaders of the Chin state had by then seized control of all of northern China, the old heartland of the Chinese people, and the Sung had been forced to flee south, where it maintained what it referred to euphemistically as a "temporary capital" at Hangchow. Though it attempted to expel the invaders, such attempts proved unsuccessful and in time it concluded a peace treaty recognizing Chin sovereignty over the northern territories and agreed to pay a yearly tribute in silver and silk.

Lu Yu's father, who had been an official in the service of the Northern Sung, was a member of a group who spoke out vociferously against the humiliation of such a settlement and called for military action to remedy it. Lu Yu took the civil service examinations, hoping to pursue a government career as his father had. But because, like his father, he advocated expulsion of the Chin invaders at a time when the government was dominated by the party of peace and conciliation, his advancement was repeatedly blocked and he failed to achieve any appreciable success in bureaucratic service. After holding a series of rather minor posts and suffering frequent dismissals and frustrations, he retired to his home in Shao-hsing in Chekiang to spend the remainder of his long life in rustic retirement.

Lu Yu was one of the most prolific of all Chinese poets, leaving behind over ten thousand poems in *shih* and *tz'u* form, as well as prose works. His poetry is marked by two major themes. One is his deep and abiding concern for the fate of his nation, expressed in the form of laments for his captive countrymen in the north and spirited calls for action to expel the hated barbarians. The other important theme is the celebration of the quiet joys of everyday life, particularly as he knew it during his years of retirement in the countryside near Shao-hsing.

In his poetry of patriotism and protest, he clearly identifies himself with Tu Fu, whose works he admired intensely. His poems on old age and the rustic life recall the works of T'ao Yüan-ming and Po Chü-i, though in sheer volume and range of detail they surpass anything produced by these earlier writers. The selection of *shih* poems below focuses mainly on these two themes in Lu Yu's poetry, as well as upon the air of independence and unconventionality that led him in his later years to adopt the literary name Fang-weng or "The Old Man Who Does as He Pleases."

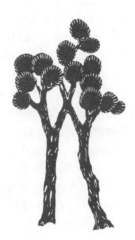

LU YU

A Trip to Mountain West Village

(Muddy wine is milky unrefined rice wine made in the last month of the year.
7-ch. regulated verse.)

Don't laugh because it's muddy — year-end wine brewed in country
      homes;
harvests were good — to make the guest linger, fowl and pork
      aplenty.
Mountains multiply, streams double back — I doubt there's even a
      road;
willows cluster darkly, blossoms shine — another village ahead!
Pipe and drum sounds tagging me — spring festival soon;
robe, cap of plain and simple cut — they honor old ways here.
From now on, if I may, when time and moonlight allow,
I'll take my stick and, uninvited, come knock at your evening gate.

Blue Rapids

(1170, ascending the Three Gorges of the Yangtze; the drumming noise made
with the oars signaled the departure of the boat. 7-ch. old style.)

A hundred men shouting at once, helping to rattle the oars;
in the boat, face to face, we can't even hear ourselves talk.
All at once the men have scattered — silence, no more scuffle;
the only sound, two winches reeling out hundred-yard towlines:
whoo-whoo, whaa-whaa — how fast the winches unwind,
boatmen already standing there on the sandy shore!

Fog lifts from reedy villages, red in the setting sun;
rain ended, from fishermen's huts the damp smoke of cooking fires.
I turn my head, look toward home, now a thousand mountains
      away;
a trip up the gorges — we've just passed rapids number one.
When I was young I used to dream of the joys of official travel;
older now, I know just how hard the going can be.

Long Sigh: Written When Spending the Night at Green Mountain Store

(5-ch. old style; in Szechwan)

One long sigh piled on another;
my travels never come to an end!
Ice and frost harry the dying year;
bird and beast cry in the sinking sun.
Sound of autumn fulling mallets fills the lonely village;
dead leaves bury the run-down inn.
White-headed, I faced a ten-thousand-mile road —
to fall into this lair of leopards and tigers.
By the roadside, marks of a fresh kill:
grease and blood stains on the bushes and thorns.
Always I've aimed for a heart of steel and stone,
forgetting family, to think of duty to my country;
but here in this place of nine parts death,
my dying would be no help to either family or state.
The heartland so long lost to invaders,
a man of spirit must drown his chest in tears.
Don't despise me for a bookish scholar —
a horse under me, I could strike the foe!

Third Month, Night of the Seventeenth, Written While Drunk

(7-ch. old style; 1173, in Szechwan)

Years ago feasting on raw whale by the eastern sea,
white waves like mountains flinging me their beauty and awe;
last year shooting tigers, south mountain autumn,
coming home at night, thick snow plastered on my sable coat;
this year — so worn and broken it really makes you laugh;
hair flecked gray, ashen face — ashamed to look at myself!
Who'd think, given some wine, I could still raise a fuss,
yanking off my cap, facing men, a big shout for every one?
Traitorous barbarians still not crushed, my heart never at peace;
the lone sword by my pillow sings out its clanging cry.
In a fallen-down posthouse I wake from dreams, the lamp about to
      go out;
tapping at the window, wind and rain — third watch by now.

After Getting Drunk, I Scribble Songs and Poems in Grass Script — Written as a Joke

(1173, at a post in Chia-chou in Szechwan; the "vermilion tower" is the government office. 7-ch. old style.)

Head poking from a vermilion tower, all eight directions cramped;
one dip of green wine and I go on for a hundred cups,
washing away the humps and hills, cliffs and crags of my heart,
cleansing myself so I can shape verses passionate, windy and free.
Ink at first spurts out like the ire of demons and gods;
characters all at once grow lean, formed like fallen dragons;
now a rare sword, drawn from its sheath, flashes a snowy blade;
now a great ship, cleaving the waves, speeds its gusty mast.

Paper gone, I fling down the brush with a lightning-and-thunder
    crash;
womenfolk flee in astonishment, little boys run and hide.
Once I drafted a proclamation to chide the western realm;
whirr, whirr, the sound of my brush stirred in the hall of state.[1]
Then one day I turned my steps from court and suddenly ten years
    passed;
west I skimmed over the Three Pa, to the far end of Yeh-lang.
Mountains and rivers remote and wild, their customs strange;
luckily there's fine wine, the kind to put me in a trance.
In the midst of drunkenness I pull the cap from my head;
I permit no trace of frost to invade this green-black hair.
Gains and losses of a man's life — truly a piddling matter;
who says old age is so full of sorrow and woe?

Border Mountain Moon

(Vermilion gates in line three refers to the mansions of nobles and high officials;
the kettles in line five were pounded at night in army camps to signal the hour.
7-ch. old style, *yüeh-fu.*)

Fifteen years ago the edict came: peace with the invader;
our generals fight no more but idly guard the border.
Vermilion gates still and silent; inside they sing and dance;
stabled horses fatten and die, bows come unstrung.
From garrison towers the beat of kettles hurries the sinking moon;
lads who joined the troops at twenty, white-haired now.
In the sound of the flutes who will read the brave man's heart?
Above the sands emptily shining, moon on warrior bones.
Spear-clash on the central plain — these we've known from old.
But when have traitorous barbarians lived to see their heirs?
Our captive people, forbearing death, pine for release,
even tonight how many places stained with their tears?

1. A reference to the time when, on the behalf of the prime minister, the poet drafted
a dispatch to be sent to the Hsi-hsia state of Central Asia.

Idle Thoughts

(7-ch. regulated verse)

Thatch gate works all right but I never open it,
afraid people walking might scuff the green moss.
Fine days bit by bit convince me spring's on the way;
fair winds come now and then, wrapped up with market sounds.
Studying the Classics, my wife asks about words she doesn't know;
tasting the wine, my son pours till the cup overflows.
If only I could get a little garden, half an acre wide —
I'd have yellow plums and green damsons growing all at once!

Vegetable Garden

(1181, in retirement in Shao-hsing; one *mou* is about one-seventh of an acre. 5-ch. old style.)

The old mountain man is learning to garden,
laughing at himself, wondering how he'll do.
Rocky barren ground, barely three *mou* —
for the heavy work I count on the two hired men.
Square plots laid out like a chessboard;
after a light shower, soil looks like melted butter.
We've hacked and cleared till all the brush and thorns are gone,
plowed and hoed till there're no more stones or clods,
laid a log bridge across the ditch,
built a little tower with broken tiles we gleaned,
on the unused land, set up poles for melons,
with the energy left over, planted a taro patch.
Like strands of silk — the thin greens growing;
like duck meat — the mushy steamed gourd.
Things such as these now I've learned to understand —
it was not for bream that I came back east.[1]

1. When the poet-official Chang Han (258?-319?) resigned his post in the capital and retired, he said it was because he longed for the bream he used to eat back home in the south.

In a Boat on a Summer Evening, I Heard the Cry of a Water Bird. It was Very Sad and Seemed to Be Saying, "Madam Is Cruel!" Moved, I Wrote This Poem.

(1183; Lu Yu was recalling his first wife whom he married when he was about twenty and divorced shortly afterwards, apparently because his mother found fault with the girl. For a poem in *tz'u* form on the subject, see p. 371. 5-ch. old style.)

A girl grows up hidden in far-off rooms,
no glimpse of what may lie beyond her wall and hedge.
Then she climbs the carriage, moves to her new lord's home;
father and mother become strangers to her then.
"I was stupid, to be sure, yet I knew
that Madam, my mother-in-law, must be obeyed.
Out of bed with the first cock's crowing,
I combed and bound my hair, put on blouse and skirt.
I did my work, tidied the hall, sprinkling and sweeping,
in the kitchen prepared their plates of food.
Green green the mallows and goosefoot I gathered—
too bad I couldn't make them taste like bear's paws.[1]
When the least displeasure showed in Madam's face,
the sleeves of my robe were soon damp with tear stains.
My wish was that I might bear a son,
to see Madam dandle a grandson in her arms.
But those hopes in the end failed and came to nothing;
ill-fated, they made me the butt of slander.
Driven from the house, I didn't dare grumble,
only grieved that I'd betrayed Madam's kindness."
On the old road that runs along the rim of the swamp,
when fox fire glimmers through drizzling rain,
can you hear the voice crying "Madam is cruel!"?
Surely it's the soul of the wife sent home.

---

1. Bear's paws are the epitome of delicious food.

Autumn Thoughts

(1186, when Lu Yu was acting governor of Yen-chou. 5-ch. old style.)

Mornings up before the rooster calls;
evenings, never home till crows have gone to rest;
orders and commissions heaped on my desk,
napping and eating in the midst of them.
Flailing a whip, I press for tax payments,
squiggling my writing brush, face red with shame —
the bright day passes in a frenzy of action,
but what solace does this bring to the helpless and poor?
Leaves have fallen, the angling woods are bare;
trim and pretty as a hairdo — hills south of the valley.
It's not that I don't have my cup of wine for comfort,
but when will this press of business ever slacken?

The Merchant's Joy

(7-ch. old style, *yüeh-fu*)

The wide wide Yangtze, dragons in deep pools;
wave blossoms, purest-white, leap to the sky.
The great ship, tall-towered, far off no bigger than a bean;
my wondering eyes have not come to rest when it's here before me.
Matted sails: clouds that hang beyond the embankment;
lines and hawsers: their thunder echoes from high town walls.
Rumble rumble of ox carts to haul the priceless cargo;
heaps, hordes to dazzle the market — men race with the news.
In singing-girl towers to play at dice, a million on one throw;
by flag-flown pavilions calling for wine, ten thousand a cask;
the Mayor? the Governor? we don't even know their names;
what's it to us who wields power in the palace?
Confucian scholar, hard up, dreaming of one square meal;

a limp, a stumble, prayers for pity at His Excellency's gate;
teeth rot, hair falls out — no one looks your way;
belly crammed with classical texts, body lean with care —
See what Heaven gives me — luck thin as paper!
Now I know that merchants are the happiest of men.

Written in a Carefree Mood

(1192, in Shao-hsing; the mummers of line four are villagers dressed up in costume
who go from house to house at the beginning of spring driving out evil spirits. 5-
ch. regulated verse.)

Old man pushing seventy,
in truth he acts like a little boy,
whooping with delight when he spies some mountain fruits,
laughing with joy, tagging after village mummers;
with the others having fun stacking tiles to make a pagoda,
standing alone staring at his image in a jardiniere pool.
Tucked under his arm, a battered book to read,
just like the time he first set off for school.

The Stone on the Hilltop

(5-ch. and 7-ch. old style)

Autumn wind: ten thousand trees wither;
spring rain: a hundred grasses grow.
Is this really some plan of the Creator,
this flowering and fading, each season that comes?
Only the stone there on the hilltop,
its months and years too many to count,

knows nothing of the four-season round,
wearing its constant colors unchanged.
The old man has lived all his life in these hills;
though his legs fail him, he still clambers up,
now and then strokes the rock and sighs three sighs:
how can I make myself stony like you?

Harp Song —
To Send to Chi-ch'ang Shao-ch'ing

(5-ch. old style, *yüeh-fu*)

Not that the tree in my garden does not bloom,
but with frost-fall, its ten thousand leaves wither;
not that you would put me aside, my friend,
but as distance parts us, we grow naturally estranged.
In the night I get up, sighing,
open the box, dig for your old letters.
They're dark with dust and the bugs have chewed them,
lines missing, words about to fade.
I read them once and my face flushes,
read them again and tears begin to flow.
Roll them up, put them back in the box —
better to leave them for the silverfish to eat!

Feeling Sorry for Myself

(1197; in the fifth month of this year, the poet's wife died at the age of seventy-
one. 7-ch. old style.)

Morning rain, evening rain, little plums turned yellow;
in house to the east, house to the west, orchids for sale smelling
         sweet;

old white-headed widower mourning in an empty hall,
wailing not for the dead alone — feeling sorry for himself as well,
teeth like battered clogs, hair resembling frost —
going by his looks, how can he last much longer?
Lean on my stick, try to get up, but I fall back on the bed each time;
death draws near me, hardly a wall away.
Ten thousand affairs of the world all dim and far removed,
my only thought to advance in virtue — that's what I work at now.
If I follow the two brothers to starve on Shou-yang Mountain,
a thousand years, bones rotted, I'll still have the fragrance of a good
       name.[1]

Sitting Outdoors

(1198; the poet was receiving a government pension in the form of grain. 7-ch.
regulated verse.)

Cap tipped back, propped by a window, still can't settle down;
haul out the cane of Ch'iung bamboo, take a turn in the garden.
Clear autumn coming on — dew soaks the grass;
bright moon not yet risen — stars crowd the sky.
Barges shove through lock gates, racing for dawn markets;
men on treadmills watering fields — no night's sleep for them!
Plain people sweating like this for one square meal,
and I sit eating government dole — wince whenever I think of it.

---

1. Po Yi and Shu Ch'i, brothers in ancient times who chose to starve to death on
Shou-yang Mountain rather than compromise with the evil of the world, are familiar
symbols of stern integrity and fidelity to one's ideals.

My Village Home

(5-ch. regulated verse)

Living's getting harder day by day —
my house just goes on staying half finished.
Flapping like butterflies — torn window paper;
cracked like a turtle shell — dried mud walls.
In a light rain the cow pen turns soggy;
a touch of frost and the mill shed feels cold.
But the late grain at least is spared from insects —
neighbors and I all sigh with relief.[1]

Sending Tzu-lung Off to a Post
in Chi-chou

(1202; Tzu-lung was the poet's second son, who was on his way to the post of judge in Chi-chou in Kiangsi. 5-ch. old style.)

I'm old and you're going away —
you have no choice, I know.
From the carriage I see you off,
brushing away tears I can't hold back.
Who likes to say good-bye?
But we're poor and have to do these things.
You will brave the billows of Hsü,[1]
from there cross Lake P'eng-li,
waves alive with boat-swallowing fish,
forests shrill with one-legged goblins.

1. A note by the poet says: "This year the late grain was badly damaged by insects — only our village was spared."

---

1. High waves on the Ch'ien-t'ang River, where the body of the loyal minister Wu Tzu-hsü was cast in ancient times. According to legend, he became the god of the waves and his anger causes the tidal bore that rages up the river.

Rice you eat in the fields — what inn will cook it?
Scull of your lone boat — by what banks will it rest?
A judge — better than T'ang times;
at least you'll be spared the whip.[2]
Line up and bow with the others — no shame in that;
to slack your job — that's the only disgrace.
You'll be an official of Chi-chou;
see you drink no more than Chi-chou water!
When you know where every penny goes,
who can find excuse for talk?
Set aside a little for A-hsi's wedding,
find a good tutor for Yüan-li.[3]
I can keep myself in food;
don't worry about fancy things for me.
My robe wears through? — let the elbows stick out;
shoes come apart? — leave the toes showing;
out the gate I may be laughed at;
back home, I'll sleep better for it.
Lord Yi, a man of name and station,[4]
solid — stands out like a mountain peak;
his family and ours have been friends for generations —
perhaps he'll grant you an interview.
If so, count that honor enough —
in no way must you seem to be courting favor!
Again there's Yang Ch'eng-chai;[5]
no one these days his match for integrity;
the kind who hears one stupid word
and spends three days washing out his ears.
You may go and see how he's getting on,
but end it there — no further talk!
Hsi-chou I've known for years,

2. In T'ang times the head of the local government could whip his subordinate officials, but this was forbidden under the Sung.

3. Tzu-lung's daughter and eldest son respectively.

4. Lord Yi is Chou Pi-ta, friend of the poet and former prime minister, who was living in retirement at Chi-chou.

5. The poet and statesman Yang Wan-li, also living in retirement.

Ching-ssu comes from our home town;[6]
not only do they excel in letters;
in action and character equally fine.
Study and learn all you can from them—
achievement lies in piling up!
"Benevolence," "righteousness"—take them where you find them;
in practice they make the gentleman.
Three years and you'll be home again;
who knows—I may still be here.
There are carp in the rivers where you're going—
give them a letter to carry now and then.[7]

I Had Occasion to Tell a Visitor about an Old Trip I Took Through the Gorges of the Yangtze

(1205; the poet is recalling the time in 1170 when he traveled up the Yangtze to a post in K'uei-chou; Chien-p'ing is a little east of K'uei-chou. There were many non-Chinese peoples living in the region. 5-ch. old style.)

Long ago I made that journey, fall rain coming down lightly,
reached the east wall of Chien-p'ing just as gates were closing.
Host at the inn met me with greetings, words rambling on and on,
his young wife grinding and cooking in her cheap white robe.
Old boatmen who work the river, some drunk, some sobered up;
merchants from Shu, peddlers of the gorges, clever at closing a deal;
soon lamps went dark, people getting ready for bed,
though outside we could still hear boats tying up, baggage being
    unloaded from horses.
Mountains steep, rivers treacherous, barbarian tribes close by;
often I saw their mallet-shaped hairdos mingling with city folk.
Now, counting on my fingers, I find it's been forty years!—
sad memories held in my heart, truly from another incarnation.

6. Ch'en Hsi-chou and Tu Ssu-kung (Ching-ssu) were friends of the poet who were apparently serving as officials in Chi-chou.

7. An allusion to an old *yüeh-fu* ballad that tells of a gift of a pair of carp, in the belly of one of which was found a letter.

Farm Families

(5-ch. regulated verse, 2 from a set of 6)

1.

Snug — the robe sewn from coarse cotton;
red — the fire kindled from dry sticks.
Meager talents I give to the countryside;
simple learning I teach the young boys:
for sheep you want a pen that's high,
for chickens, a closely woven basket.
Farm families have joys of their own,
not in a class with those of kings.

2.

It's late, the children come home from school;
braids unplaited, they ramble the fields,
jeering at each other — guess what's in my hand!
arguing — who won the grass fight after all?
Father sternly calls them to lessons;
grandfather indulgently feeds them candy.
We don't ask you to become rich and famous,
but when the time comes, work hard in the fields!

Sitting Up at Night

(7-ch. *chüeh-chü*)

Spinners' lights from house to house brighten the deep night;
here and there new fields have been plowed after rain.
Always I feel ashamed to be so old and idle.
Sitting close by the stove, I hear the sound of the wind.

To Show to My Sons

(1209; Lu Yu's deathbed poem. The Nine Provinces are the divisions of China in ancient times. 7-ch. *chüeh-chü*.)

In death I know well enough all things end in emptiness;
still I grieve that I never saw the Nine Provinces made one.
On the day the king's armies march north to take the heartland,
at the family sacrifice don't forget to let your father know.

Other Sung Poets

T HE early Sung poets, much like their counterparts in the early T'ang, for the most part simply carried on the fashions that had prevailed in the decades preceding, particularly, in the case of the Sung writers, the ornate and sentimental style associated with Li Shang-yin and his imitators. With the appearance of men such as Wang Yü-ch'eng (954-1001), Mei Yao-ch'en (1002-1060) and Ou-yang Hsiu (1007-1072), however, a wholly new kind of poetry began to take shape, plainer in diction, broader in subject matter and far more serious in intent.

Ou-yang Hsiu, a statesman, thinker, and cultural leader in many fields, perhaps did most to publicize the new style, though his less famous contemporary and lifelong friend, Mei Yao-ch'en, was undoubtedly the finer poet. Mei, who spent his life in minor government posts, employed a deliberately simple and low-keyed style to describe the events of his personal life and the social ills of the time, producing works that in power and immediacy of appeal rival the finest products of the T'ang. It is no accident that these creators of a new style of Sung poetry such as Mei and Ou-yang often drew their inspiration from the works of Tu Fu, Han Yü, and Po Chü-i, though at the same time they achieved a calmness, even sunniness of outlook quite uncharacteristic of earlier poetry. This note of optimism is most ingenuously revealed in the poem in my selection entitled "Song of Delight" by the philosopher Shao Yung (1011-1077), though in less obvious form it underlies the work of Mei

Yao-ch'en and Ou-yang Hsiu as well. Both, like Shao Yung, were strong supporters of Neo-Confucianism, the leading intellectual movement of the period.

Su Shih or Su Tung-p'o, whose work represents perhaps the finest flowering of this new poetic movement, has already been treated in the preceding chapter. Another important figure of the time was the statesman Wang An-shih (1021-1086), who is famous for the controversial government reforms that he instituted during his period in power. The poetry of his younger days reflects his concern with social and political problems and devotion to Confucian ideals, though as a poet he is more admired for the intimate and reflective works written after his retirement from public life.

Huang T'ing-chien (1045-1105), a disciple of Su Tung-p'o who shared with Su an interest in Ch'an or Zen Buddhism, wrote poetry that is studiedly unemotional in tone and fastidious in its choice of language. Though it was highly influential in its time and continued in succeeding centuries to enjoy a certain vogue in Buddhist circles, it never won wide popularity. More typical of Sung poetry as a whole are the works of Yang Wan-li (1127-1206) and Liu K'o-chuang (1187-1269), with their colloquial tone and attention to the details of everyday life. This ability to discover poetry even in the drab and undramatic aspects of life, to employ simple language and imagery and a rather matter-of-fact approach to create works of surprising power and beauty, is in fact one of the crowning achievements of Sung poetry. As one late Sung poet put it, writing of Lu Yu, another poet who, as we have seen, excelled in the depiction of genre scenes:

> Using what is plain and simple, he fashioned subtle lines;
> taking the most ordinary words, he changed them into wonders.[1]

---

1. Tai Fu-ku (b. 1167), "Reading the *Chien-nan shih-kao* by Mr. Fang-weng."

WANG YÜ-CH'ENG *(954-1001)*

Journey to a Village

(7-ch. regulated verse)

My horse threads a mountain trail through bamboos just yellowing;
I let him go the long road — the country holds my eye.
Countless valleys, taking voice, fill with echoes of evening;
a few peaks, speechless, stand in the slanting sun.
Leaves fall from the quince tree, the color of rouge;
buckwheat flowers open — fragrant white snow.
What's this? My poem done, I'm suddenly lost in thought —
this village bridge, these meadow trees are like the ones back home!

OU-YANG HSIU *(1007-1072)*

Written for the Pavilion of the Drunken Old Man at Ch'u-chou

(5-ch. old style)

Forty — that's not so old!
Drunken Old Man is just a name I have.
In drunkenness I forget all things —
how then can I keep track of my age?
I love the water below the pavilion
that comes from between the jumbled peaks,
its voice seeming to fall from the sky,

pouring down in front of the rainy eaves,
flowing into the cliff-bound ravine
to feed the bubbling of hidden springs.
Its roar doesn't drown out human voices;
its clear tone is not that of flutes and strings;
not that I don't love pipes and strings,
but musical instruments are too much bother.
So from time to time I take some wine
and walk the long way to these swirling waters.
Wild birds eye my drunkenness,
valley clouds persuade me to take a nap;
mountain flowers only know how to laugh,
they haven't learned to talk with me yet.
And then the wind comes from the cliffs,
blowing me back to sobriety.

Calligraphy Practice

(5-ch. old style)

Practicing calligraphy, not noticing night had come,
I only wondered why the west window was so dark.
My tired eyes were blurry to begin with,
I can't tell if the ink is thick or thin.
All man's life has this same unawareness —
he toils and slaves, not really minding,
when all he gets is an empty name,
a thing that shines the space of an hour.
There's a truth here not confined to calligraphy practice;
let me write it in big letters for future warning!

Distant Mountains

(5-ch. *chüeh-chü*)

Mountain colors, whether near or far —
I watch the mountains, walking all day.
Peaks, knolls shift with every angle;
a stranger walks by, ignorant of their names.

SHAO YUNG *(1011-1077)*

Song on Being Too Lazy to Get Up

(7-ch. *chüeh-chü*)

Half remembering, yet not remembering, just waked up from a
      dream;
almost sad, but not sad, a time when I'm feeling lazy,
I hug the covers, lie on my side, not wanting to get up yet —
beyond the blinds, falling petals fly by in tangled flurries.

Arriving in Lo-yang Again

(7-ch. *chüeh-chü*)

Those years, I was a green-youthed wanderer;
today I come again, a white-haired old man.
From those years to today makes one whole lifetime,
and in between, how many things have had their day and gone!

Thoughts on T'ien-chin Bridge

(7-ch. *chüeh-chü*)

The countless great lords and statesmen of past regimes —
later ages know them merely as a list of names.
Only the water under T'ien-chin Bridge
goes on year after year, making the same sound.

Song of Delight

(5-ch. old style)

Be happy, be happy again,
be glad and be glad once more!
Fine fellows to be my friends,
beautiful sights to fill my view,
good wine for my drink,
good food for my fare,
born, grew up, and now I grow old
all in a time of perfect peace!

MEI YAO-CH'EN *(1002-1060)*

My Neighbor to the South, the Office Clerk Hsiao, Came in the Evening to Say Good-bye

(5-ch. old style)

Remember a while ago we happened to meet,
met – and were like old friends?
You said you lived in a different alley, but the house is right in back
of mine;
behind the wall, lamplight shines through;
under the fence we share the same well.
You ask me over, serve me fish for dinner;
sometimes when you call I'm too poor to offer wine.
But it's settled you're to leave tomorrow,
and here's a whole cask to ladle from.
The night is long — suppose you do get drunk!
Once on the road, there'll be no use looking back.

Back from Green Dragon, Presented to Hsieh Shih-chih

(Hsieh Shih-chih was a nephew of the poet's first wife. 7-ch. old style.)

Away from you three or four years,
tall and skinny exactly as before,
only your beard a bit bushier and blacker,
in learning long ago a shoulder above me;
and I — old now, no more use,
white hair stringy, the top about to go —
the things I write are out of tune with the times;
a peaked wife, babies bawling, no more money —

luckily with the Classics I can while away the bright days;
wealth and power — why aim for the blue sky?
Drinking wine these days, I never take much;
before the cup's filled again my belly starts to churn.
Last night you and I drank and joked;
a few rounds and I'd nodded off.
Cocks crow, dogs bark, in my ears a buzzing;
I raise my head — the whole room spins around.
Up, I pull at my headcloth but it won't stay straight.
Hoist sail, let's be off to the gray sea's border!
or better, climb a whale and ride ten thousand li —
but I have no lightning, no whip of crackling thunder;
courage stumbles, my heart quails — should I take a nap?
In dreams at once I come to a rush-grown shore.
I'll not be staying to drink with you again,
and who can manage to die drunk like the banished immortal?[1]

Sharing Lodging with Hsieh Shih-hou in the Library of the Hsü Family and Being Much Bothered by the Noise of Rats

(5-ch. old style)

The lamp burns blue, everyone asleep;
from their holes the hungry rats steal out:
flip-flop — a rattle of plates and saucers;
clatter-crash! — the end of my dream.
I fret — will they knock off the inkslab on the desk?
worry — are they gnawing those shelves of books?
My little son mimics a cat's miaowing,
and that's a silly solution for sure!

1. Li Po, who was said to have drowned when he drunkenly attempted to embrace the reflection of the moon in a river; see p. 213.

Shih-hou Pointed Out to Me That from Ancient Times There Had Never Been a Poem on the Subject of Lice, and Urged Me to Try Writing One

(5-ch. old style)

A poor man's clothes — ragged and easy to get dirty,
easy to get dirty and hard to keep free of lice.
Between the belt and the lower robe is where they swarm,
ascending in files to the fur collar's margin.
They hide so cleverly, how can I ferret them out?
dining on blood, making themselves at home —
My world too has its sallies and withdrawals;
why should I bother to pry into yours?

Sad Remembrance

(Memories of the poet's first wife, a daughter of a relatively well-to-do family, who died the previous year. 5-ch. old style.)

From the time you came into my house
you never seemed to mind being poor,
every evening sewing till midnight,
lunch ready a little past noon.
Ten days and nine we ate pickles;
one day — a wonder — we dined on dried meat.
East and west for eighteen years,
the two of us sharing bitter and sweet,
counting all along on a hundred years' love —
who'd have thought you'd be gone in one night!
I still remember when the end came,
how you held my hand, not able to speak —
this body, though it lives on,
at the last will join you in dust.

Out and Back on the Fifteenth Night of the First Month

(On the night of the fifteenth, the first full moon of the new year, the people of the capital dressed in their best clothes and packed the streets, amusing themselves at street stalls and entertainments. The year before, the poet's wife and second son had died, leaving him with a small son and daughter to raise. 5-ch. old style.)

If I don't go out I'll only mope;
a stroll outside might ease my mind.
Rich man, poor man, each with his companion —
I alone feel no special joy.
Growing older, my spirits quickly flag;
I start to go and already feel depressed.
Back home I face my boy and girl;
before they speak the sour smell of grief is in my nose.
Last year they went out with their mother,
aping her with smears of lipstick and rouge;
now she's gone to the springs below
and dirt is on their faces, their clothes in rags.
But I remember that you are still young
and hide my tears — I can't let you see them.
I push the lamp aside, lie facing the wall,
a hundred worries cramped in my chest.

The Dappled Horse

(5-ch. old style)

The boat moored, lunch in a lonely village;
on the far bank I see a dappled horse,
in lean pasture, gaunt with hunger;
scruffy birds flocking down to peck his feed.
Pity is powerless — I have no bow;
again and again I try to pelt them with clods
but I haven't the strength to manage a hit,
face sweaty and hot with chagrin.

Marrying Again

(5-ch. old style)

Some days ago I remarried,
delighting in now, sorrowful for the past;
someone to entrust the household to,
no more my lone shadow under the moon.
Force of habit — I call the wrong name;
as of old, something weighing on my heart.
How lucky I am — gentle and mild:
to have found two women with natures like this!

Aboard a Boat at Night, Drinking with My Wife

(5-ch. old style)

The moon appears from the mouth of the sheer bluff,
its light shining behind the boat over there.
I sit drinking alone with my wife;
how much better than facing some dreary stranger!
The moonlight slowly spreads over our mat,
dark shadows bit by bit receding.
What need is there to fetch a torch?
We've joy enough in this light alone.

At Night, Hearing Someone Singing in the House Next Door

(5-ch. old style)

Midnight: I still haven't gotten to sleep
when I hear faint sounds of singing next door.
I picture to myself the red lips moving;
the dust stirs on the rafters, I know.[1]
She makes a mistake and laughs to herself.
I get up to listen and put on my robe;
put on my robe, but the song has ended.
The moon in the window shines a little while longer.

An Offering for the Cat

(Written on a river journey. 5-ch. old style)

Since I got my cat Five White
the rats never bother my books.
This morning Five White died.
I make offerings of rice and fish,
bury you in mid-river
with incantations — I wouldn't slight you.
Once you caught a rat,
ran round the garden with it squeaking in your mouth;
you hoped to put a scare into the other rats,
to clean up my house.
When we'd come aboard the boat
you shared our cabin,
and though we'd nothing but meager dried rations,
we ate them without fear of rat piss and gnawing —

---

1. Allusion to a famous singer of Han times whose voice was so beautiful that the very dust on the rafters stirred in response.

because you were diligent,
a good deal more so than the pigs and chickens.
People make much of their prancing steeds;
they tell me nothing can compare to a horse or donkey —
enough! — I'll argue the point no longer,
only cry for you a little.

Lunar Eclipse

(When a lunar eclipse occurred, it was the custom to make an offering of wheat cakes and pound on bronze mirrors to scare away the evil influences that were swallowing up the moon; cassia hare is another name for the moon. 5-ch. old style.)

The maid comes into the hall
bringing word of the weird event:
in a sky made of blue glass,
the moon like a piece of blackened crystal;
now when it ought to be ten parts round,
only a thumb-length of brightness showing!
My wife is off with baked wheat cakes,
the children make a racket pounding on mirrors,
and though such beliefs are foolish and shallow,
I honor in them the spirit that seeks to save.
Night deepens and the cassia hare comes forth,
crowds of stars trailing it down the west.

WANG AN-SHIH *(1021-1086)*

Confiscating Salt

(Salt was a government monopoly and the officials made every effort to prevent
people living on the seacoast from boiling water and extracting salt for private
profit. The poem attacks the government for depriving the people of a possible
livelihood and competing with them for profit. 7-ch. old style.)

From the local office, orders flying thicker than comb's teeth:
along the seacoast, salt confiscation stricter than ever.
Poverty moans and sobs under a broken roof
while boatloads of inspectors patrol back and forth.
Islands of the ocean, from times past lean and barren;
island folk struggling just to keep alive:
boil sea water or starve to death;
who can sit unmoving, not try to escape?
And now they say there are pirates hereabouts
who murder traveling merchants, scuttle their boats —
The life of one subject weighs heavier than the realm!
What true man would vie with others for a hairbreadth's gain?

Impromptu; Late Spring at Pan-shan

(Pan-shan or "Halfway-to-the-Mountain" was the place where the poet lived in
retirement, so called because it was halfway between Nanking and Mt. Chung. 5-
ch. regulated verse.)

Late spring has snatched away the blossoms,
left me this cool shade instead,
the sloping road quiet under its covering of shadows,
the garden cottage deep in intertwining green.
Bench and mat whenever I want a little rest,
walking stick and shoes for visiting secluded spots —
otherwise I've only the north mountain birds
that pass this way, leaving their lovely notes behind.

Written on the Wall of
Pan-shan Temple

(5-ch. old style)

Cold days sit where it's warm,
hot days walk in the cool.
All beings — no different from Buddha;
Buddha — just the same as all beings.

Twenty Poems in Imitation of Han-shan
and Shih-te

(The second of the series; on Han-shan and Shih-te, see p. 259. 5-ch. old style.)

Once I was a cow, a horse;
the sight of hay and bean stalks pleased me;
another time I was a woman;
men were what I liked to see.
And if in truth I am this I,
it will be like this always.
But if, unresigning, I love and hate,
I know I will become the slave of things.
Solemn, solemn, the man of full stature
will not look on things as self.

By the River

(5-ch. *chüeh-chü*)

River waters ruffled in the west wind,
river blossoms shedding their late red;
sorrows of parting, borne on the transverse flute,
are blown far away east of the tangled hills.

Written for My Own Amusement

(5-ch. old style)

I shut the door, hoping to drive off sorrow,
but to the very end sorrow refused to go.
Let a spring breeze come along, though, and then what happens?
I could beg sorrow to linger and sorrow would never stay!

Fresh Flowers

(5-ch. old style)

Old age has little joy,
less when you're lying sick in a bed.
Dip water, fix fresh flowers,
take comfort from this drifting scent;
drifting scent gone in a moment;
and I — will I be here for long?
Fresh flowers and an old I —
so! — best forget each other.

HUANG T'ING-CHIEN *(1045-1105)*

Song of the Clear River

(7-ch. old style)

River gulls bob and toss in reed-flower autumn;
eighty-year-old fisherman, not a worry in a hundred:
by clear dawn he works the scull, picking lotus pods,
in evening sun hauls in the net, letting the boat drift.
His little boys are learning to fish — not bad at all;
his old woman, white-haired, has pleasures still ahead.
The whole family, wine-drowsy, sleep beneath the thatch,
their boat on the cold sand where night tides run out.

Once More Following the Rhymes of Pin-lao's Poem "Getting Up After Illness and Strolling in the Eastern Garden"

(5-ch. old style)

West wind slaughters the lingering heat,
deadly as General Ho Ch'ü-ping,
unclogging ditches to flood the lotus pond,
sweeping leaves, brightening up the bamboo lane.
In the midst, a man calm and sedate
knows for himself the nature of perfect understanding;
the monkey of the mind, just now waking up,
gives a laugh — all six windows wide open![1]

---

1. In Buddhist writings the mind is often compared to a monkey romping in the trees of desire; the "six windows" are the six organs of sense, the eye, ear, nose, tongue, body, and mind.

To Go with Shih K'o's Painting of an Old Man Tasting Vinegar

(Shih K'o is a tenth-century painter noted for his treatment of humorous and supernatural subjects; the painting, as we know from other sources, actually depicted an elderly couple. Master Wu is the famous T'ang painter Wu Tao-tzu. 7-ch. old style.)

Old lady Shih, braving acerbity, pokes in her three-foot beak;
old man Shih, vinegar-tasting, face in a hundred wrinkles:
who knows how it feels to scrunch up your shoulders, shivering
      clear to the bone?
A painting not to be surpassed even by the brush of Master Wu!

CH'EN SHIH-TAO *(1053-1102)*

Cold Night

(5-ch. regulated verse)

A long time in one place and I always think of moving;
then I run into the same trouble and I'm sorry I made the change.
I raise the wick of the cold lamp but the flame is out,
rake up what's left of the fire but it's turned to ashes.
Icy water drips a while and then stops;
windy blinds flap open and shut.
I know well enough what writing should avoid,[1]
but thoughts come, and sorrow just somehow appears.

---

1. In a 7-ch. regulated verse addressed to one Li Chang, Wang An-shih stated, "Writing should particularly avoid too frequent sorrow."

YANG WAN-LI *(1127-1206)*

Sitting at Night on
the Moonlit Terrace

(7-ch. regulated verse)

Fall days are not entirely free of heat,
but fall nights are clear right through to dawn.
So the old man for several evenings running
has been sitting outdoors until the third watch.
The wind blusters, stars bright one moment, gone the next;
clouds scud by, the moon greeting them, sending them off.
You chase after delights, chase in vain,
then when you think there're no delights, suddenly they come!

Cold Fly

(7-ch. *chüeh-chü*)

Noted outside the window: a fly, the sun on his back,
rubbing his legs together, relishing the morning brightness.
Sun and shadow about to shift — already he knows it,
suddenly flies off, to hum by a different window.

Keng-tzu (1180), First Month, Fifth Day,
Dawn: Crossing by the Ta-kao Ferry

(7-ch. *chüeh-chü*)

River and hills beyond the fog — I peer but can't make them out.
Only the dogs and chickens tell me there's a village ahead.
In the ferryboat, thick on the planks, frost like snow,
my straw sandal stamping the first print in it.

Relaxing in the Evening in My Study,
the Wo-chih-chai

(5-ch. old style)

I shut the door but can't sit down,
open the window, stand in a breath of cool.
Groves of trees shade the bright sun,
the ink stone on my desk gives off a jade-green glow.
I let my hand wander over scrolls of poems,
softly humming three or four verses.
The first scroll I pick up pleases me greatly,
the second suddenly makes my spirit sink.
Throw it aside — I can't go on reading!
I get up and wander around the chair.
The ancients had their mountains of sorrow,
but my mind is calm and clear as a river.
Those people are no concern of mine —
why should I let them break my heart?
The mood is over and instead I laugh;
a lone cicada urges on the evening sun.

LIU K'O-CHUANG *(1187-1269)*

Leaving the City

(7-ch. *chüeh-chü*)

I stop for a short rest at the wine seller's west of the city;
where green shade is deepest, crows are cawing.
The proprietor sighs — Sir, you're too late —
blossoms are all gone from the trellis of flowering thorn.

From "Ten Poems Recording Things that Happened at the Year's End"

(7-ch. *chüeh-chü*)

A beggar in patched robe stands in my doorway;
how would he know I'm hard pressed to get through the years
      remaining?
The dyer, the wine woman — I haven't paid them yet,
and then I've got to send my boy some money for his school.

Weeping for Hsüeh Tzu-shu

(5-ch. regulated verse)

When the doctor came from Chin-t'an
he said the disease could still be cured.
No one believed it was serious;
when we heard he was dead, we thought it was a lie.
His friends are putting in order the manuscripts he left;
his wife reads off instructions for the funeral.
I gather up the books I borrowed from him
and, hiding my tears, return them to his son.

⸺⸺⸺⸺⸺⸺⸺

CHAPTER TWELVE

Lyrics in *Tz'u* Form

⸺⸺⸺⸺⸺⸺⸺⸺⸺⸺⸺⸺⸺⸺⸺

A S stated in the Introduction, the *tz'u* or "lyric meter" form came to prominence in the latter part of the T'ang dynasty and the period of disunion that followed, i.e., in the ninth and tenth centuries. In the past there was much uncertainty as to just how and when the form came into being. But at the beginning of the present century, a number of early manuscripts were found sealed in a cave at Tun-huang in northwestern China, and among these were the texts of some five hundred anonymous works in *tz'u* form, many of them dating from the eighth century. These texts seem to indicate that the *tz'u* was a popular song form that originated among the singing girls and musicians who entertained in the wineshops and brothels, probably developing out of the type of folk songs and popular ditties we have seen in chapter 6. Some of the *tz'u* were written to fit native Chinese melodies, others to tunes imported from Central Asia. In time, poets of the educated class, who in the course of their social life frequented the entertainment districts, developed an interest in the form and tried their hand at composing works in it. By the ninth century, the form had gained wide popularity among scholar-poets, who refined it and enlarged its scope. My selection opens with four anonymous works from the Tun-huang manuscripts, followed by poems by known poets of the T'ang, Five Dynasties Period, and Sung. The texts of the Tun-huang works are often damaged or faulty, and the translations are hence tentative in places.

Unlike the *shih,* which usually uses lines of uniform length, the *tz'u* is in most cases marked by lines of varying lengths, the particular number and length of the lines being dictated by the tune that the lyric is designed to fit. The various metrical patterns continued in later times to be known by the title of the tune they fitted, and are so identified in the selection that follows, though later poets who employed the patterns did not necessarily intend their works to be sung. In addition to prescribed line lengths, the metrical patterns called for a fixed tonal sequence and rhyme scheme. Many of the poems, as will be seen, are in two stanzas.

The early *tz'u,* not surprisingly in view of their origin, are often mildly erotic or have a folksong quality. The treatment tends to be impressionistic and deliberately fragmented, the diction delicate, decorative, at times a trifle precious, the mood wistful or brooding. As in earlier love poetry in *shih* form, the beautiful woman neglected or abandoned by her lover is a frequent theme.

One of the first important poets to work extensively in the *tz'u* form was Wen T'ing-yün (812-872), whose works in mood and decor often resemble the love poetry of late Six Dynasties times. Even more renowned is Li Yü (937-978), the last ruler of a kingdom called Southern T'ang that maintained a precarious existence in southeastern China after the breakup of the T'ang empire in 907. He succeeded to the throne in 961 and ruled from his capital in Nanking until 975, when his state was overthrown by the first emperor of the Sung and he was taken captive to the Sung capital in the north. In his hands the *tz'u* form acquires a more personal note, his later poems dealing not with the conventionally sorrowing ladies of earlier lyrics, but with the very real pains of his own captivity and his unendurable longing for the past.

In Sung times the lyric form reached its peak of popularity and excellence. Most of the major poets of the time wrote in the form, some of them employing it almost exclusively. Among the latter is Li Ch'ing-chao (1084?-c.1151), the devoted wife of a scholar-official and one of China's best known women poets. The Sung poets further broadened the content of the lyric meter, often using it to treat events in their daily lives and at times injecting a more philosophic or patriotic note. Nevertheless, the main concern of the *tz'u,* as contrasted with the *shih,* continued to be things felt rather than things observed, interior rather than external worlds.

I have grouped all my *tz'u* selections together in the chapter that follows, though some are by poets such as Ou-yang Hsiu, Su Tung-p'o, or Lu Yu, whose works in *shih* form have appeared earlier. The reader should consult these earlier appearances to see how the *tz'u* lyrics fit into the poet's career and artistic development as a whole. To aid identification of the poems, which in most cases have no titles, I have wherever possible used the translations of the tune titles as they appear in Wu-chi Liu and Irving Yucheng Lo, *Sunflower Splendor: Three Thousand Years of Chinese Poetry* (New York: Doubleday 1975), where many more examples of *tz'u* in translation may be found. One should keep in mind that the tune title refers simply to the metrical pattern of the poem and in most cases has nothing to do with the poem's content.

ANONYMOUS

Four *Tz'u* from Tun-huang

Tune: "Eternal Longing"

I.
He was a traveler west of the river,
with wealth and eminence rare in this world.
All day long in vermilion towers
..... dancing and singing songs.[1]

The cup filled again and again, till he's drunk as mud;
lightly, lightly trading golden goblets,
wearing out the day tasting joys, pursuing pleasures —
Some people are rich and never go home.

2.
He was a traveler west of the river;
only he knew how lonely he was,
dust and dirt covering his face,
all day long being cheated by others.

Morning after morning standing by the west gate of the market,
the wind blowing the tears that came down in two streams,
gazing toward his native land so many roads away —
Some people are poor and never go home.

---

1. Two characters are missing at the beginning of the line; the vermilion towers are multistoried houses of entertainment.

3.
He was a traveler west of the river,
then he took sick, lay an inch away from death.
Still he stayed on, looking for news,
though as time went by it seemed he'd have to depart.

The villagers dragged him to the west side of the road —
his father and mother knew nothing about it —
tied a tag on his body with his name written on it —
Some people die and never go home.

Tune: "Magpie on the Branch"

4.
I can't stand the wily magpie and all his extravagant stories!
He brings me good news, but what proof does he ever have?
One of these times when he flies by, I'll grab him, capture him live,
shut him up in a golden cage to put a stop to his chatter!

With the best of intentions I went to her, delivered my good news —
who'd have thought she'd shut me up in a golden cage?
I only hope her soldiering husband comes home soon
so she'll lift me up, turn me loose to head for the blue clouds!

WEI YING-WU *(b. 736)*

Tune: "Flirtatious Laughter"

Milky Way
Milky Way
at dawn stretching on and on over the autumn city:
one who is sorrowful rises, gazes at it, thinking of him —
south of the river, north of the border — so far apart!
far apart
far apart
the same Milky Way for both of us, but roads between cut off!

LIU YÜ-HSI *(772-842)*

"Bamboo Branch Song"

(Patterned after a folk song of the region of Shu, present-day Szechwan.)

Red blossoms of mountain peach crowd the uplands,
spring waters of Shu rivers buffet the mountains as they flow.
Crimson blossoms so quickly fading, like my lover's ardor;
flowing waters so endless, like the sorrow I feel.

WEN T'ING-YÜN *(812-872)*

Tune: "Deva-like Barbarian"

On the many-leafed bedscreens, gold flickers and fades.[1]
Her cloudy locks threaten to shroud the fragrant snow of her cheeks.
Lazily she rises, paints her moth eyebrows,
fiddles over her makeup, endlessly combing and washing.

She catches her flowery form in mirrors front and back,
reflecting her flowery face now in one, now in the other.
On her newly donned embroidered gauze jacket
are pairs and pairs of golden partridges.

Tune: "Deva-like Barbarian"

In her ornate tower by bright moonlight always she thinks of him.
Strands of willow languid as her thoughts, spring that saps one's
        strength —
outside the gate the grass grows deeper and deeper.
"When I saw you off, I heard your horses neighing."

1. The "gold" may be the morning sun shining in on the lazy sleeper.

On her patterned quilt, a pair of gold kingfishers.
The scented candle dwindles, shedding tears.
Blossoms fall, a nightjar cries.
By the green-gauze window she loses her way in remnants of a
      dream.

Tune: "Dreaming of the South"

She stops combing her hair,
leans alone from the upstairs window that looks out over the river:
a thousand sails pass by, but none of them are his.
She stares and stares at the slanting sunshine, the water flowing far
      away,
brokenhearted by white-weeded shoals.

WEI CHUANG *(836-910)*

Tune: "Deva-like Barbarian"

People all say the southland's better —
for a traveler, the southland's the place to grow old,
springtime waters bluer than the sky,
painted boats where you listen to the rain and doze —

Beside the wine-warmer, someone like the moon,
pale arms two drifts of frozen snow.
"You're not that old — don't go home —
go home and your heart is bound to break!"

Tune: "Lotus-leaf Cup"

I remember that year, under the blossoms,
late at night
when I met her the first time,
a lakeside room, painted blinds on the west side lowered,
and I held her hand, making secret promises —

Dismayed at dawn orioles, the leftover moon,
we said good-bye —
and since that time, all word cut off,
the two of us live now in different lands,
with no way at all to meet!

Tune: "The Taoist Priestess"

Last night at midnight
by my pillow in a dream distinctly I saw her,
and in all the talk that followed,
her peach blossom face, just as it used to be,
repeatedly lowered eyes under willow leaf eyebrows —

Half ashamed, half delighted,
she made as though to go, yet kept on lingering —
And when I woke up and knew it was a dream,
the pain was more than I could bear!

KU HSIUNG *(fl. 928)*

Tune: "Telling of Innermost Feelings"

Long nights when he neglects me — where's he gone?
No word at all,
my scented room shut tight,
eyebrows puckered,
the moon about to set —
How can he *do* this, not come to see me!

I loathe this lonely coverlet!
If I could exchange my heart,
somehow make it your heart,
maybe *then* you'd know how much I care!

LI YÜ *(937-978)*

Tune: "The Fisherman"

(From early times in Chinese literature the solitary fisherman has been idealized as a symbol of perfect freedom.)

1.
Wave blossoms for my delight, a thousand sheets of snow;
peach blossoms wordless, the regiments of spring:
one pot of brew,
one pole and line —
in this world we live in, how many men like me?

2.
One scull in the spring wind, one leaf of a boat;
one thread of silk line, one light hook:
blossoms fill the shore,
wine fills the jug —
ten-thousand-acre waves — I roam them as I please!

Tune: "Deva-like Barbarian"

Blossoms bright, the moon dark, shadowed in thin mist,
tonight's just right for making my way to you —
In stocking feet she goes out by the scented stairs,
holding in her hand her gold-threaded slippers.

On the south side of the painted hall she sees him,
clings to him for a time, trembling —
It's so hard for me to slip away,
tonight you may love me any way you please!

Tune: "Pure Serene Music"

Since we parted, spring half over;
everywhere I look, grief overwhelms me.
Below the steps, fallen plum petals like tumbles of snow —
I brush them off only to be covered with them again.

Wild geese arrive but bring no letters.
The road's so long, even in dreams it's hard to go home.
This pain of separation is like the spring grass —
the farther away I journey, the ranker it grows.

Tune: "Ripples Sifting Sand: A Song"

Beyond the blind, the rain rattles down,
spring moods fading away,
yet the gauze coverlet can't keep off the fifth watch cold.
In dreams I forget I'm a stranger here,
clutching at happiness for a moment —

Don't lean on the railing all alone,
before these endless rivers and mountains.
Times of parting are easy to come by, times of meeting hard.
Flowing water, fallen blossoms — spring has gone away now,
as far as heaven from the land of men.

Tune: "Song of Tzu-yeh"

Life's sorrows and regrets — who can escape them?
But I alone waste away my soul in thoughts that have no end.
To my old kingdom in dreams I return once more,
and when I wake, tears stream down in pairs.

The high tower — who's to climb it with me?
Autumn's clear vista as I've known it for so long,
but past events have turned to emptiness,
become like things in a dream.

Tune: "Crows Crying at Night"

Blossoms of the wood have scattered their spring crimson —
it came too suddenly! —
powerless before the dawn-borne rains, the night-borne winds.

Rouge-stained tears
detaining a lover, making him drunk —
will such times ever come again?
These are life's endless regrets, a river flowing endlessly east.

Tune: "Gazing at the South"

Unspeakable sorrow!
Last night my soul went dreaming
and I thought I was once again wandering in the royal gardens I
      knew,
the carriages like flowing water, their horses fine as dragons,
blossoms by moonlight, and just then a spring breeze —

MAO WEN-HSI *(10th cen.)*

Tune: "Drunk among the Flowers"

I mustn't ask about him —
I'm afraid to ask —
asking would only add to my heartache —
Spring waters swell and flood the pond,
the crested ducks follow each other around.

Last night the rain came pouring down,
toward dawn a cold spell set in,
and all I do is think of that man in his lookout tower —
how long since I've had news from the border!

OU-YANG HSIU *(1007-1072)*

Tune: "Treading on Grass"

At the post house lodge, plum flowers scattering,
by the valley bridge, willows coming out,
fragrant grass, warm wind that sways the traveler's reins:
parting grief—the farther apart, the more endless it grows,
long and unbroken like a river in spring.

Inch on inch of gentle heart,
brimming, brimming, her rouge-stained tears:
the tower so tall—don't go near, don't lean on the high railing!
At the very end of the level plain—spring hills are there,
but the traveler's even farther, beyond spring hills.

Tune: "Song of Picking Mulberry"

Ten years ago I was a visitor at the wine jar,
the moonlight white, the wind clear.
Then care and worry whittled me away,
time went by with astounding swiftness, and I grew old.

But though my hair has changed, my heart never changes.
Let me lift the golden flagon,
listen again to the old songs,
like drunken voices from those years long past.

SU TUNG-P'O *(1037-1101)*

Tune: "Song of River City"

    The year *i-mao*, 1st month, 20th day: recording a dream I had last night.

(Written in 1075. The dream was of the poet's first wife, Wang Fu, whom he married in 1054, when she was fifteen. She died in 1065, and the following year he carried her remains back to his old home in Szechwan and buried them in the family plot, planting a number of little pines around the grave mound.)

Ten years — dead and living dim and draw apart.
I don't try to remember
but forgetting is hard.
Lonely grave a thousand miles off,
cold thoughts — where can I talk them out?
Even if we met you wouldn't know me,
dust on my face,
hair like frost —

In a dream last night suddenly I was home.
By the window of the little room
you were combing your hair and making up.
You turned and looked, not speaking,
only lines of tears coursing down —
Year after year will it break my heart?
The moonlit grave,
its stubby pines —

Tune: "Prelude to Water Music"

    On mid-autumn night of the year *ping-ch'en* (1076) I drank merrily until dawn, got very drunk and wrote this poem, all the while thinking longingly of Tzu-yu.

(On Tzu-yu, see p. 302.)

Bright moon, when did you appear?
Lifting my wine, I question the blue sky.
Tonight in the palaces and halls of heaven
what year is it, I wonder?

I would like to ride the wind, make my home there,
only I fear in porphyry towers, under jade eaves,
in those high places the cold would be more then I could bear.
So I rise and dance and play with your pure beams,
though this human world — how can it compare with yours?

Circling my red chamber,
low in the curtained door,
you light my sleeplessness.
Surely you bear us no ill will —
why then must you be so round at times when we humans are
        parted?
People have their griefs and joys, their joinings and separations,
the moon its dark and clear times, its roundings and wanings.
As ever in such matters, things are hardly the way we wish.
I only hope we may have long long lives,
may share the moon's beauty, though a thousand miles apart.

Tune: "Sand of Silk-washing Stream"

Five poems written along the road to Stone Lake at Hsü-chou,
where I went to give thanks for rain. The lake is 20 li east of the
city. Though separated from the Ssu River, its water level is always
the same as that of the river and its water of the same degree of
clearness or muddiness.

(Written in 1078, when the poet was governor of Hsü-chou in Kiangsu. There
was a drought this year and Su had gone to Stone Lake, said by local lore to be the
home of a rain-making dragon, to pray for rain. When rain fell, he made a second
trip to give thanks. The first of the five poems is omitted.)

I.
Throw on rouge and powder, watch the governor pass!
In threes and fives by thorn hedge gates
they push and trample each other's red silk skirts.

Lead the old, bring the children! Like a harvest festival,
crows and hawks wheeling above the village shrine —
At dusk I met an old man lying drunk beside the road.

2.
Layer on layer of hemp leaves, jute leaves shining:
some family is boiling cocoons — the whole village smells good.
Beyond the hedge, spinning girls call invitingly.[1]

White-haired, with goosefoot staff, he raises drunken eyes —
Pick greens, grind parched grain, ease an empty belly!
Tell me, when will bean leaves turn yellow here?

3.
Flutter flutter on clothes and cap, jujube flowers fall;
village south, village north echo to spinning reels.
Half leaning on the old willow, they peddle yellow melons.

Wine-drowsy, a long road, I'm getting sleepier;
sun high, throat parched, thinking only of tea —
I'll knock on a gate and see what the villagers'll give me.

4.
Soft grasses, a plain of sedge fresh with passing rain;
horses race the light sand road but raise no dust.
When can I quit and take up plowing and planting?

Sun warm on mulberry and hemp glints like water;
wind over mugwort and moxa comes perfumed.
Your governor, long ago, lived in a place like this.

---

1. "Spinning girls" is probably the name of a singing insect, though the term may mean real girls working at their spinning.

Tune: "Immortal at the River"

Drank tonight at Eastern Slope, sobered up, drank again;
got home somewhere around third watch.
The houseboy by now is snoring like thunder:
I bang the gate but nobody answers.
Leaning on my stick, I listen to river sounds.

Always it irks me — this body not my own.
When can I forget the world's business?
Night far gone, wind calm, the river's crepe of ripples stilled:
I'll leave here in a little boat,
on far waters spend the years remaining.

Tune: "Partridge Sky"

Mountains shine through forest breaks, bamboo hides the wall;
withered grass by small ponds, jumbled cicada cries.
White birds again and again cut across the sky;
faint scent of lotus shining pink on the water.

Beyond the village,
by old town walls,
with goosefoot cane I stroll where late sunlight turns.
Thanks to rain that fell at the third watch last night
I get another cool day in this floating life.

CHOU PANG-YEN *(1056-1121)*

Tune: "Palace of Night Revels"

Leaves fall, slanting sun lights the river
that rolls its gentle ripples
on and on for a thousand miles.
On the bridge, an acid wind strikes my eyes,
I stand a long while
watching the twilight,
the lamp-lit town.

In my old house, under the cold window,
I hear countless leaves
flutter and fall from the parasol tree by the well.
I've no love for this lonely quilt, get up again and again.
Who knows that
it's for her sake
I cover this sheet with words?

LI CH'ING-CHAO *(1084?-c. 1151)*

Tune: "Song of Picking Mulberry"

Evening comes with an onslaught of wind and rain,
washing clean the heat and glare.
I put away my reed pipes,
face the flower-formed mirror, applying light makeup.

Red silk gauze so sheer my white skin shines through,
snowy-smooth, cream-fragrant:
I smile and say to my husband,
Tonight inside the light curtains, pillow and mat will be cool!

Tune: "Telling of Innermost Feelings"

Night comes and, drowsy with drink, I'm slow to shed my
        ornaments,
these plum petals stuck on a withered twig.
I wake from wine, its aroma scattering my spring sleep,
the dream grown distant — no returning there now.

No sound from anyone,
the moon still lingering,
kingfisher blinds lowered,
and once more I crush the withered stamens,
once more finger the fragrance left in them,
once more possess that time.

Tune: "As in a Dream: Song"

Always I recall the river arbor at twilight,
so muddled with wine we didn't know the way back,
excitement over, heading home by evening boat,
a wrong turn taking us deep into lotus blossoms,
and struggling to push through,
    struggling to push through,
we'd startle into flight a whole sandbar full of herons.

Tune: "Pure Serene Music"

Year after year in the snow
always we'd pick plum blossoms, drunk as we were,
shattering every cluster — what did we care? —
and their clear tears fell all over our clothes.

This year by sea's bend, sky's border,
lonely, lonely, gray invading both temples,
I watch, as evening comes, the wind rising
and know that I'll be hard put to discover a single blossom.

LU YU *(1125-1210)*

Tune: "Phoenix Hairpin"

(Said to have been written in 1155, when the poet chanced to meet his first wife in the Shen family garden in Shao-hsing. They had been happily married, but the poet's mother forced them to divorce. At the time of the meeting here, both were remarried.)

Pink tender hand,
yellow-corded wine,
city crammed with spring hues, willow by garden wall:
east winds hateful,
the one I loved, cold —
a heart all sadness,
parted how many years?
wrong! wrong! wrong!

Spring as always,
someone grown needlessly thin,
red tear stains wet the kerchief, soaking through mermaid gauze.
Peach petals falling,
stillness of a pond pavilion:
mountain-firm vows go on forever,
but a letter would be useless now —
don't! don't! don't!

HSIN CH'I-CHI *(1140-1207)*

Tune: "Ugly Rogue"

When I was young, not knowing the taste of grief,
I loved to climb the storied tower,
loved to climb the storied tower,
and in my new songs I'd make it a point to speak of grief.

But now I know all about the taste of grief.
About to speak of it, I stop;
about to speak of it, I stop
and say instead, "Days so cool — what a lovely autumn!"

GLOSSARY

Chin-t'i-shih, see Modern style *shih*.

Chüeh-chü or quatrain: a 4-line poem in *shih* form that uses a 5-ch., 7-ch., or rarely a 6-ch. line and observes the rules of tonal parallelism. The rhyme appears at the end of the 2nd and 4th line, with an optional rhyme at the end of the 1st line.

Fu, see Rhyme-prose

"Imitating the old poems" or *ni-ku:* a poem that imitates the style and mood of the early *shih* poetry of the Han and Wei period, particularly the "Nineteen Old Poems of the Han."

Ku-shih, see Old style poetry.

Lü-shih, see Regulated verse.

Mixed line form or *tsa-yen:* a poem in old style or modern style *shih* form that uses lines of mixed lengths.

Modern style *shih* or *chin-t'i-shih:* any *shih* poetic form such as *lü-shih, chüeh-chü,* or *p'ai-lü* that observes the rules of tonal parallelism, as opposed to the *ku-shih* or old style poem that does not observe such rules.

Old style poetry or *ku-shih:* term used to designate poems in *shih* form that do not observe the rules of tonal parallelism. They may be any length, though almost always consisting of an even number of lines. Lines are usually made up of 4, 5, or 7 characters, though in the *tsa-yen* or "mixed line" form, a mixture of lines of irregular lengths may be used.

P'ai-lü: poem in 5-ch. or 7-ch. line form that employs tonal and verbal parallelism in all the couplets and is of unlimited length. Unlike the *lü-shih* or regulated verse, it need not use a single rhyme throughout.

Poem without a category or *tsa-shih,* sometimes called miscellaneous poem: a poem that does not fit into any of the conventional categories such as love poem, travel poem, poem of parting, etc. It is often reflective or philosophical in tone.

Regulated verse or *lü-shih: shih* poem in 8 lines that observes the rules of tonal parallelism and uses either a 5-ch. or 7-ch. line throughout. A single rhyme is used, the rhyme appearing at the end of the 2nd, 4th, 6th, and 8th line, and optionally at the end of the 1st line. In almost all cases, the rhyme word belongs to the level tone. Strict verbal parallelism is required in the 2nd and 3rd couplet.

Rhyme-prose or *fu.* A poetic form that came to prominence in the 2nd cen. B.C. and continued in popularity for many centuries. It uses lines of varying lengths and often includes a prose preface and interludes of prose interspersed with the verse portions. The diction tends to be florid and there is extensive use of parallelism and allusion. Many of the works are descriptive and run to considerable length, others are more subjective and philosophical in tone.

Shih: a form of poetry first used in the *Shih ching* or *Book of Odes* and continuing in use today. The early *shih* is marked by lines that are predominantly 4 characters in length, with end rhyme employed, usually at the end of the even-numbered lines. Poems vary in length but almost always consist of an even number of lines. Around the first century A.D., the 4-ch. line was replaced in popularity by a 5-ch. line, often with a light caesura after the 2nd character, or a 7-ch. line with a caesura after the 4th character.

Song style: a poetic form that derives its name from the "Nine Songs" of the *Ch'u Tz'u.* It customarily uses a line of from 4 to 7 characters, broken in the middle by the insertion of a meaningless particle pronounced *hsi* in modern Chinese. Rhyme occurs at the end of most lines.

Tz'u or lyric meter: a song form characterized by prescribed rhyme and tonal sequences and the frequent use of lines of varying length. *Tz'u* were originally lyrics written to tunes imported from Central Asia, and the different metrical patterns employed in them were designated by the title of the particular tune that they fitted. Later writers of *tz'u,* though they did not necessarily intend their works to be sung, continued to use the old tune title to indicate the metrical pattern they were following.

Yüeh-fu: literally, Music Bureau, the title of a government office set up in Han times to collect folk songs. From this, the term came to designate the songs themselves. The early *yüeh-fu* songs or ballads are often irregular in form, using lines of varying lengths. Later songs and poems in folk song style tend to use regular lines of 5-ch. or 7-ch. length. Early *yüeh-fu* and later poems in *yüeh-fu* style frequently deal with the lives and hardships of the farmers or soldiers on border duty and express direct or indirect criticisms of government policy. Romantic love is another important theme in *yüeh-fu* style poems, the poet usually adopting the persona of a young woman.

A SELECTED BIBLIOGRAPHY ON CHINESE POETRY FROM EARLY TIMES TO THE THIRTEENTH CENTURY

The following is a selected bibliography of works in English on Chinese poetry of the period covered in the anthology. For fuller listings, see the bibliography in *Sunflower Splendor*. I wish to thank my friend Professor Marsha Wagner of Columbia University for assisting me in compiling the bibliography.

General Anthologies and Reference Works:

Birrell, Anne. *New Songs from a Jade Terrace: An Anthology of Early Chinese Love Poetry*. London: Allen & Unwin, 1982.

Bynner, Witter, and Kiang Kang-hu. *The Jade Mountain*. New York: Knopf, 1929. New York: Doubleday reprint, 1964; Vintage reprint, 1972.

Chang, H. C. *Chinese Literature 2: Nature Poetry*. New York: Columbia University Press, 1977.

Ch'en, C. J., and Michael Bullock. *Poems of Solitude*. London: Abelard-Schuman, 1960.

Frankel, Hans. *The Flowering Plum and the Palace Lady: Interpretations of Chinese Poetry*. New Haven: Yale University Press, 1976.

Frodsham, J. D., and Ch'eng Hsi. *An Anthology of Chinese Verse: Han Wei Chin and the Northern and Southern Dynasties*. Oxford: Clarendon Press, 1967.

Hightower, James Robert. *Topics in Chinese Literature: Outlines and Bibliographies*. Cambridge: Harvard University Press, 1962.

Liu, James J. Y. *The Art of Chinese Poetry*. Chicago: University of Chicago Press, 1962.

—— *The Interlingual Critic: Interpreting Chinese Poetry*. Bloomington: Indiana University Press, 1982.

Liu, Wu-chi, and Irving Yucheng Lo. *Sunflower Splendor: Three Thousand Years of Chinese Poetry*. New York: Doubleday, 1975.

Miao, Ronald C., ed. *Studies in Chinese Poetry and Poetics*, vol. 1. San Francisco: Chinese Materials Center, Inc., 1978.

Payne, Robert. *The White Pony*. New York: John Day, 1947.

Rexroth, Kenneth. *One Hundred Poems from the Chinese*. New York: New Directions, 1959.

Rexroth, Kenneth, and Chung Ling. *The Orchid Boat: Women Poets of China*. New York: McGraw-Hill, 1972.

Waley, Arthur. *Chinese Poems*. London: Allen & Unwin, 1946. Included in *Translations from the Chinese*. New York: Vintage Books, 1971.

Watson, Burton. *Early Chinese Literature*. New York: Columbia University Press, 1962.

—— *Chinese Lyricism: Shih Poetry from the Second to the Twelfth Century*. New York: Columbia University Press, 1971.

Chapter One: The Book of Odes

Karlgren, Bernhard. *The Book of Odes*. Stockholm: Museum of Far Eastern Antiquities, 1950.

McNaughton, William. *The Book of Songs*. New York: Twayne Publishers, 1971.

Pound, Ezra. *The Classic Anthology as Defined by Confucius*. Cambridge: Harvard University Press, 1954.

Waley, Arthur. *The Book of Songs*. London: Allen & Unwin, 1937.

Wang, C. H. *The Bell and the Drum: Shih Ching as Formulaic Poetry in an Oral Tradition*. Berkeley: University of California Press, 1974.

Chapter Two: The Ch'u Tz'u

Hawkes, David. *Ch'u Tz'u, The Songs of the South*. London: Oxford University Press, 1959.

Waley, Arthur. *The Nine Songs: A Study of Shamanism in Ancient China*. London: Allen & Unwin, 1955; San Francisco: City Lights Books, 1973.

Yang, Hsien-yi, and Gladys Yang. *Li Sao and Other Poems of Chu Yuan.* Peking: Foreign Languages Press, 1953.

Chapter Four: Poems of the Han and Wei

Kent, George W. *Worlds of Dust and Jade: 47 Poems and Ballads of the Third Century Chinese Poet Ts'ao Chih.* New York: Philosophical Library, 1969.

Chapter Five: T'ao Yüan-ming

Acker, William. *T'ao the Hermit: Sixty Poems by T'ao Ch'ien.* London: Thames & Hudson, 1952.
Chang, Lily Pao-hu, and Marjorie Sinclair. *The Poems of T'ao Ch'ien.* Honolulu: University of Hawaii Press, 1953.
Hightower, James Robert. *The Poetry of T'ao Ch'ien.* Oxford: Oxford University Press, 1970.

Chapter Six: Chin, Six Dynasties and Sui Poets

Frodsham, J. D. *The Murmuring Stream: The Life and Works of Hsieh Ling-yün.* 2 vols. Kuala Lumpur: University of Malaya Press, 1967.
Holzman, Donald. *Poetry and Politics: The Life and Works of Juan Chi* (A.D. *210-263).* Cambridge: Cambridge University Press, 1976.
Marney, John. *Liang Chien-wen Ti.* Boston: G. K. Hall, 1976.

Chapter Seven: Major T'ang Poets I: Wang Wei, Li Po, Tu Fu

Chang, Yin-han, and Lewis C. Walmsley. *Poems by Wang Wei.* Rutland, Vermont: Tuttle, 1958.
Robinson, G. W. *Poems of Wang Wei.* Harmondsworth: Penguin, 1973.
Wagner, Marsha L. *Wang Wei.* Boston: G. K. Hall, 1981.
Yip, Wai-lim. *Hiding the Universe, Poems by Wang Wei.* New York: Grossman, 1972.
Yu, Pauline. *The Poetry of Wang Wei: New Translations and Commentaries.* Bloomington: Indiana University Press, 1980.

Obata, Shigeyoshi. *The Works of Li Po*. New York: Dutton, 1922.

Waley, Arthur. *The Poetry and Career of Li Po*. London: Allen & Unwin, 1950.

Alley, Rewi. *Tu Fu: Selected Poems*. Peking: Foreign Languages Press, 1962.

Davis, A. R. *Tu Fu*. New York: Twayne Publishers, 1971.

Hawkes, David. *A Little Primer of Tu Fu*. Oxford: Clarendon Press, 1967.

Hung, William. *Tu Fu: China's Greatest Poet*. Cambridge: Harvard University Press, 1952.

Chapter Eight: Major T'ang Poets II: Han Yü, Po Chü-i, Han-shan

Owen, Stephen. *The Poetry of Meng Chiao and Han Yü*. New Haven: Yale University Press, 1975.

Levy, Howard S. *Translations from Po Chü-i's Collected Works*. 2 vols. New York: Paragon, 1971.

Waley, Arthur. *The Life and Times of Po Chü-i*. London: Allen & Unwin, 1949.

Snyder, Gary. "The Cold Mountain Poems of Han-shan," *Evergreen Review*, (1958), 2(6): 69-80. *Evergreen Review Reader 1957-1967*. New York: Grove Press.

Watson, Burton. *Cold Mountain: 100 Poems by the T'ang Poet Han-shan*. New York: Grove Press, 1962; Columbia University Press, 1970.

Chapter Nine: Other T'ang Poets

Chan, Marie. *Kao Shih*. Boston: G. K. Hall, 1978.

Frodsham, J. D. *The Poems of Li Ho*. Oxford: Clarendon Press, 1970.

Graham, A. C. *Poems of the Late T'ang*. Baltimore: Penguin, 1965.

Kroll, Paul. *Meng Hao-jan*. Boston: G. K. Hall, 1981.

Liu, James J. Y. *The Poetry of Li Shang-yin: Ninth-Century Baroque Chinese Poet*. Chicago: University of Chicago Press, 1969.

Nienhauser, William H. et al. *Liu Tsung-yüan*. New York: Twayne, 1973.

Owen, Stephen. *The Poetry of the Early T'ang*. New Haven: Yale University Press, 1977.

—— *The Great Age of Chinese Poetry: The High T'ang*. New Haven: Yale University Press, 1981.

Chapter Ten: Two Major Sung Poets: Su Tung-p'o, Lu Yu

Yoshikawa, Kōjirō. *An Introduction to Sung Poetry.* Translated by Burton Watson. Cambridge: Harvard University Press, 1967.

Lin, Yutang. *The Gay Genius: The Life and Times of Su Tungpo.* New York: John Day, 1947.

Watson, Burton. *Su Tung-p'o: Selections from a Sung Dynasty Poet.* New York: Columbia University Press, 1965.

—— *The Old Man Who Does As He Pleases: Poems and Prose by Lu Yu.* New York: Columbia University Press, 1973.

Chapter Eleven: Other Sung Poets

Chaves, Jonathan. *Heaven My Blanket, Earth My Pillow: Poems from Sung-Dynasty China by Yang Wan-li.* New York: Weatherhill, 1975.

—— *Mei Yao-ch'en and the Development of Early Sung Poetry.* New York: Columbia University Press, 1976.

Schmidt, J. D. *Yang Wan-li.* Boston: G. K. Hall, 1976.

Chapter Twelve: Lyrics in Tz'u Form

Chang, Kang-i Sun. *The Evolution of Chinese Tz'u Poetry: From Late T'ang to Northern Sung.* Princeton: Princeton University Press, 1980.

Fusek, Lois. *Among the Flowers: The Hua-chien-chi.* New York: Columbia University Press, 1982.

Hu, P'in-ch'ing. *Li Ch'ing-chao.* New York: Twayne Publishers, 1966.

Liu, James J. Y. *Major Lyricists of the Northern Sung.* Princeton: Princeton University Press, 1974.

Lin, Shuen-fu. *The Transformation of the Chinese Lyrical Tradition: Chiang K'uei and Southern Sung Tz'u Poetry.* Princeton: Princeton University Press, 1978.

Lo, Irving Yucheng. *Hsin Ch'i-chi.* New York: Twayne Publishers, 1971.

Soong, Stephen C. *Song Without Music: Chinese Tz'u Poetry.* Hong Kong: Chinese University Press (A Renditions Book), 1981.

Wixted, John Timothy. *The Song-Poetry of Wei Chuang (836-910 A.D.).* Occasional Paper No. 12, Center for Asian Studies, Arizona State University, 1979.

INDEX OF POETS

TRANSLATIONS FROM THE ORIENTAL CLASSICS

STUDIES IN ORIENTAL CULTURE

COMPANIONS TO ASIAN STUDIES

INTRODUCTION TO ORIENTAL CIVILIZATIONS

NEO-CONFUCIAN STUDIES

MODERN ASIAN LITERATURE SERIES

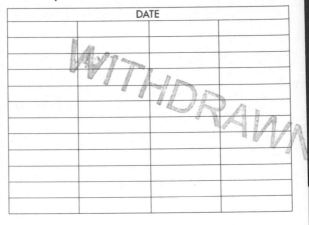

DATE		

WITHDRAWN